Palgrave Macmillan Studies in Banking and Financial Institutions

Series Editor: **Professor Philip Molyneux**

The Palgrave Macmillan Studies in Banking and Financial Institutions are international in orientation and include studies of banking within particular countries or regions, and studies of particular themes, such as corporate banking, risk management, and mergers and acquisitions. The focus of the books is research and practice, and they offer up-to-date and innovative studies on contemporary topics in banking that will have global impact and influence.

Titles include:

Steffen E. Andersen
THE EVOLUTION OF NORDIC FINANCE

Seth Apati
THE NIGERIAN BANKING SECTOR REFORMS
Power and Politics

Vittorio Boscia, Alessandro Carretta and Paola Schwizer
COOPERATIVE BANKING IN EUROPE: CASE STUDIES

Roberto Bottiglia, Elisabetta Gualandri and Gian Nereo Mazzocco (*editors*)
CONSOLIDATION IN THE EUROPEAN FINANCIAL INDUSTRY

Dimitris N. Chorafas
CAPITALISM WITHOUT CAPITAL

Dimitris N. Chorafas
SOVEREIGN DEBT CRISIS
The New Normal and the Newly Poor

Dimitris N. Chorafas
FINANCIAL BOOM AND GLOOM
The Credit and Banking Crisis of 2007–2009 and Beyond

Violaine Cousin
BANKING IN CHINA

Vincenzo D'Apice and Giovanni Ferri
FINANCIAL INSTABILITY
Toolkit for Interpreting Boom and Bust Cycles

Peter Falush and Robert L. Carter OBE
THE BRITISH INSURANCE INDUSTRY SINCE 1900
The Era of Transformation

Franco Fiordelisi and Ornella Ricci (*editors*)
BANCASSURANCE IN EUROPE
Past, Present and Future

Franco Fiordelisi
MERGERS AND ACQUISITIONS IN EUROPEAN BANKING

Franco Fiordelisi, Philip Molyneux and Daniele Previati (*editors*)
NEW ISSUES IN FINANCIAL AND CREDIT MARKETS

Franco Fiordelisi, Philip Molyneux and Daniele Previati (*editors*)
NEW ISSUES IN FINANCIAL INSTITUTIONS MANAGEMENT

Kim Hawtrey
AFFORDABLE HOUSING FINANCE

Jill M. Hendrickson
REGULATION AND INSTABILITY IN U.S. COMMERCIAL BANKING
A History of Crises

Otto Hieronymi (*editor*)
GLOBALIZATION AND THE REFORM OF THE INTERNATIONAL BANKING AND MONETARY SYSTEM

Sven Janssen
BRITISH AND GERMAN BANKING STRATEGIES

Alexandros-Andreas Kyrtsis (*editor*)
FINANCIAL MARKETS AND ORGANIZATIONAL TECHNOLOGIES
System Architectures, Practices and Risks in the Era of Deregulation

Caterina Lucarelli and Gianni Brighetti (*editors*)
RISK TOLERANCE IN FINANCIAL DECISION MAKING

Roman Matousek (*editor*)
MONEY, BANKING AND FINANCIAL MARKETS IN CENTRAL AND EASTERN EUROPE
20 Years of Transition

Philip Molyneux (*editor*)
BANK PERFORMANCE, RISK AND FIRM FINANCING

Philip Molyneux (*editor*)
BANK STRATEGY, GOVERNANCE AND RATINGS

Imad A. Moosa
THE MYTH OF TOO BIG TO FAIL

Simon Mouatt and Carl Adams (*editors*)
CORPORATE AND SOCIAL TRANSFORMATION OF MONEY AND BANKING
Breaking the Serfdom

Victor Murinde (*editor*)
BANK REGULATORY REFORMS IN AFRICA

Anders Ögren (*editor*)
THE SWEDISH FINANCIAL REVOLUTION

Özlem Olgu
EUROPEAN BANKING
Enlargement, Structural Changes and Recent Developments

Ramkishen S. Rajan
EMERGING ASIA
Essays on Crises, Capital Flows, FDI and Exchange Rate

Allesandro Roselli
FINANCIAL STRUCTURES AND REGULATION: A COMPARISON OF CRISES IN THE UK, USA AND ITALY

Yasushi Suzuki
JAPAN'S FINANCIAL SLUMP
Collapse of the Monitoring System under Institutional and Transition Failures

Ruth Wandhöfer
EU PAYMENTS INTEGRATION
The Tale of SEPA, PSD and Other Milestones Along the Road

The full list of titles available is on the website:
www.palgrave.com/finance/sbfi.asp

Palgrave Macmillan Studies in Banking and Financial Institutions
Series Standing Order ISBN 978-1-4039-4872-4
(*outside North America only*)

You can receive future titles in this series as they are published by placing a standing order. Please contact your bookseller or, in case of difficulty, write to us at the address below with your name and address, the title of the series and the ISBN quoted above.

Customer Services Department, Macmillan Distribution Ltd, Houndmills, Basingstoke, Hampshire RG21 6XS, England

Bank Regulatory Reforms in Africa

Edited by

Victor Murinde

palgrave macmillan

AERC CREA

First published 2012 by
PALGRAVE MACMILLAN

Palgrave Macmillan in the UK is an imprint of Macmillan Publishers Limited, registered in England, company number 785998, of Houndmills, Basingstoke, Hampshire RG21 6XS.

Palgrave Macmillan in the US is a division of St Martin's Press LLC, 175 Fifth Avenue, New York, NY 10010.

Palgrave Macmillan is the global academic imprint of the above companies and has companies and representatives throughout the world.

Palgrave® and Macmillan® are registered trademarks in the United States, the United Kingdom, Europe and other countries.

ISBN 978–0–230–31333–0

This book is printed on paper suitable for recycling and made from fully managed and sustained forest sources. Logging, pulping and manufacturing processes are expected to conform to the environmental regulations of the country of origin.

A catalogue record for this book is available from the British Library.

A catalog record for this book is available from the Library of Congress.

10 9 8 7 6 5 4 3 2 1
21 20 19 18 17 16 15 14 13 12

Printed and bound in Great Britain by
CPI Antony Rowe, Chippenham and Eastbourne

Contents

Figures

Tables

Foreword

This book is based on papers that were presented at the Twelfth Senior Policy Seminar (SPS XII) of the African Economic Research Consortium (AERC), which took place in Mombasa, Kenya, on 22–24 March 2010. Leading public policymakers, monetary and financial economists, professional bankers and advisors from central banks across Africa gathered for sober reflection on one topical subject – bank regulatory reforms in Africa. The seminar was opened by the Hon. Wycliffe Ambetsa Oparanya, Minister for Planning and National Development, Government of Kenya. Professor Njuguna Ndungu, Governor of the Central Bank of Kenya, delivered the opening keynote address.

The three days of intense discussions focused on how to enhance bank competition and intermediation efficiency across Africa. This region-wide meeting brought together 71 economic policymakers and advisors drawn from the highest levels of government and representing 22 countries in the continent.

In the wake of the recent financial crisis, which has created enormous regulatory risks, some changes in the content of banking regulation are crucial and any positive transformations are likely to produce encouraging results. The regulatory system in many African countries has evolved in the recent past, notably through progressively more detailed capital requirements and increasing demands that banking organizations enhance their own risk-management systems. However, with respect to the structure of the implementation of bank supervision and regulation, major changes are still in the works that will probably rearrange and consolidate financial oversight and extend the powers of African central banks.

The AERC Senior Policy Seminar in Mombasa provided a structure for the honest exchange of experiences. The arrangement turned on syntheses of relevant research findings presented by senior scholars. Each session then featured a brief summary of the presentation and a floor discussion by the policymakers themselves.

Wrapping up the debates was a working session in which participants identified additional key areas of research to generate findings that they would like to utilize in policy formulation. This atmosphere generated spirited interaction among the participants and helped the policymakers to fine-tune their own approaches as they applied the lessons and details of AERC-supported economic policy research from elsewhere in the continent. Besides this specific immediate result, the seminar improved the prospects for cooperative policy research between policymakers and researchers. The outcomes of the consultations served as inputs for AERC's policy research agenda and helped with the identification of structures and methods intended to promote collaboration among policymakers and researchers, both within individual countries and across the continent.

The media coverage was impressive. The seminar elicited significant interest from the local, regional and international media organizations, which covered the event very well. In Kenya they included the *Daily Nation*, Nation Television (NTV), the *Standard*, Kenya Broadcasting Corporation (KBC) and FM stations like Kiss FM, as well as Xinhua, a Chinese international media organization. At the meeting, journalists were also involved in long interviews with the key presenters and participants, and they too were given extensive coverage in the local newspapers. Ahead of the meeting, a piece on the seminar and about AERC was published in the *Daily Nation*, the *Standard* and the *East African*. These are high-profile media outlets with extensive readership and circulation that covers the East African region. Other promotional materials prepared for the seminar included an AERC documentary, which was screened at the AERC publications desk and distributed to some of the participants.

Let me thank the contributors, who carried out thorough research work to sustain the debate on bank regulation in Africa. Also, I wish to thank all colleagues inside and outside the AERC, resource staff as well as participants, and importantly the Office of the Chief Economist of the African Development Bank, which made SPS XII and this book possible. It is my hope that this volume and the knowledge it contains will generate serious interest in Basel III and associated issues of bank regulation in Africa.

William Lyakurwa
Executive Director, African Economic Research Consortium

Contributors

Louis Kasekende is Deputy Governor, Bank of Uganda.

Kupukile Mlambo is Advisor, Office of the Chief Economist and Vice-President, African Development Bank.

Victor Murinde is Director of the African Development Institute at the African Development Bank; at the start of this project, he was Professor of Development Finance, Birmingham Business School, University of Birmingham, United Kingdom.

Francis M. Mwega is Professor of Economics, University of Nairobi, Kenya.

Abraham Mwenda is Managing Director and Chief Executive Officer, Development Bank of Zambia.

Njuguna Ndungu is Governor, Central Bank of Kenya.

Sunil S. Poshakwale is Professor of International Finance, Cranfield School of Management, Cranfield University, United Kingdom.

Binsheng Qian is Lecturer in Finance, Cranfield School of Management, Cranfield University, United Kingdom.

Taoufik Rajhi is Chief Training Officer, African Development Institute, African Development Bank.

Hatem Salah is Professor of Economics and Banking, Ecole Supérieure de Commerce de Tunis, University of Manouba, Tunisia.

Tianshu Zhao is Lecturer in Banking, University of Stirling, United Kingdom.

1
Keynote: Progress with Bank Regulation Reforms in Kenya

Njuguna Ndungu

1.1 Introduction

I am delighted to be with all of you here in Mombasa and to speak on 'Bank Regulatory Reforms in Africa: Enhancing Bank Competition and Intermediation'. But before I make my remarks, let me take this opportunity to thank the African Economic Research Consortium (AERC) for their invitation to give the keynote address at this seminar. This is indeed a timely topic as we continue to assess the effects of the global financial crisis and find long-term solutions to mitigate and prevent recurrence. I am informed that approximately 70 senior policymakers from more than 20 countries in Sub-Saharan Africa (SSA) are in attendance. This signals the importance of this seminar and the policy spin-offs it will generate.

At the outset, I would like to recognize the important role that the AERC has played in strengthening local capacity for managing economies within SSA. The AERC has contributed to advanced policy research and graduate training in economics. Most institutions of policy in SSA today are led by AERC alumni. I am happy to be part of this group myself.

This seminar is taking place at a time when countries in Africa are taking stock of the second- and third-round effects of the global financial crisis. You will agree with me that the crisis, which initially hit African countries with stronger financial linkages to international capital markets, significant trade relations with the Western world and rich natural resources, set the stage for challenging times in policy making and implementation.

Africa's prospects in the post-crisis period are contingent on the behaviour of policymakers. Indeed, there is need for better regulation that can readily identify emerging vulnerabilities, properly price risks and strengthen incentives for prudent behaviour. It is tempting after the crisis to call for more regulation *but we should emphasize better regulation*. Second, we should emphasize building strong institutions. Globally, the remedial actions taken by governments to deal with the crisis have borne fruit and the green shoots of recovery are beginning to sprout.

For us here in Kenya, we remain committed to fostering a stable market-based financial system as mandated by law. An efficient financial system collects and collates deposits from micro-savers and channels them to investors. This is the intermediation process. This process allows economic agents to evaluate the risks and prices in the market and align their investment portfolio and investment gestation.

The Kenyan case is both interesting and a policy strategy challenge. It reflects an example of segmented markets. But the cost of credit and interest rates spread remains high. The spread is a major challenge in the banking sector because it acts as an impediment to expansion of credit and development of financial intermediation and signals inefficiency in the sector.

The challenge for a policymaker is to develop a financial sector that answers to the challenges of the economy. In order to address market inefficiencies, the Central Bank and other stakeholders have undertaken significant reforms for the banking sector. These reforms include the operationalization of the credit reference bureaux, payment systems improvements, opening of new currency centres, automation of trading system for treasury bonds and the activation of horizontal repos. I wish to highlight these initiatives.

1.2 Operationalization of credit referencing mechanism

The Banking (Credit Reference Bureau) Regulations were operationalized on 2 February 2009. This will facilitate the sharing of credit information by institutions licensed under the Banking Act. This link will allow the industry to build information capital that is critical in the credit market. It will also enhance access to credit by SMEs and individuals that have been constrained by lack of physical collateral.

Further, the Banking Sector will be able to address the problem of non-performing loans at the origination point as credit history of applicants will be taken into account during the credit appraisal process.

1.3 Licensing of deposit-taking microfinance institutions

The Microfinance Act was operationalized effective May 2008. Currently, one institution has been licensed and eight applications for licences are being processed. With the unique business models of microfinance institutions mainly targeted at the lower end of the market, bringing them under the purview of the Central Bank will not only give them a legal basis in dealing with depositors but will also boost access to formal financial services by the populace. Deposit-taking microfinance institutions are free to be community-based or nationwide.

1.4 The National Payments System

The National Payments System sits at the centre of the financial system. It is imperative that payments systems are secure and efficient. The Central Bank continues with its initiatives to modernize the national payments system. Accordingly, from 1 October 2009, value capping was effected with all payments above Ksh.1 million being made through the Real Time Gross Settlement System (RTGS). This initiative enhanced the security and efficiency of high value payments.

1.5 MPESA[1]

The celebrated MPESA falls under this category of reforms. As we have seen this market unfolding, MPESA account holders have soared to nine million, total transactions surpassed Ksh.48 billion a month (or averaging Ksh.1.6 billion a day) and agents increased to 17,000 in the last three years.

1.6 Monetary policy

On the monetary policy front, the Central Bank of Kenya has observed that, despite signalling efforts by the Monetary Policy Committee to bring down the rates of interest by lowering the Central Bank Rate (CBR), banks have not responded accordingly. Further, the failure of the banking system to extend the maturity of their loan products is a consequence of the characteristic nature of not only their deposits, which are largely short term, but also their assessment and pricing of risk.

To support economic development, there is need for the development of banking products that support long-term lending. These development banking products will play a significant role in influencing a downward trend in commercial banks lending rates. The Central Bank will therefore explore how development banking products can be introduced into the market to enhance the monetary policy transmission mechanism and lengthen the maturity profile of commercial bank term loans.

1.7 Developments in the bond market

The Central Bank has successfully raised funds for infrastructure development for the Government through infrastructure bonds. These infrastructure bonds have not only facilitated financing of the Government's infrastructure programme but also set the pace for the issuance of similar bonds by corporate entities such as KENGEN and Safaricom. This, coupled with automated trading in the Nairobi Stock Exchange, will be important for a vibrant bond market. In addition, to deepen and widen the bond market, the Central Bank implemented the following measures:

- *Issuance of benchmark bonds*: The Bank together with Market Leaders Forum adopted 2, 5, 10, 15 and 20 year maturities as benchmark bonds. This move has not only firmed up the yield curve, but has improved pricing, reflected through improved secondary market trading.
- *Reopening of benchmark bonds*: This has increased trading activities in the secondary market.
- *The shape and position of the Yield*: The vibrant bond market has led to a downward shift in the Yield Curve with an upward gentle slope reflecting stability. This has created reliable pricing benchmark for corporates, many of which raised required capital via issuance of corporate bonds in 2009/10. It is also a useful tool in pricing credit facilities as it signals the direction of interest rates.

You will recall that the Central Bank of Kenya (CBK), the Nairobi Stock Exchange (NSE) and the Capital Markets Authority collaborated in the automation of trading of Treasury Bonds through the NSE. The main objective of this initiative was to make bonds trading secure and efficient, and to create a vibrant market. The expected improvement in market activity will also improve market liquidity and encourage more investors to participate in the bond market.

1.8 Operationalization of the horizontal repos

We have introduced the Interbank Master Repurchase Agreement, otherwise known as the horizontal repo, which is aimed at deepening the capital and money markets and enhancing the intermediation process. I am happy to note that the horizontal repo as a tool of redistributing liquidity in the market has also provided a useful barometer on the status of liquidity in the banking sector. The horizontal repo is an additional facility for commercial banks to use alongside the vertical repo which is an instrument between commercial banks and CBK.

1.9 Other initiatives

The changing market dynamics in the Kenyan Banking Sector have made it necessary for the Central Bank to reinvent itself and become proactive in detecting opportunities and threats to financial sector stability. With a view not only to enhance intermediation and the competitiveness of the banking sector but also to increase efficiency and access, the Central Bank has been in the forefront in encouraging various financial services providers, such as:

- *mobile phone money transfer providers*, such as M-PESA
- *Savings and Credit Co-operatives (SACCOs) and Agency Banking models*
- *Shariah compliant banking products* – we have seen the introduction of two Shariah compliant banks and growing interest in a number of institutions seeking to offer Shariah compliant products.

We have now started to realize the dividends of the reforms we have undertaken in the financial sector. Kenya now has a healthy, sound and strong banking system. The size of the banking system has been enhanced in terms of deposits mobilized, credit growth and competition. Specifically:

- Deposit accounts have increased from 2.6 million (end 2005) to 8.4 million (end 2009) and deposits have doubled from Ksh.545 billion (US$7.2 billion) to Ksh.1065 billion (US$14 billion) in the same period.
- Lowering barriers to entry, via removal of minimum balances, has supported financial reach.

- Banks have taken their services to the customers due to increasing competition and improvements in the delivery channels. Banks are opening and re-opening branches in areas with none or few branches.

Efficiency is achieved when there are strong institutions with requisite capacity to satisfy market needs while complying with statutory and prudential requirements.

One of the main challenges of monetary policy has been the presence of currency outside banks. In March 2008, it was Ksh.9 billion above the Central Bank target. However, in March 2010 it was Ksh.4.9 billion below CBK target as a result of banks' increased coverage of rural and low income areas.

Financial sector reforms are far from being accomplished. Given the changing dynamics of the economy and its growing complexities, the financial industry has to remain responsive and supportive of the broader economic ambitions and agenda. All the major players and stakeholders in the banking system will have to strive for continuity; broaden and deepen reforms; build and sustain the already implemented reforms; and fill the remaining gaps. The growing competition, along with increasingly diversified services both across the regions and sectors, as well as improved access to customer-base on the back of progressive reliance on technology, are the harbingers of the changing and efficient intermediation role of banks in the days ahead.

The Central Bank, like others in the region, is committed to reforms in the banking industry towards enhanced competitiveness. In line with this, the Central Bank has earmarked amendments to the Banking Act and Microfinance Act going forward. The amendments to the Banking Act and Microfinance Act are expected to further enhance efficiency and competitiveness of our financial sector. The CBK, in collaboration with the Government and market players, will enhance its efforts in addressing other structural rigidities that contribute to market inefficiencies, to take stock of developments as well as other emerging constraints.

Before I conclude, let me once again take this opportunity to reiterate the critical role of the financial sector in Africa's economic development. This potential can only be realized when African policymakers implement reforms to remove binding constraints in the sector. I am sure that in this gathering we have the capacity to identify those constraints to unleash Africa's potential.

Finally, I do hope that you will find time in your busy schedules to enjoy our world reknowned beaches. I wish you fruitful deliberations.

Note

1. The word MPESA stands for M-PESA, where M denotes mobile and PESA is a Swahili word for money; hence MPESA is a loose acronym for 'mobile money' – it refers to an electronic money transfer service using a cell phone, which is an innovative popular practice in Kenya.

2
Bank Regulation in Africa: From Basel I to Basel II, and Now at a Crossroads

Victor Murinde

2.1 Introduction

The regulation and supervision of banking is a very topical issue, especially with respect to African economies that have small banking units (e.g. microfinance banks in Chad and Ethiopia) and large wholesale banks (e.g. investment banks in Botswana and Namibia) but tend to offer a limited range of financial instruments, predominantly deposits and loans. As highlighted in the paper by Kasekende et al. (2010), commercial banks continue to dominate the financial sector in Africa and non-bank financial institutions play a negligible role, except for public sector provident funds. In many African countries, capital markets remain peripheral as a vehicle for raising capital. However, as banking systems expand and offer a wider range of financial instruments, as in South Africa, Kenya, Nigeria and other large economies, how should bank supervision and regulation respond? Consider this dictum from Adam Smith:

> Though the principles of the banking trade may appear somewhat abstruse, the practice is capable of being reduced to strict rules. To depart upon any occasion from those rules, in consequence of some flattering speculation of extraordinary gain, is almost always extremely dangerous, and frequently fatal to the banking company which attempts it.
>
> (Adam Smith, *Wealth of Nations*, Book V, Chapter 1, part iii)

In modern parlance, the above dictum mimics some elements of 'narrow banking': the creation of banking institutions focused on the traditional functions, namely deposit-taking from individuals and small- and medium-sized enterprises (SMEs), and payment systems for institutions (see Kay, 2009). Perhaps Adam Smith refers to a period when there were no formal banks in Africa, except probably in South Africa and Egypt; but, arguably, banking co-exists with commerce, even in rudimentary modes. The transition in bank regulation in Africa takes us back to the period before Basel I, namely to the dictum by Adam Smith, then to Basel I and then on to Basel II. Basel II has been problematic for Africa, as is argued further on, and recently the bank regulatory waters have been muddied by the financial crisis, which was generated outside Africa.

The crises in Asia, Mexico and Russia, and the global financial crisis can be attributed not simply to monetary issues or subprime mortgages, but mainly to the spread of contagion effects exacerbated by weak regulatory environments (see Brana and Lahet, 2009; Goodhart, 2008; Han et al., 2003; Jackson, 1999; Mizen, 2008; Radelet et al., 1998; Sharma, 2001; Sojli, 2007). Although the latest crisis affected banks globally more than any in the past, the serial occurrence of these crises seems to suggest that regulators must do something fundamental to stop this recurring cycle (see Brunnermeier et al., 2009), especially for developing economies which are most vulnerable to contagion but have no 'voice' in the architecture of bank regulation. In addition, the financial crisis exposed the inadequacy of the Basel rules. As Kay (2009: 7) observed: 'Basel capital adequacy rules proved worse than useless'. Globally, capital adequacy rules not only failed in their objectives, but also generated 'regulatory arbitrage', involving an explosion of asset securitization and the use of off-balance sheet vehicles (SIVs and conduits) intended to evade the rules. So, given the global financial crisis and some criticisms of Basel II, Africa is at the crossroads of bank regulation, contemplating where to go next. As observed by Brownbridge and Kirkpatrick (2002), the key questions for policymakers are related to the specific methods of bank regulation and supervision that can work best in existing economic environments. This is the challenge for Africa today: trying to recover from the financial crisis, encumbered with Basel II that lost its credibility during the crisis, and aiming for regulation that will encompass specific features of banking such as microfinance institutions and credit to SMEs.

This chapter highlights key trends in bank regulation in Africa, especially the transition from Basel I to Basel II, and hazards a conjecture on the future path for an effective regulatory regime for Africa countries. The rest of the chapter is structured in four sections. Section 2.2 presents a holistic perspective of bank regulation in terms of flow of funds and bank regulatory framework. It is shown that bank regulation not only revolves around financial intermediation, but also involves institutional, legal and political environments. Section 2.3 highlights the evolution of the banking revolution in Africa, including the transition from Basel I to Basel II. The challenges facing bank regulation and supervision[1] in Africa, now at a crossroads, are discussed in Section 2.4, and some recommendations are proposed in Section 2.5.

2.2 Bank regulation in a flow-of-funds context

We invoke the flow-of-funds framework to underpin the role of bank regulation in ensuring the functionality of banks and capital markets in relation to households, companies, the government and the external sector, in the sense that a '... main function of the flow of funds accounts is to reveal the sources and uses of funds that are needed for growth...' (Klein, 2000: ix). See also the surveys in Green et al. (2005). Importantly, in this framework banks matter if they are well regulated.

It is argued that bank regulation ensures the arrival and use of timely and accurate information in flow-of-funds transactions that take place in an economy, mainly involving exchanges of assets and liabilities. These transactions generate flows of funds from one agent to another and from one sector to another. In Table 2.1, flow-of-funds accounts show net transactions in financial instruments among the key economic sectors (Green and Murinde, 1998). Each row (i) represents an asset, and each column (j) a sector. Each cell (i,j) in the matrix shows net purchases (+) or sales (−) of asset i by sector j during the unit time period. The row sums of the matrix are zero as net purchases of an asset must equal net sales, and each column (j) sums to the j'th sector's surplus or deficit, that is, its net acquisition of financial assets (NAFA). When households and companies make consumption and investment decisions, changes in the stocks of assets and liabilities are tracked through identities, which state that the current stock is equal to the sum of the previous period's stock, net flows into or out of the stock through transactions, changes in valuation (capital gains or losses), and depreciation of the pre-existing stock. Net flows into or out of a stock correspond to entries in the flow-of-funds account for any given sector. Entries for non-reproducible assets, such as land, reflect flows (purchases and sales) that do not enter into the current account. However, one sector may sell land to another to augment its funds in order to purchase other assets. Intangible assets are also included in any complete representation of flow of funds.

The behaviour of banks in response to a regulator, or any agent, may influence the portfolio behaviour of the household sector and the company sector, and the role of flow of funds in interest rate determination.[2] Hence, flow-of-funds models seek to explore why agents in a particular sector hold specific assets and why the agents choose to substitute assets in their portfolio. Also, as shown by Moore et al. (2006a,b), stochastic policy simulations within a flow-of-funds model can shed light on the type of banking sector reforms that influence outcomes for households, companies, banks and government.[3] As Fleming and Giugale (2000) emphasize, a key advantage of the flow of funds is that it imposes internal consistency on analyses and forecasts, and provides an exposition of the complete financial implications of policy or other changes. Hence, the framework in Table 2.1 revolves around the banking sector, but this sector can play its role only when it is well regulated and there is financial stability.

In the context of bank regulation, the flow of funds provides a holistic perspective on the implications of effective regulation and supervision. First, the framework underpins the sources and uses of funds between the household, company and banking sectors, on the one hand, and the foreign sector, on the other hand. The banking sector provides financial intermediation from the household sector to the company sector. Financial instruments (such as deposit and loan interest rates), financial reforms and bank regulation influence the size of intermediation. Therefore, in a flow-of-funds context, the main implication for bank regulation is the centrality of the financial intermediation role, so that there must be a stable source of funding for all types of banks, including

Table 2.1 Bank regulation ensures functionality of flow of funds

	Household sector	**Company sector**	**Bank sector**	**Government sector**	**Foreign sector**
	H	P	B	G	F
1. *Income–expenditure*					
1.1 Income (Y)	Y^H	Y^P			
1.2 Taxes (T)	T^H	T^P		T^G	
1.3 Consumption (C)	C^H	C^P		C^G	C^F
1.4 Investment (I)	I^H	I^P		I^G	I^F
Net acquisitions (S)	S^H	S^P		S^G	S^F
2. *Assets and liabilities: Balance-sheet accounts*					
2.1 Capital (K)	K^H	K^P		K^G	K^F
2.2 Loans (L)	L^H	L^P	L^B	L^G	
2.3 Domestic money (M)	M^H	M^P	M^B	M^G	
2.4 Foreign money (R)				R^G	R^F
Net worth (W)	W^H	W^P	W^B	W^G	W^F

commercial banks and investment banks. For example, it is very important for banks to maintain capital ratios to avoid liquidity and solvency risks. If commercial banks ignore the basic principle of the deposits ratio and over-rely on money-market financing, liquidity crises may soon occur in banks once market confidence is lost. The crisis may be further complicated by the loss of market confidence through compounding liquidity problems, as in the recent financial crisis.

Further, from a holistic perspective, the framework of bank regulation must encompass the main sectors in the flow of funds indicated in Table 2.1. Barth et al. (2006) provide a framework for bank regulation that covers the institutional issues.

The dichotomy of the public-versus-private-interest view of regulation presents two contending theories of bank regulation (see Barth et al., 2006). However, the overall regulatory framework also recognizes the key roles played by the institutional environment, political factors and legal considerations.

In the case of the public interest theory, bank regulation seeks to protect and benefit the public at large as consumers of banking services. This requires that regulation should aim to secure innovative and good quality services at low prices through the promotion of competition (Kay, 2009). This view is based on the argument that markets are prone to fail. In theory, unregulated banking markets can yield undesirable results, such as financial crises. The work by Nobel laureate Joseph Stiglitz (2001) is consistent with the public interest view of bank regulation. Stiglitz's main message is that credit markets fail to operate optimally when all parties to a transaction do not have the same level of information (the problem of 'asymmetric information'), leading to undesired outcomes which could be improved, in theory, by government regulation.[4] Hence, the argument is that effective bank regulation can foster the development of a properly functioning banking system, which can have positive effects on savings, intermediation and economic growth (see also, Matthews et al., 2007). Bank regulation aims to improve intermediation efficiency, protects banks from negative externalities, such as financial crises, and protects the public from such problems as loan sharks and ponzi schemes. The question of bank efficiency in Africa is explored through case studies on Kenya, Zambia, Egypt and Algeria.

The private interest view, or the Chicago theory, suggests that regulation does not protect the public at large, but only the interest of specific groups. The Nobel laureate George Stigler (1982) argues that, in practice, some regulations protect firms, organizations and professional and occupational groups, instead of the general public they were intended to protect. Stigler's view causes some economists to be sceptical about the ability of regulators to correct market failure. In general, it cannot be taken for granted that governments will act in the interests of society as a whole. Governments may act at the behest of interest groups or firms, taking actions that enrich them, or they may act for the benefit of government employees or policymakers (see Barth et al., 2004, 2006; Beck et al., 2006).

In practice, the relationship between the government and the central bank in African countries has been largely umbilical. Bank regulation serves to ensure the survival of the government (the sovereign), finance the government, and sometimes finance cronies or the wealthy who have familial, political or corrupt connections with the government. Governments and their cronies have a 'grabbing hand' and political leaders look more to their personal interests than to the interests of the public. Perhaps it is plausible to argue that, in the context of Africa, although the weight of the public-versus-private interest in bank regulation varies over time, there is reasonable evidence to support the private interest view in some cases. This suggests that central banks that have very strong supervisory powers will attract political interference and possibly corruption. Indeed, Barth et al. (2006) find that domestic political factors shape bank regulations and their effectiveness.

It is useful to distinguish between microprudential and macroprudential regulation.[5] The former relates to factors that affect the stability of an individual bank or financial institution, while the latter refers to factors which affect the stability of the financial system as a whole, such as systemic problems. It follows that the nature and stance of microprudential regulation tend to be influenced by bank-specific characteristics, such as size and leverage, but they may also be influenced by how strongly the bank is linked to the rest of the banking system. In the case of macroprudential regulation, changes in the business cycle may influence changes in bank performance, and macroprudential regulation is required to reduce the adverse effects of these cycles on bank performance and the banking system in general. It has been proposed that counter-cyclical capital charges provide the way forward for future bank macroprudential regulation (see Brunnermeier et al., 2009; Jefferis, 2009). According to Brunnermeier et al. (2009), regulators should increase the existing capital adequacy requirements (based on an assessment of inherent risks) by two multiples; the first is related to above average growth of credit expansion and leverage, while the second multiple on capital charges should be related to the mismatch in the maturity of assets and liabilities (e.g. including adjustments to mark-to-market accounting).

However, since the global financial crisis, it has been argued that a review of macroprudential regulation should encompass the broader aspects of financial services regulation, such as depositor protection or deposit insurance, and the safety of the payment system. Depositor insurance schemes raise funds through levies on other authorized firms. While these funds are usually not sufficient to cover the failure of large banking institutions, or a banking crisis, they are adequate for small deposit-taking institutions, so that the costs of bank failure are not passed on to the general public. Government bailouts of 'too large to fail' banks in the global financial crisis (in the UK and US but rarely in Africa) have created a problem where taxpayers act as unpaid insurers of most transactions in wholesale banking.

Overall, in the holistic context of the flow of funds (Table 2.1) and the framework of bank regulation, it may be argued that if bank regulation is weak or poorly implemented, sectoral outcomes will suffer and the standard of living may be seriously retarded. This is worrying in the sense that if African countries get bank regulation and supervision wrong, asset creation will suffer, intersectoral flows of funds will stagnate, savings and investments will slow down, the government sector may crowd out the private sector and, consequently, particularly low living standards will languish. The question is: What is the 'right' bank regulation and supervision regime for African countries? Should African regulators apply the Basel II standards simply because 'rich countries do it'?

2.3 Evolution of bank regulation in Africa and transition from Basel I to Basel II

Arguably, the regulation of banks in Africa has evolved through three overlapping phases. The first was the pre-1960s colonial phase. Colonies and territories were served by currency boards as precursors for central banks; examples include the East African Currency Board (1919–1966) and the West African Currency Board (1912–1968). Regulation of banking business was mainly controlled from abroad. Commercial banks were mainly foreign owned, and these banks were regulated by the home country (Kirkpatrick et al., 2008). On the whole, regulation did not address public interest issues. For example, there was widespread market failure and local entrepreneurs could not access bank credit. The entrepreneurs, as Hyuha and Ddumba (1992) cite in an example from Uganda, were presumed to lack adequate business acumen, good credit histories and acceptable collateral. Rather, the type of bank regulation seems to have perpetuated the status quo, thus pointing to an aspect of regulatory failure in the context of bank intermediation among local entrepreneurs.

In the second phase, post-independence 1960s–1970s, national central banks replaced currency boards and assumed limited bank regulation, in addition to issuing national currencies and introducing monetary policy. Importantly, the new central banks intervened to address market failure by launching state-owned development banks (notably, agricultural development banks, industrial development banks and cooperative banks) to finance specific sectors. At the pan-African level, the African Development Bank (AfDB) was established in 1964 to finance long-term developmental projects. In the 1970s, regulation was invoked to attain nationalization; some countries (e.g. Uganda and Tanzania) introduced state-owned commercial banks, mainly by nationalizing foreign banks. Governments used the banks to direct credit to local entrepreneurs (Brownbridge and Harvey, 1998). However, the banks experienced principal-agent problems, especially where managers were political protégés and credit was allocated through political peddling, testimony to the private interest view of bank regulation discussed in Section 2.2. Consequently, banks suffered bad loans from government-owned agricultural and manufacturing enterprises. In Ghana, for example, 47 per cent of non-performing bank loans in 1977 were attributed to government enterprises (Brownbridge and Harvey, 1998: 64). Corruption and fraud contributed to banks' impaired loan portfolios. Although the state-owned banks were technically insolvent in some countries, there was no banking crisis in terms of banks closing down or depositor runs. These banks remained liquid and operational because they had a government guarantee.

The third phase, the Basel regime, includes the transition from Basel I to Basel II. When Basel I, also known as the 1988 Basel Accord, was initiated by the Basel Committee in 1988 and enforced by the Group of Ten (G-10) in 1992, the emphasis was on a set of minimal capital requirements for banks in order to address credit risk. Banks' assets were classified and grouped into five categories according to credit risk, carrying risk weights of zero (e.g. home country sovereign debt), 10, 20, 50 and up to 100 per cent. It was required that banks with an international presence hold capital equal to 8 per cent of their risk-weighted assets. African countries were not among the architects of the Basel Accord but, like most other countries, they adopted, at least in name, the principles prescribed in Basel I. However, in general, the efficiency with which the Basel I principles were enforced in Africa, and even within nations of the Group of Ten, varied considerably.

African countries left Basel I because it became apparent that the regulatory regime was no longer 'fit for purpose'. For example, the diagnosis and prediction of bank failures using capital requirements and early warning systems were increasingly becoming a key concern for bank regulators. Maimbo (2002) notes that bank failures in Zambia in the mid-1990s brought into question the ability of the central bank to diagnose the financial condition of banks or act promptly in implementing corrective action. However, it appears that in the transition from Basel I to Basel II, African countries jumped from the frying pan into the fire. For example, Basel II does not address the key financial risks faced by banks operating in African countries, specifically the local banks that are instrumental in financing SMEs, and microfinance banks, especially when there are too many to regulate effectively.

Because of the limitations of Basel I, the Basel Committee on Banking Supervision revised and extended the 1988 Basel Capital Accord to form Basel II. Basel II has three pillars: Pillar I on minimum capital requirements; Pillar II on the supervisory review process; and Pillar III on market discipline (Cornford, 2008). The first pillar is structured around Basel I *credit risk* considerations, but develops more extensive procedures for computing minimum bank capital requirements for *market risk* and regulatory capital requirements for *operational risk*. The requirements for minimum regulatory capital for *credit risk* are calculated using two approaches, namely the Standardized Approach (SA) and the Internal Ratings-based Approach (IRBA). The SA measures credit risk based on external credit assessments provided by external credit assessment institutions, such as credit rating agencies (e.g. Moody's, S&P and Fitch Ratings) or export credit agencies. The version of SA that is most used is the Simplified Standardized Approach (SSA), which relies on only one of the simplest options available under the SA. The IRBA has two versions: the foundation version (FIRBA), by which banks calculate the probability of default on the basis of their own ratings but rely on bank supervisors for measures of the other determinants of credit risk; and the advanced version (AIRBA), under which banks estimate their own measures of all the determinants of credit risk, including stated loss and exposure. Pillar 1 has been amended to enable banks to set minimum capital requirements for *market risks*, which may arise from adverse changes in interest rates, exchange rates and the prices of stocks and financial instruments, and could affect the bank's portfolio of tradable assets. Two alternative ways are used to set minimum capital levels for market risk: banks may use their internal risk management models (IM), or they may use a standardized methodology under which capital requirements are estimated separately for different categories of market risk. There are three options with respect to regulatory capital requirements for *operational risk*, from the simplest to the most sophisticated. The simplest is the Basic Indicator Approach (BIA), where the capital charge is a percentage of banks' gross income; the Standardized Approach for Operational Risk (SAOR), where the capital charge is the sum of percentages of banks' gross income from specified operations or, alternatively, for two of the main bank operations, namely retail and wholesale banking, of percentages of loans and advances. The most sophisticated is the Advanced Measurement Approach (AMA), where banks estimate the required capital using their own internal systems for measuring operational risk.

The second pillar sets rules for supervisory review of capital adequacy. It focuses on enhancing official supervisory practices and ensures that supervisory agencies have the power to scrutinize and discipline banks. The rules covered by Pillar 2 include setting supplementary levels of minimum regulatory capital for risks which are not covered at all, or covered inadequately by Pillar 1. The third pillar envisions greater market discipline of banks through policies that force banks to disclose accurate, transparent information.

In general, considerable debate surrounds the validity of these pillars. Barth et al. (2006) present a comprehensive database on the banking regulations of more than 150 countries. It offers the first comprehensive cross-country assessment of the impact of bank regulation on the operation of banks, and assesses the validity of the Basel Committee's influential approach to bank regulation. Their research, conducted at a time of heated debate on Basel II, throws some light on the three main pillars. For example, with respect to Pillar 1, the evidence does not suggest that capital regulations have a significant impact on bank development, efficiency, stability or corruption (see Mullineux et al., 2003). This finding is attributed to the harmonization of national capital regulations which makes it difficult to establish a relationship between capital regulations and bank performance. However, the lack of clear evidence on the beneficial effects of current capital regulations may reflect the inadequacy of the Basel I capital regulations and the need for implementing Basel II, or it may well be the case that banks tend to evade capital regulations. Regarding the second pillar of Basel II, it is found that strengthening official supervisory powers tends to make things worse, not better. Unless the country is 'top ten' in terms of the development of its political institutions, the evidence suggests that strengthening official supervisory powers damages bank development and leads to greater corruption in bank lending without any compensating positive effects. Regarding the third pillar, on market discipline, it is found that regulations requiring informational transparency and which strengthen the ability and incentives of the private sector to monitor banks tend to promote sound banking. Hence, Barth et al. (2006) conclude that strengthening capital standards or empowering supervisors do not boost bank efficiency, reduce corruption in lending or reduce banking system fragility. Rather, what is more promising is to introduce reforms that place far more emphasis on policies that promote market discipline, such as disclosure requirements and transparency in the banking sector and better private-sector monitoring of banks, rather than on regulations that often tend to translate into discretionary abuse (see also Barth et al., 2004, 2006; and Beck et al., 2006).

In addition, the global financial crisis has provoked some questions about whether the existing bank regulatory systems are 'fit for purpose'. The argument is that the regulation of banks must do more than instil best practice amongst bankers, or converge regulatory capital to prudential capital. Brunnermeier et al. (2009) observe that current bank regulatory systems are imperfect because they implicitly assume that the whole banking system can be made safe by simply trying to ensure that individual banks are safe. Banks and other financial institutions try to improve their safety by behaving in ways that collectively undermine the system. For example, an individual bank may try to sell an asset when the price of risk increases but if many banks act in a similar manner, the asset price will collapse, forcing institutions to take even further steps to rectify the situation, and leading to generalized declines in asset prices and increased correlations and volatility in asset markets. This type of endogeneity of risk is more pronounced when there is a common denominator, such as a financial crisis, which destabilizes banks individually and engenders bank fragility (a perverse effect, contrary to the intended result of 'financial stability').

Another issue raised by Basel II is the role of ratings agencies. The global financial crisis has shown that granting regulatory significance to ratings by private agencies for Basel II was a disastrous mistake; it stimulated extensive regulatory arbitrage. The widespread consensus is that these ratings should no longer play any role in financial services (see Kay, 2009). The agencies should not be regulated, rather, their role is to inform investors in the marketplace instead of regulators.

It is not surprising that progress with Basel II in Africa has been rather slow. In a survey on how countries are progressing with the adoption of Basel II, Cornford (2008) found that, as of mid-2008, only 12 countries in Africa intended to adopt Basel II, out of a total of 17 countries that responded to the survey.

The dynamics and status quo of African countries are also interesting. As shown in Table 2.2, the results obtained by Cornford (2008) suggest that not many African countries had been converted to adopting Basel II by 2008, compared to the initial survey conducted by the BIS (2004). In terms of Pillar 1, the results in the table show that the African countries that responded to the survey intended to adopt the SA for credit risk and the BIA for operational risk, which is consistent with earlier surveys in 2004. But there seems to be an increase in the percentage of countries intending to introduce both the SA and the FIRBA for credit risk, and the BIA and the SAOR for operational risk by 2009. The same finding

Table 2.2 Percentages of African country respondents to survey on Basel II

Pillar 1			
Credit risk	Standardized approach (SA)	Foundation version of the internal ratings-based approach (FIRBA)	Advanced version of the internal ratings-based approach (AIRBA)
2007	17	0	0
2009	58	25	8
Operational risk	Basic Indicator Approach (BIA)	Standardized Approach for Operational Risk (SAOR)	Advanced Measurement Approach (AMA)
2007	17	17	0
2009	42	33	17
Pillar 2	Percentage response (out of the 12 African countries that responded)		
2007	25		
2009	75		
Pillar 3	Percentage response (out of the 12 African countries that responded)		
2007	17		
2009	75		

Source: Cornford (2008: 5).

is obtained with respect to Pillars 2 and 3. The figures in Table 2.2 also show that a higher percentage of African countries intended to introduce Pillars 2 and 3 by 2009, which suggests a widespread tendency by the respondents to prioritize the implementation of Basel II with respect to strengthening supervisory capacity and disclosure standards. There are many reasons why most African countries have been slow in implementing Pillars 2 and 3, namely limitations on supervisory capacity; lack of historical data, which is a big problem for the adoption of the IRBA as well as to risk-based supervision and capital management more generally; and problems regarding transparency and financial reporting. However, the data in the above table implies that most respondents perhaps did address these problems, given that there was an increase in the percentage of countries intending to adopt the FIRBA for credit risk and Pillars 2 and 3 by 2009. Of course, caution must be exercised with these results: a response of 32 per cent (17 countries out of 53) is not impressive for generating an African position; the survey reports up to 2009 and a more recent survey are required to update this information.

In order to identify a clear direction at the crossroads, future research on Africa should explore the determinants of bank supervisory and regulatory choices in selected groups of African countries. Current knowledge seems to suggest that countries with more open, competitive, democratic political systems that have effective constraints on executive power tend to adopt an approach to bank supervision and regulation that relies more on private monitoring, imposes fewer regulatory restrictions on bank activities and the entry of new banks, and has less of a role for government-owned banks. By contrast, countries with more closed uncompetitive autocratic political institutions that impose ineffective constraints on the executive tend to rely less on private monitoring, impose more restrictions on bank activities and new bank entry, and create a bigger role for government banks. These findings underscore the difficulty in deriving uniform best practice guidelines globally.

2.4 Africa at the bank regulatory crossroads?

African countries were encouraged to adopt Basel II with no empirical evidence to support the choice. So, in the debate outlined above focusing on Africa, there are three main questions. First, does Basel II suit the needs of African banks? Second, how can Africa have bank supervisors with state-of-the-art risk modelling skills but without the

Table 2.3 Central bank as supervisory authority

Central bank only	Multiple bank supervisors, including the central bank	Central bank, not supervisory authority
Botswana	Morocco	Algeria
Burundi	Nigeria	Benin
Egypt		Burkina Faso
Gambia		Cameroon
Ghana		Central African Republic
Lesotho		Chad
Libya		Côte d'Ivoire
Namibia		Gabon
Rwanda		Guinea Bissau
South Africa		Kenya
Sudan		Madagascar
Swaziland		Mali
Tunisia		Niger
Uganda		Senegal
Zimbabwe		Togo

Source: Barth et al. (2006) updated.

accompanying higher compensation? The biggest challenge to African banks and regulators is the measurement and management of credit. Third, what do African banks need?

There is also the question of whether the central bank is still the supervisory authority in African economies. As shown in Table 2.3, which is updated from Barth et al. (2006), there appear to be three main categories: the group of African countries where the central bank is the only regulatory and supervisory authority; the group of countries where there are multiple bank supervisors, including the central bank; and the group where the central bank is not the supervisory authority and possibly a quasi-autonomous agency is the supervisory authority. It is interesting that the majority of African countries fall in the first and third categories, which represent polar cases of the public-versus-private view of bank regulation in Africa.

Globally, bank regulation has become merely one component of financial services regulation, and a range of the regulatory functions which used to be the responsibility of self-regulating agencies have been nationalized and are performed by public agencies. Examples include stock exchanges and the control systems of banks. The information on Africa in Table 2.3 seems to point to the same development, which is not ideal because these regulatory functions (which have been nationalized elsewhere in the world) are not more effectively performed by public agencies. As noted by Kay (2009), the main issue is whether the greater power of enforcement that comes from the authority of the public agency does offset the informational disadvantage experienced by an external regulator.

In addition, it should be taken into consideration that the global crisis developed during the transition from Basel I to Basel II for many African countries, thus aggravating a process that was rather slow, mainly because of resource constraints and data requirements. The global financial crisis has, therefore, complicated the transition from Basel I to Basel II for most African economies, which raises the question: how does Africa adopt the very tools that proved impotent in the face of the global financial crisis?

Jefferis (2009) summarizes the viewpoints of African central bankers on the implications of the global financial crisis for bank regulation, drawing on a report of the key findings of a survey commissioned by AfDB and GTZ about selected African central banks in Eastern and Southern Africa. Key issues include the impact of changing the international supervisory environment of African regulators; cross-border supervisory issues; new challenges, for example, macroprudential supervision; adequacy of voice; role of governments in the financial sector; and capital account liberalization.

Given the crisis, the process of moving beyond the standardized approach of Pillar 1 of Basel II is more problematic. But there are also human capital needs to be able to deal with new models and collect required data, given the paucity of the expertise in many central banks in Africa. In addition, except for Nigeria and South Africa, the lack of local credit rating agencies is a major problem. Moreover, risk weights have gone up globally and this will reduce lending to Africa, and counter-cyclical capital requirements make Basel II adoption even more challenging. Higher capital requirements for African banks may not be a major concern because capital requirements exceed Basel I requirements in most countries.

There is also *the locus of regulation*; there are some transnational regulation issues arising from cross-border supervision, especially non-convergence of national and international regulation (for example by foreign banks). The evidence is that cross-border banking in Africa is growing in importance involving foreign banks from Europe, the US and India as well as intra-African banking groups from South Africa, Nigeria, Kenya and Morocco, among others (Murinde and Ryan, 2003). The key to effective cross-border supervision is information symmetry by sharing data between home–host supervisors, and cooperation (by drawing up memoranda of agreement, for example). However, some risks may persist, such as small countries which may be marginalized by banks from larger countries. Regional collaboration initiatives have not been explored, for example between SADC and EAC.

In addition, African central banks have not fully adopted macroprudential supervision responsibilities, which involve supervision at systemic level (financial stability) to complement the supervision of institutions. Macroprudential supervisory units do exist, but there are many practical challenges facing them, including: identifying macroprudential indicators to be monitored; gathering data and models to be used for stress tests; pinpointing the critical trigger levels to justify intervention; and capacity building to link research and the regulatory or supervisory functions of the central bank. Many African countries are being encouraged to follow the example of South Africa, which has a fully-fledged financial stability department that is distinct from bank regulation.

There is also the issue of lack of 'voice' in the Basel II revisions: the interests of poor and small African countries are not sufficiently represented in global forums where key decisions are being made. Only South Africa represents Africa on the BIS and Basel Committee. There is limited regular consultation between South Africa and the 14 member countries of SADC, and Africa relies on the IMF to represent the African voice.

But there are also problems related to recent changes in the structure of banking in Africa that make the regulatory crossroads very perplexing, for example the emergence of Islamic banking. As Murinde (2010) points out, the first modern experiment with Islamic banking in Africa was in Egypt in 1963, and by 1967 there were nine Islamic banks. Islamic banking assets in North Africa, West Africa and East Africa grew rapidly in the 1980s–1990s, and by early 2010 Islamic banks were operating in 38 out of 53 African countries, while the banking system is almost wholly Islamized in the Sudan. Unlike conventional banks, which rely on interest rates for asset pricing, Islamic banks in Africa use some novel financial instruments in their operations, underpinned by Islamic law (*Shariah*) that prohibits the payment of interest on bank deposits or loans, which is regarded as usury. Also forbidden is investment in enterprises that involve alcohol, pork or gambling, which makes it akin to ethical investments (see Khalil et al., 2002). Some of these instruments are tailored to fulfil risk management and monitoring roles or even a poverty reduction role, as in Senegal. However, many central banks in Africa have yet to develop adequate capacity to supervise and regulate Islamic banking (either Islamic financial institutions or Islamic windows).

2.5 Concluding remarks: the way ahead

This chapter highlights some landmarks in the evolution of bank regulation in Africa, especially the transition from Basel I to Basel II, and hazards a conjecture on the future path for an effective regulatory regime, post-crisis. The chapter invokes a flow-of-funds framework to provide a holistic perspective of bank regulation: the argument is that the regulation not only revolves around financial intermediation, but it also involves institutional, legal and political environments. The main lessons are threefold. First, African countries have achieved the transition of their regulations from Basel I to Basel II but post-crisis the countries are stuck at a crossroads – it is important to involve these countries actively in the ongoing architecture of Basel III. Second, the participation of these countries is not merely for the sake of stakeholder ownership, but also for wider implications such as mitigating the spectre of regulatory arbitrage. Third, one key lesson from the failure of Basel I and Basel II in Africa and elsewhere is that the proposed Basel III regime must go beyond market risk concerns; it must represent development-enabling regulation. For example, simple regulatory tools for microfinance banking not only ensure financial stability but they also reinforce social protection.

In general, it is useful to recognize why it was necessary to move from Basel I to Basel II, and also what the international regulatory system offers for banks globally. In addition, it is important to note three further points. First, the Bank for International Settlement (BIS) has no legislative authority, thus Basel II constitutes a set of recommendations for national regulators to tailor the Basel II pillars to country needs for bank regulation and supervision. Second, Basel II is not 'one size fits all'; it tries to meet different risk requirements in different countries, as can be seen from the options available under Pillar 1, for example. Third, the Basel Committee has attempted to offer a consultative process throughout the transition from Basel I to Basel II; for example, the consultation at the time of writing is about strengthening the resilience of the banking sector and the international framework for liquidity risk measurement standards, with monitoring and input required from country regulators and the public by 16 April 2010. However, Kay (2009: 9) sums it up very well:

> The lesson of the failure of the Basel accords is not that the regime should be elaborated beyond the 400 pages of text in the current accords. It is that the whole system should be swept away, and the responsibility for capital adequacy and risk management be put back where it belongs – in the hands of the executive of banks, who should then carry heavy and exclusive responsibility for failure of control. There must be a better way. There is. It involves a combination of tighter, but more narrowly focused, regulation and a larger role for competition and market forces.

African countries must leave the crossroads for an alternative model of bank supervision that virtually amounts to Basel III. The current framework (Basel II) has always been controversial but the global financial crisis provides the basis for Africa and other developing countries to come out with a strong voice that tells the Basel Committee to start over again. Importantly, the 'voice' has to be convincing, so it behoves all of us, policymakers and researchers alike, to produce waterproof evidence as to how and why the bank regulation dilemma in Africa has to be addressed by a new standard.

The evidence should address the following areas:

- The most immediate action is to secure access for Africa to the G-20 meetings in Korea in November 2010 so that Africa is represented and can effectively participate in the development agenda of these meetings. This action recognizes that while the G-20 goes beyond the initial G-8 in membership and mandate, Africa and other lowest income countries are still excluded from participation and setting the agenda of the G-20, as well as directly shaping the intensity of the debate on procedures and policy strategies for the key development challenges. The G-20 has to show that the transition from G-8 governance of the world marks a genuine step forward; the G-20 cannot be dominated by 20 countries which represent the bulk of GDP but not most of the world's population which are in the world's poorest countries. They strive for development opportunities, including adequate financing.
- The other immediate action relates to *Africa's voice in post-crisis bank regulatory reform*, to secure Africa's access to, and voice in, the ongoing international architecture of bank regulation in terms of the proposed enhancements of the Basel II framework and the framework for adherence to international standards by the Financial Stability

Board (FSB). The financial crisis severely tested the Basel II framework that integrated traditional bank lending and capital market activities, especially during the transition from Basel I to Basel II in many African countries. Although the crisis has slowed the momentum of regulatory reforms in Africa, it has not derailed ongoing work. But the rules of the regulatory game are changing globally and African countries are articulating what they need from the new bank regulation architecture. It is useful to note that Africa had no say in past regulatory reforms, and recent reforms of international regulatory bodies leave African countries virtually voiceless (e.g. Africa has 1/44 members of the FSB). The AfDB and African Economic Research Consortium (AERC) commend the African Committee of 10 (C-10), which represents African finance ministers and central bank governors, as an effective representation in the ongoing work of Basel reform and the innovations in the FSB. The C-10 is active post-crisis and represents the best efforts by African countries to deal with the peculiarities of financial regulation and the development financing agendas of these countries. It is hoped that the AfDB, as Secretariat of the C-10, would facilitate Africa's inputs into the discussion on banking regulation reforms that are coordinated by the FSB and the Basel Committee.

- The other important next step is towards enhancing *Africa's role in sharing information for transnational regulation*. Africa takes seriously this role, which arises from cross-border supervision, to reduce information asymmetry and non-convergence of national and international regulation, especially where large foreign banks are heavily involved in small poor economies. Specifically, Africa cannot effectively regulate foreign bank subsidiaries without strong information-sharing with home regulators. Here, the key to effective cross-border supervision is information symmetry by sharing data between home–host supervisors and cooperation, by exploring mechanisms such as a Memorandum of Understanding (MoU). As a lead, the US should sign MoUs to share information among US and host-country African supervisors. This point arises from research evidence which shows that cross-border banking in Africa is growing in importance (e.g. foreign banks from Europe, US, India and intra-African banking groups, from South Africa, Nigeria, Kenya, Morocco and so on). The point also arises from the experience in Africa that, before the financial crisis, Africa was repeatedly hit by the collapse of global banks (BCCI, Meridien) due to inadequate home-country regulation, poor communication of problems by regulatory authorities, and attempts by banks to hide problems in bank branches in low income countries, including Africa. Also, past African banking crises have been exacerbated by the export of bank capital to tax havens.

- Another key issue relates to *risk weighting in the design of new regulatory architecture*. The financial crisis exposed the unreliability of risk weights produced by the key rating agencies (S&P, Moody's and Fitch Ratings) as a market-discipline component of bank regulation. Bank risk was undervalued. Post-crisis, the issue of regulating credit rating agencies to avoid exacerbating financial instability is on the table for discussion, especially in African countries that do not have the capacity to generate their own risk rating metrics. A key unresolved issue is how to measure and assign risk weights to the mix of banking services, in both small and large banking markets. Specifically for Africa, regulation needs to allow for flexibility in remodelling risk-weighted assets, especially where foreign banks dominate; for example, giving project finance a higher risk weight as opposed to residential mortgage lending may influence how credit is allocated in the real economy and hence address the issue of making access to finance easier in Africa. African researchers should continue to look into this issue and produce prototype models, information notes and policy briefs in order to inform the ongoing discussions within the C-10 and the broader international forums.
- What institutional, political and legal settings favour effective bank regulation and supervision in Africa? The work by Barth et al. (2006) provides striking evidence from data across the world that strengthening the discretionary powers of prudential supervisors in countries with weak institutional environments leads to lower level of bank development, greater corruption in lending and banks that are less safe and sound. The message to policymakers in Africa is that *'best practice' for advanced countries may not work for developing countries*; in this context, simply following the Basel II recommendation of strengthening supervisory powers has to accompanied by substantial progress in institutional development and political setting.
- Regarding the design of the interbank market in specific African countries: how does this market work? Barth et al. (2006) conclude that regulation works best when it facilitates market forces. Hence, the most relevant part of Pillar III of Basel II for Africa is the interbank market. Bank regulatory policies that enable private markets to better monitor banks and that encourage private actors to 'discipline' banks are associated with desirable outcomes, specifically, the interbank market provides the market discipline component of regulation,

in addition to its apparent role in managing liquidity and hence monetary policy. Studies that document the microstructure of the interbank market in Africa (e.g. nature of participants, prices, quantities, information arrival, transaction costs) and how the market is evolving, are very timely. Moreover, this market is most strategic in maintaining the interbank confidence. One lesson from the financial crisis is that when the interbank market in the UK and US went comatose, government intervention could not resuscitate the market.

- What aspects of microprudential and macroprudential regulation work best, separately or jointly, in specific case studies in Africa? Barth et al. (2006) find that about the same number of countries (69) set up their central banks as the sole bank supervisory agency as those who do not provide the central bank with any supervisory power (61). Hence, the central bank is not always the supervisor authority. Quasi-autonomous bank regulation and supervision is good for Africa to minimize the 'private interest view' of regulation. Effective bank regulation and supervision should achieve the microprudential role, mainly through 'market discipline', and the macroprudential role of financial stability to reduce systemic risk through a quasi-government agency. Would this approach resolve the 'too big to fail' problem, as many large banks are emerging in large African countries? To be of any value for banks in African economies, a new regulatory regime must encompass this dual role.
- What types of information asymmetry characterize the banking market in Africa? The lesson from Stiglitz (2001) is that the nature of information asymmetries matters and hence there is a role for the public view of regulation. If the agents in the banking market have the same level of information, or 'symmetric information', the central bank does not have to intervene in the market. However, in Africa, information asymmetries are more pronounced in specific banking areas, such as microfinance institutions, hence it is not possible to regulate effectively all microfinance institutions in countries where there are too many and pose the greatest prudential risk to their customers, as noted by Brownbridge and Kirkpatrick (2002). Identification of information asymmetries should help in generating a consolidated set of core principles for regulating microfinance institutions, including tools for monitoring unsafe and unsound practices and exit policies.
- Simplicity does it: the 'narrow banking' model for Africa? Let us remind ourselves about the Adam Smith dictum, because sometimes human nature tends to take very complex models such as Basel II

as simply the most effective when, in fact, what is required is a simple formula. In instances where the banking systems are very simple and basic (e.g. Group C), why do we need VaR models for which we cannot collect the data, let alone run the model competently? The narrow banking model is likely to keep depositors' funds safely tucked away from rogue traders (those who chase some flattering speculation of extraordinary gain), increase competition and refocus regulators on protecting retail customers and essential services from the fallout of failure which characterized the outbreak of the global financial crisis. So, essentially, the narrow banking model breaks up the banks into the category of banks that accept retail deposits and access the payment system, and the 'casino' category for financial markets. More importantly for Africa, narrow banking might facilitate lending to SMEs.

- The payment systems in Africa comprised the most likely casualty in case of bank contagion during the global financial crisis. The payment systems in most African countries are mainly unregulated and are driven by banks in the OECD, whether they use Real Time Gross Settlement (RTGS), Batch Payment System (e.g. BACS), the Card System (usually VISA and Mastercard) or the cash system. Innovations, such as M-PESA in Kenya, which is a mobile phone-based payment system, should be self-regulated.
- There is also the issue of a *contingent fund for future financial crises.* In particular, the issue is that African countries are not in a position to finance large bailout plans in the event of major bank failures. One proposal under discussion is to introduce a financial transactions tax on bank balance sheets in order to build a fund against the contingent liability that could arise when banks fail. The proposal may be appealing for Africa for two reasons. First, for African economies the option of bank bailouts is not only inadequate but also not feasible. Second, Africa recognizes the need to be part of the international harmonization of financial transactions tax in order to eliminate the possibility of banks getting involved in regulatory arbitrage and tax arbitrage, especially by global banks which are too big to fail, and may threaten the stability of banking systems in small economies.

All in all, it is useful to highlight at least three observations that require urgent attention. First, African countries have amended their regulation from Basel I to Basel II but post-crisis the countries are stuck at a crossroads – going back to Basel I or Basel II is not an option and yet most of the emerging themes for Basel III are merely tangential to the concerns of developing economies. It is important to involve these countries actively in the ongoing architecture of Basel III. Second, the participation of these countries in the architecture of Basel III is not merely for the sake of stakeholder ownership, but also for wider implications such as sharing of information and coordinated enforcement of rules to mitigate the spectre of regulatory arbitrage – a major re-occurrence under Basel I and Basel II was that some banks would migrate across countries seeking to exploit differences in enforcement of the rules. Third, one key lesson from the failure of Basel I and Basel II in Africa and elsewhere is that the proposed Basel III regime must go beyond market risk concerns; it must represent development-enabling regulation. For example, in African countries, where microfinance and financing of small and medium enterprises are core activities to break away from poverty, simple regulatory tools for microfinance banking not only ensure banking stability but they also reinforce social protection mechanisms in force.

Notes

1. The terms regulation and supervision are used interchangeably; strictly, they are not. Supervision is wide ranging, tends to grow in scope and is subject to regulatory capture, whereas regulation is more focused (see Kay, 2009).
2. See, in particular, Tobin and Brainard (1968), Green (1992), Green and Murinde (1998, 2004, 2005).
3. The implementation of flow-of-funds accounts in official statistics follows the UN System of National Accounts (United Nations, 1968 and 1993).
4. Broadly, there are three types of market failure in banking: (a) fraud; (b) systemic risk; and (c) information asymmetry.
5. These two are consistent with the 'twin peaks' model by Taylor (2009), which sets out two fundamental objectives for financial regulation. The first is to ensure the stability and soundness of the financial system or 'systemic protection', while the second is 'consumer protection' or protecting individual depositors, investors and policy holders to the extent that they cannot reasonably be expected to protect their own interests.

References

Barth, J.R., G. Caprio, Jr. and R. Levine. 2004. 'Bank regulation and supervision: What works best?' *Journal of Financial Intermediation*, 12: 205–48.

Barth, J.R., G. Caprio, Jr. and R. Levine. 2006. *Rethinking Bank Regulation: Till Angels Govern*. Cambridge: Cambridge University Press.

Beck, T., A. Demirguc-Kunt and R. Levine. 2006. 'Bank supervision and corruption in lending'. *Journal of Monetary Economics*, 53: 2131–63.

Brana, S. and D. Lahet. 2009. 'Capital requirement and financial crisis: The case of Japan and the 1997 Asian crisis'. *Japan and the World Economy*, 21: 97–104.

Brownbridge, M. and C. Harvey. 1998. *Banking in Africa – The Impact of Financial Sector Reform since Independence*. Oxford: James Currey Ltd.

Brownbridge, M. and C. Kirkpatrick. 2002. 'Financial regulation and supervision in developing countries: An overview'. *Development Policy Review*, 20(3): 243–5.

Brunnermeier, M., A. Crockett, C. Goodhart, A.D. Persaud and H. Shin. 2009. *The Fundamental Principles of Financial Regulation*. Geneva & London: ICMB & CEPR.

Cornford, A. 2008. Introduction to Basel 2: the Current State of Play. Paper prepared for the G24 Technical Group Meeting, 8–9 September. UN Headquarters, Geneva.

Fleming, A.E. and M.M. Giugale. 2000. *Financial Systems in Transition*. Singapore: World Scientific.

Goodhart, C.A.E. 2008. 'The background to the 2007 financial crisis'. *International Economics and Economic Policy*, 4: 331–46.

Green, C.J. 1992. 'The flow of funds'. In P. Newman, M. Milgate and J. Eatwell (eds.), *The New Palgrave Dictionary of Money and Finance*. London: Macmillan.

Green, C.J. and V. Murinde. 1998. 'Modelling the macroeconomic policy framework for an emerging market economy'. *The Manchester School*, 66: 302–30.

Green, C.J. and V. Murinde. 2004. 'Flow of funds: Implications for research on financial sector development and the real economy'. *Journal of International Development*, 15: 1015–36.

Green, C.J. and V. Murinde. 2005. 'Flow of funds: the relationship between finance and the macroeconomy'. In C.J. Green, C.H. Kirkpatrick and V. Murinde (eds.), *Finance and Development: Surveys of Theory, Evidence and Policy*. Cheltenham: Edward Elgar.

Green, C.J., C. Kirkpatrick and V. Murinde. 2005. *Finance and Development: Surveys of Theory, Evidence and Policy*. Cheltenham: Edward Elgar.

Han, K.C., S.H. Lee and D.Y. Suk. 2003. 'Mexican peso crisis and its spillover effects to emerging market debt'. *Emerging Markets Review*, 4(3): 310–26.

Hyuha, M. and J.S. Ddumba. 1992. 'Financial decline in Uganda'. Paper presented to the Uganda Economics Society, 20 November.

Jackson, K.D. 1999. *Asian Contagion: The Causes and Consequences of a Financial Crisis*. Boulder, Co: Westview Press.

Jefferis, K. 2009. 'The new world of banks, governments, regulation and supervision – viewpoints from African central banks'. Paper presented at Catham House Seminar on Financial Systems Reforms: The Implications for Non-G20 Countries, 15 October.

Kasekende, L., K. Mlambo and V. Murinde. 2010. 'A comparative overview of bank regulatory experiences and impact on bank competition and intermediation efficiency in Africa'. AERC SPS-XII Mombasa, 22–24 March.

Kay, J. 2009. *Narrow Banking: The Reform of Banking Regulation*. London: CSFI.

Khalil, A., C. Rickwood and V. Murinde. 2002. 'Agency contractual problems in profit-sharing financing practices by Islamic banks'. In M. Iqbal and D. Llewellyn (eds.), *Islamic Banking and Finance: New Perspectives on Profit-Sharing and Risk*. Cheltenham: Edward Elgar.

Kirkpatrick, C.H., V. Murinde and M. Tefula. 2008. 'The measurement and determinants of X-inefficiency in commercial banks in sub-Saharan Africa'. *European Journal of Finance*, 14(7): 625–39.

Klein, L.R. 2000. 'Preface'. In A.E. Fleming and M.M. Giugale (eds.), *Financial Systems in Transition*. Singapore: World Scientific.

Maimbo, S.M. 2002. 'The diagnosis and prediction of bank failures in Zambia, 1990–98'. *Development Policy Review*, 20(3): 261–78.

Matthews, K., V. Murinde and T. Zhao. 2007. 'Competitive conditions among the major British banks'. *Journal of Banking and Finance*, 31(7): 2025–42.

Mizen, P. 2008. 'The credit crunch of 2007–2008: A discussion of the background, market reactions, and policy responses'. *Federal Reserve Bank of St. Louis Review*, 90(5): 531–67.

Moore, T., C.J. Green and V. Murinde. 2006a. 'Financial reforms and stochastic policy simulations: A flow-of-funds model'. *Journal of Policy Modelling*, 28: 319–33.

Moore, T., C.J. Green and V. Murinde. 2006b. 'Portfolio behaviour in a flow-of-funds model of the household sector'. *Journal of Development Studies*, 41: 675–702.

Mullineux, A.W., V. Murinde and A. Pinijkulviwat. 2003. 'Financial reform in Thailand'. In M.J.B. Hall (ed.), *The International Handbook on Financial Reform*. Cheltenham: Edward Elgar.

Murinde, V. 2010. 'Banks and credit markets in Africa'. In E. Aryeetey and L. Kasekende (eds.), *The African Companion*. Oxford: Oxford University Press.

Murinde, V. and C. Ryan. 2003. 'The implications of WTO and GATS for the banking sector in Africa'. *The World Economy*, 26(2): 181–207.

Radelet, S., J.D. Sachs, R.N. Cooper and B.P. Bosworth. 1998. 'The East Asian financial crisis: Diagnosis, remedies, prospects'. *Brookings Papers on Economic Activity*, 1: 1–90.

Sharma, S. 2001. 'The missed lessons of the Mexican peso crisis'. *Challenge*, 44(1): 56–89.

Sojli, E. 2007. 'Contagion in emerging markets: the Russian crisis'. *Applied Financial Economics*, 17(3): 197–213.

Stigler, G.J. 1982. 'The Process and Progress of Economics', Nobel Memorial Lecture, 8 December.

Stiglitz, J.E. 2001. 'Principles of financial regulation: A dynamic portfolio approach'. *World Bank Research Observer*, 16: 1–16.

Taylor, M.W. 2009. *Twin Peaks Revisited: A Second Chance for Regulatory Reform*. London: CSFI.

Tobin, J. and W.C. Brainard. 1968. 'Pitfalls in financial model building'. *American Economic Review Paper and Proceedings*, 58: 99–122.

United Nations Department of Economics and Social Affairs. 1968. *A System of National Accounts*. Studies in Methods, Series F, No. 2. United Nations, New York.

United Nations Department of Economics and Social Affairs. 1993. *Revised System of National Accounts*. Studies in Methods, Series F, No. 2, United Nations, New York.

3
Comparative Overview of Bank Regulatory Experiences and the Impact on Bank Competition and Intermediation Efficiency in Africa

Kupukile Mlambo, Louis Kasekende and Victor Murinde

3.1 Introduction

It is widely acknowledged by researchers as well as policymakers and practitioners that there is a positive relationship between finance and growth. Claessens and Laeven (2004), Green et al. (2005), Levine and Demirgüç-Kunt (2009) and Kirkpatrick et al. (2008) present evidence with respect to African economies. The link between finance and growth is especially important at this stage of financial globalization, when African countries are trying to recover from the first-round effects of the global financial crisis that started in late 2007 with the subprime mortgage crisis in the United States. The paradox is that, notwithstanding the positive finance–growth nexus, the financial sector in Africa featured the main contagion vehicles of the global financial crisis, namely the capital and foreign exchange markets.

Moreover, it is well known that competition in the financial services sector in Africa has important implications, especially for enhancing productive efficiency, financial stability and effective regulation and supervision of the banking sector. These implications have possible positive spillover effects into the rest of the economy, or indeed from one African country to the rest of the continent.[1] The argument is that competition stimulates productivity growth, either through general technical progress or through improved efficiency, or both. It is also argued that competition exacerbates the moral hazard problem of financial institutions, especially banks. The main lesson for policymakers is that, in order to achieve a highly competitive banking sector, African countries must undertake some fundamental reforms, especially with respect to bank regulation and supervision. But, the question is: what type of reforms and with what dynamics?

The recent financial crisis has highlighted the need for regulation in a liberalized global finance environment. This regulation primarily concerns the banks which were, to a great extent, the root cause of the crisis, through granting and, subsequently, securitizing subprime loans to risky borrowers. The issue of banking regulation is acute, particularly in countries where bank intermediation is dominant, as is the case with many African counties.

This chapter provides a comparative overview of bank regulatory experiences and the impact on bank competition and intermediation efficiency, based on national case studies from Africa.[2]

3.2 Overview of financial sector in Africa

During the late 1980s and 1990s many African countries started implementing financial sector reforms as part of overall economic reforms, the objective being to build financial markets which were more efficient, robust and deeper. The first phase of these reforms focused on changing policy, including liberalizing interest rates and removing quantitative controls, lifting barriers to entry and privatizing state-owned financial institutions. While these reforms liberalized financial markets, they did not deal adequately with structural and institutional issues (Evans, et al., 2002; Matthews, et al., 2007). Oligopolistic structures, combined with inadequate regulation and supervision of financial markets, allowed interest rate spreads to widen and limited efficiency gains. In the second phase of reforms, the focus shifted to strengthening the financial infrastructure (especially the regulatory frameworks, including the supervisory capacity of the banking system) and emphasizing central bank independence. Recently, more emphasis is being put on corporate governance issues, including enhancing transparency and accountability, improving information and disclosures requirements, investor education and better accounting and auditing standards that meet international requirements.

Overall, the financial sector has been improving since the implementation of reforms. Although still very low, financial depth has increased, with liquid liabilities as a share of GDP, as a measure of financial depth, increasing from 36 per cent in 2000 to 42 per cent in 2008 (see Table 3.1). The comparative figure for East Asia was 141 per cent of GDP. The ratio

Table 3.1 Key financial indicators for selected African countries

	Private credit/ GDP (%)			Liquid liabilities/ GDP (%)			Bank NPLs/ total loans (%)		Market capitalization (%)		
	2000	2007	2008	2000	2007	2008	2000	2007	2000	2007	2008
Algeria	6	13	13	38	60	58	–	–	–	–	–
Botswana	14	20	22	23	43	44	2	–	16	48	27
Egypt	59	51	43	83	96	88	14	–	29	107	53
Ghana	14	18	–	28	34	–	12	6	10	16	21
Kenya	28	27	26	38	44	38	33	23	10	50	32
Morocco	51	70	80	74	105	106	18	8	29	101	76
Nigeria	12	25	33	22	28	36	23	8	9	52	23
South Africa	134	164	80	54	48	69	3	1	154	294	178
Tunisia	73	72	73	58	64	67	22	17	15	15	16
Tanzania	5	15	16	20	28	30	–	–	3	–	6
Zambia	9	12	15	24	23	24	24	11	7	21	–
SSA	61	71	40	36	35	42	–	–	90	149	–
East Asia	101	99	100	117	137	141	–	–	47	159	58

Source: World Bank, World Development Indicators Database; see World Bank (2010).

of private sector credit to GDP, which is a proxy for bank intermediation, increased between 2000 and 2007 but declined in 2008. At the individual country level, South Africa's financial markets dwarf those of other African countries, with the possible exception of North African countries. South Africa also has one of the largest stock markets in the world, with a market capitalization of 178 per cent in 2008, compared with an average market capitalization of 58 per cent for Asia.

African financial markets are now much freer and the banking system has improved through stronger balance sheets and capital bases, while risk management has been enhanced. For countries where data is available, the quality of bank loans has improved (see Table 3.1). In Nigeria, where bank restructuring and consolidation was recently implemented, the share of non-performing loans in total loans declined from 23 per cent in 2000 to 8 per cent in 2007. Table 3.2 shows the efficiency and stability indicators for selected African and Brazil, Russia, India and China (BRIC) countries. The net interest margin, which is a proxy for efficiency, shows an improvement in countries such as Botswana, Kenya, Nigeria, Tanzania and Zambia. The bank cost-to-income ratio, which is another efficiency measure, but from the cost side, improved in Algeria, Kenya, Nigeria, South Africa and Zambia.

A useful measure of bank soundness is the z-score, where a higher score implies a lower probability of insolvency risk. In general, African

Table 3.2 Bank performance indicators for selected African countries and BRICs

	Net interest margin (%)		**Bank cost-income ratio (%)**		**Bank z-score**	
	2000	**2007**	**2000**	**2007**	**2000**	**2007**
Algeria	3.7	6.4	50.6	45.8	9.5	8.2
Botswana	8.1	5.2	43.9	53.2	12.8	13.6
Egypt	2.2	2.1	47.9	53.3	7.9	5.0
Kenya	7.6	6.5	74.9	56.0	7.0	6.1
Nigeria	8.4	5.4	61.5	54.7	3.6	11.6
South Africa	4.7	7.2	57.9	55.2	9.5	5.0
Tanzania	7.8	6.5	76.3	78.2	3.8	6.8
Zambia	12.0	9.1	68.8	54.0	6.6	6.6
BRICs						
Brazil	10.5	14.1	81.6	69.3	4.2	6.2
Russia	7.5	6.0	85.3	66.3	1.9	6.6
India	3.2	2.8	60.0	47.7	6.1	8.8
China	2.1	2.6	68.3	39.7	13.7	15.7

Source: Murinde (2009).

banks are sound, with relatively higher z-scores than some of the BRICs. However, the z-scores for some of Africa's more developed countries, such as South Africa, Egypt and Algeria, deteriorated between 2000 and 2007. In comparison, bank soundness in the BRICs improved over the same period.

As a result of the reforms introduced in the 1980s and 1990s, African financial systems have been able to weather the full impact of the financial crisis. However, as Table 3.1 shows, in countries with relatively more developed financial systems, such as South Africa and Egypt, the impact of the financial crisis has been stronger, with some of the financial ratios, including private sector credit to GDP and market capitalization, showing a decline between 2007 and 2008. In Egypt the market capitalization ratio halved in the two years, falling from 107 per cent to 53 per cent, while in South Africa it fell from 294 per cent to 178 per cent.

In relative terms, Africa's financial sector remains small. In global terms, Africa accounted for 0.71 per cent of bank assets, 0.2 per cent of debt securities and 1.3 per cent of equities in 2008 (see Table 3.3). By comparison, Asia accounted for 12 per cent of global bank assets, 16 per cent of global equities and 5.8 per cent of debt securities. Relative to

Table 3.3 Indicators of capital market size in 2008 (US$ billion)

	Equity	Bonds	Bank assets	Total
Africa	444.5	155	693.1	1292.6
EU	7262.8	29137	46802.4	83202.2
North America	12771.1	32164	16528.7	61463.8
Japan	3209	11478	10027	24714
Latin America	1456.6	1808.1	2189.8	5454.5
Asia	5326.7	4832.9	11708.4	21868
Total emerging countries	8558.9	7815.4	18020	34394.3
World	33513.1	83529.6	97381.4	214424.1
Share of emerging market (%)				
Africa	5.19	1.98	3.85	3.76
Latin America	17.02	23.14	12.15	15.86
Asia	62.24	61.84	64.97	63.58
Share of world market (%)				
Africa	1.33	0.19	0.71	0.6
EU	21.67	34.88	48.06	38.8
North America	38.11	38.51	16.97	28.66
Japan	9.58	13.74	10.3	11.53
Latin America	4.35	2.16	2.25	2.54
Asia	15.89	5.79	12.02	10.2

Source: IMF World Economic Outlook Database (October 2009).

\frica's capital markets are also small, on average accounting for per cent of GDP in 2008, compared with a global average of 352 per cent, and an Asian average of 245.7 per cent. Banks also dominate the financial markets, accounting for half of the capital market assets.

The financial sectors in most African countries still face a number of challenges. These include lack of competition, weak corporate governance systems and low outreach. Despite financial liberalization, the banking sector remains oligopolistic, leading to inefficient pricing of financial assets and low rates of deposit. The recent experience in Nigeria, where bank restructuring and consolidation was not accompanied by governance reforms, has brought to the fore issues of corporate governance. Furthermore, the recent financial crisis has highlighted the shortcomings of existing regulatory frameworks and has underscored the need for further reflection on the role of central banks. Also, fewer Africans have personal bank accounts or are able to access finance, partly as a result of costly banking services.[3]

3.3 Case Study of banking sector reforms in four middle-income countries

In practical terms, regulation comprises several distinct types of measures, with the following as the most long-standing measures: structural measures, relating to access to the banking market (approval, minimum capital and implementation conditions); type of activity (deposit bank, investment bank); and geographic jurisdictions of activities and the size of institutions (restricted acquisition of holdings). Deregulation in the 1980s reduced the reliance on direct measures such as ceiling interest rates and loan size management, and replaced them with prudential measures which do not undermine the market mechanism, such as prudential ratios and sufficient equity capital.

In the four middle-income countries studied, namely South Africa, Nigeria, Egypt and Algeria, banking regulation and reform have evolved unevenly (World Bank database, updated June 2008). For example, South Africa presents a case of gradual restructuring of the banking sector, which led to South African banks spawning the financial services sector in the rest of Africa. In its recent reforms, Nigeria bravely designed and implemented a shock-treatment type of banking sector reform, which amounts to a 'big bang'. The banking sector reforms in Egypt give mixed signals in terms of effort and success, which seems to suggest that the country should take it one step further. Algeria is characterized as a slow reformer; arguably it is high time for the country to embrace full financial restructuring, given the efforts it has made so far and considering the need to mitigate the adverse effects of the raging global financial crisis.

In general, there is no 'one-size-fits-all' approach to financial reforms. The banking sector reforms in South Africa were not only comprehensive but also carefully structured over a long period. Strong banks have emerged, which have gone global. This gradual approach offers important lessons for the rest of the continent. But it is interesting that the big bang approach adopted by Nigeria has also worked, suggesting that, in some economies, shock treatment can achieve results very rapidly.

3.3.1 Banking and financial sector reforms in South Africa[4]

The key feature of the banking sector reforms in South Africa is the gradualness of the process that spanned almost two decades, including complementary reforms in the capital market as well as insurance services (see Table 3.4 for the chronological sequence of the major banking sector reforms).

Furthermore, South African banking institutions adopted their own internal policies to provide for greater participation in social regeneration programmes. It would appear that these reforms have created new opportunities and challenges. Financial liberalization brought about greater competition for traditional domestic South African banks, especially with foreign bank entry. However, at the same time, the banks were exposed to volatile international capital movements. South African banks were forced to adopt a more open and global attitude in the daily management of their activities.

After the opening up of South Africa's financial system in 1994, international participation in the local banking industry increased significantly, rising from 3 per cent in 1994 to 9.5 per cent of total banking sector assets by the end of October 2004. There are now more than ten foreign banks with formally established branches or subsidiaries in South Africa, and more than 60 international banks with representative offices in the country. These foreign banks provide enhanced competition for the South African banks, particularly in the fields of wholesale banking and international trade financing as well as in the market for foreign exchange. In addition, electronic commercial banking, automated teller machines (ATMs), Internet and mobile banking, and issuance of debit and credit cards are some of the innovations that have surged. Hence, it may be argued that the reforms that encouraged foreign banks to operate in South Africa have improved the overall

Table 3.4 Chronology of key banking sector reforms in South Africa

Year	Specific reforms aimed at bank competitiveness
1991	Risk-based capital requirements, in line with EU directives, are introduced for banks
1996	Accounting and financial reporting by banks are required to conform to Generally Accepted Accounting Principles
1998	The South African Reserve Bank (SARB) changes its operational procedures for providing banks with short-term liquidity: an auction system is introduced where banks can tender on a daily basis for liquidity provided by the SARB
1999	SARB introduces certain limits on banks' deposits in the Cash Reserve Contra Accounts (CRCA), which effectively limits the possibility for banks to use the monthly averaging of required reserve holdings
2001	Consolidated accounting rules for financial conglomerates (to avoid double counting of regulatory capital) are made mandatory for banking groups
2001	New securitization notice adopted under Basel II. Securitization is broadened to allow banks to act as originator, sponsor or repackager in a securitization scheme; also, the minimum prescribed capital requirement for all banks and mutual savings associations is raised from 8% (as stipulated under Basel I) to 10%
2002	The Banks Act, 1990, is amended to compel all banks to establish sound risk management and corporate governance principles and to restrict certain investments made by banks (e.g. equity)
2003	Banks are required to develop a risk matrix to verify clients' identities, as per the Finance Intelligence Centre Act (FICA), making legislation against money laundering more effective
2004	Section 50 of the Banks Act prescribes that a controlling company must not invest more than 40% of the controlling company's share capital and reserve funds
2005	The South African banking market is opened for foreign banks. South African banks, in turn, are allowed to establish branch offices, subsidiaries and representative offices in many countries around the world
2006/ 2007	The National Credit Act becomes operational on 1 June 2007, with the aim of enabling all South Africans to have access to credit at affordable rates as well as protecting them from predatory lending. The National Credit Regulator and the National Consumer Tribunal are created to ensure enforcement
2007	The Banking Association of South Africa unveils a code of conduct, agreed to by all major consumer lending banks, setting out a standard according to which banks undertake to adhere to lending practices
2008	SARB implements Phase I of the Integrated Cash Management System (ICMS) to improve efficiency; also, all South African banks start operating under Basel II

Source: Kasekende et al. (2009).

quality of service in the banking sector, and lower interest rates or higher deposit rates have increased in order to attract customers.

South Africa has established a relatively well-developed banking system that compares favourably with those in many developed countries and that distinguishes South Africa from many other emerging-market countries (see Mboweni, 2004). The South African banking system has remained stable and its banks are adequately capitalized, partly as a result of financial consolidation (see Tables 3.5 and 3.6). Banks maintained capital-adequacy ratios above the minimum requirement of 10 per cent, from 11.4 per cent in December 2001 to 12.8 per cent in December 2007. Growth in the total balance sheet remained strong during 2007 and 2008. In South African Rand terms, banking sector assets increased by 84 per cent between 2003 and 2007, and by 24 per cent in 2008, but declined by 6.4 per cent in 2009. Loans and advances, along with investment and trading positions, were the main contributors to the increase in banking sector assets between 2003 and 2008, accounting for 73.8 per cent of total assets. Overall, loans and advances remained robust in 2008, but declined in 2009, falling from R1871 billion in 2008 to R1853 billion in 2009, partly as a result of the global financial crisis.

Growth in mortgage loans relative to other assets has been strong, increasing from R684.9 billion at the end of December 2006 to R853.8 billion at the end of December 2007, R966.9 billion at the end of December 2008 and R994.1 billion at the end of December 2009. Overdrafts and loans increased from R383.5 billion at the end of December 2006 to R474.4 billion at the end of December 2007, increasing to R566.8 billion at the end of December 2008, but decreasing to R552.7 billion at the end of December 2009.

Despite the global financial crisis, profitability ratios remained strong. The return on regulatory capital amounted to 18.1 per cent at the end of December 2007, compared with 18.3 per cent at the end of December

Table 3.5 Financial services indexes in South Africa, 2007

Type of index	Q2	Q3	Q4
Financial services index	97	98	98
Retail banking and specialized finance confidence index	100	94	95
Investment banking and specialized finance confidence index	100	100	100
Investment management confidence index	97	99	97
Life insurance confidence index	90	100	100

Source: Kasekende et al. (2009).

2006, while the return on assets equalled 1.4 per cent at the end of both December 2006 and December 2007. The efficiency ratio improved from 58.8 per cent at the end of December 2006 to 56.9 per cent at the end of December 2007, compared with 64.2 per cent in 2001. The liquid assets held exceeded the statutory liquid-asset requirement throughout 2007. The average daily amount of liquid assets held in December 2007 represented 112.5 per cent of the statutory liquid-asset requirement (in December 2006 this was 111.2 per cent).

However, during 2007 credit risk ratios deteriorated, with non-performing loans (NPLs) increasing from R18.8 billion at the end of December 2006 to R29.4 billion at the end of December 2007 (expressed as a percentage of total loans and advances, from 1.1 per cent at the end of December 2006 to 1.4 per cent at the end of December 2007). The increase in interest rates, together with other adverse developments in the South African and international economic environments, contributed to this deterioration. In addition, growth was somewhat distorted by securitization transactions that occurred during the year. Foreign currency loans and advances registered a decrease between 2006 and 2009, falling from R191.7 billion at the end of December 2006 to R190.4 billion at the end of December 2007, R177.5 billion at the end of December 2008 and R163.8 billion at the end of December 2009.

Table 3.6 shows that the banking sector in South Africa was strong, stable, and financially sound during 2001–2007, perhaps because of the financial sector reforms: all indicators for capital adequacy, liquidity, earnings and profitability, sensitivity to market risk and asset quality performed much better than the stated threshold or benchmark.

3.3.2 Banking and financial sector reforms in Nigeria

In contrast to the gradualist approach to banking reform in South Africa, Nigeria embarked in 2004 on a big bang style of banking sector reform aimed at enhancing the competitiveness of banks.[5] The reforms included raising the minimum capitalization requirement for banks to 25 billion Nigerian Naira by December 2005; a phased withdrawal of public funds from banks, which took effect in July 2004; and a consolidation of banking institutions through mergers and acquisitions. In addition, bank regulation was revamped by incorporating and adopting a risk-focused and rule-based regulatory framework; adopting zero tolerance in the area of information reporting; introducing an electronic financial analysis and surveillance system (e-FASS) for automated submission of returns by banks and other financial institutions;

Table 3.6 Financial soundness indicators for South African banking sector, 2001–2007

	Mean (%)	**Standard deviation (%)**	**Threshold (%)**	**Actual (%)**	**Signal**
Capital adequacy					
Regulatory capital to risk-weighted assets	12.65	0.65	12.00	12.78	No
Regulatory tier 1 capital to risk-weighted assts	9.25	0.56	8.69	9.48	No
Earning and profitability					
Return on assets	1.01	0.34	0.67	1.36	No
Return on equity	13.01	4.52	8.49	18.11	No
Interest margin to gross income	50.37	11.12	39.25	58.51	No
Non-interest expenses to gross income	64.28	11.32	75.60	48.64	No
Liquidity					
Liquid assets to total assets	4.56	0.24	4.32	4.63	No
Liquid assets to short-term liabilities	8.89	0.71	8.18	8.71	No
Sensitivity to market risk					
Aggregate net open position in foreign exchange to capital	1.65	0.76	2.41	0.69	No
Asset quality					
Non-performing loans to total loans and advances	2.20	0.86	3.06	1.38	No
Specific provisions to total loans and advances	1.52	0.45	1.07	0.86	Yes
Share of mortgage advances in private sector credit	43.06	3.46	46.52	48.95	Yes

Source: Kasekende et al. (2009).

collaborating with the Economic and Financial Crimes Commission (EFCC) in the establishment of the Financial Intelligence Unit (FIU) and the enforcement of anti-money laundering and other economic crime measures; and strictly enforcing the contingency planning framework for systemic banking distress during 2008. To expedite distress resolution, the formation of an asset management company has been announced recently. The new reforms also emphasized the liability of the boards of failed banks.

Table 3A.1 presents performance indicators for the main banks in Nigeria after the introduction of the reforms. It is notable that, after the big bang, all bank performance indicators for each major bank satisfied high-quality benchmarks for return on equity, capital strength, asset size and soundness. In addition, following financial consolidation, the depth of the financial sector increased as credit to the private sector rose from 26.2 per cent in 2006 to 67.8 per cent in 2007. There was also an increase in savings from ₦1082.0 billion in 2006 to ₦2949.8 billion in 2007, of which commercial banks held 76 per cent of the funds while other savings institutions – such as life insurance funds, pension funds and microfinance banks – accounted for 24 per cent. During the same period, the number of bank branches increased from 3468 to 4579 across all the states in the country. Consequently, the number of bank employees went up. By the end of 2008, the financial sector had become a significant employer in Nigeria.

An important element of the programme was reforming the payments system and the interbank money market. Payment system reforms were put in place when seven banks were appointed as settlement banks for the clearing of cheques. During the financial restructuring, the value and volume of clearing cheques increased significantly as more individuals shifted to non-cash transactions. To promote the efficient use of cheques, fines and prosecution were to be enforced in the case of dishonoured cheques. The introduction of the Central Bank of Nigeria (CBN) Inter Bank Fund Transfer system for the transfer of funds amongst banks increased the value of transactions by 56 per cent. The non-payment of interest on the standing deposit facility also instilled confidence and encouraged banks to place and borrow funds among themselves and discount houses.

Electronic commerce also expanded with the increased use of ATM machines, the introduction of Point of Sale (POS) terminals, issuance of debit and credit cards, and Internet and mobile banking innovations, as shown in Table 3.7.

The financial reforms also saw an increase in the number of mergers and acquisitions (M&A), involving 60 banks, which resulted in 24 stronger and bigger banks. Also, some banks acquired other financial institutions such as stock-broking houses in order to offer wholesale/universal banking products. The emergence of strong and big banks appears to have, over time, created some competition. While initially interest rate spreads widened, in 2008 they narrowed drastically as financial institutions tried to offer lower rates on loans and higher savings rates on deposits in order to attract more customers. Banks also invested

Table 3.7 Market share of e-payment market by type of transaction (in per cent)

	2006	2007
ATMs	73.35	88.5
Web (internet)	3.51	7.1
POS	23.04	4.3
Mobile	0.11	0.1

Source: Central Bank of Nigeria (2008).

in research and development to ensure that the level of services offered was of an international standard with more focus on personal banking. In order to give concessions to banks that were raising fresh funds from the capital market to reduce the cost of funds and ensure a seamless transition, regulatory authorities had to give concessions to banks.

However, despite the improvement of the banking sector in Nigeria following the restructuring and consolidation exercise, in 2009 concerns began to emerge that the banking system was suffering from stress. As a result of bank consolidation and high oil prices, banks became highly liquid and with the real sector lagging behind, this liquidity found its way to the capital markets. Investors borrowed from banks to invest in Nigeria's stock market. At the same time, there appears to have been some corporate governance problems and sometimes outright abuses through the use of Special Purpose Vehicles set up by some CEOs to lend money to themselves in order to manipulate the stock price.[6] Regulatory lapses at the central bank have also been highlighted as another weakness, especially with regard to regulating margin lending activity which became a serious problem as the financial crisis began to deepen and stock prices started falling.[7]

Recently, the CBN announced a four-pronged strategy to deal with the challenges in the financial sector, namely: (i) enhancing the quality of banks; (ii) establishing financial stability; (iii) enabling healthy financial sector evolution; and (iv) ensuring that the financial sector contributes to the real economy.

3.3.3 Banking and financial sector reforms in Egypt

Egypt is an interesting contrast to banking sector reforms in South Africa and Nigeria. The Egyptian banking industry is amongst the oldest and largest in Africa. Banking reform started in the early 1970s, but the first stage of the modern financial sector reforms occurred during 1990–1996 and was aimed at full liberalization of the banking sector in order to make the banks efficient and competitive. The foreign exchange market was liberalized in February 1991 and banks were allowed to set foreign exchange rates for trading foreign currencies. In 1992 interest rate ceilings were abolished for the private and public sectors, and lending limits to these sectors were eliminated in 1992 and 1993, respectively. The second stage of the reforms (1996–2001) continued with the liberalization of prices, and included privatization and deregulation.

The third stage of the reforms (2002–2007) included the introduction of the Financial Sector Assessment Programme (FSAP) in 2002, which highlighted key priorities for financial sector reform in banking and non-banking, and the financial sector Development Policy Loan (DPL) in 2005, which included enhancements for the investment climate. In 2002, the Central Bank of Egypt (CBE) required banks to raise their capital adequacy ratios to meet Basel II standards. The minimum capital requirement for all banks was raised to LE500 million (approximately $87 million), following the Banking Law in 2003. Subsequently, some banks merged; for example in 2005, the Banque Misr with Banque du Caire, and the National Société Generale Bank (NSGB) with Misr International Bank. It is to be noted that Egypt has been a member of the WTO since 30 June 1995 and made commitments to General Agreement on Trade in Services (GATS) in 1997. As a result of its banking reform, Egypt no longer limits foreign bank entry into the domestic banking market. Several foreign banks have majority shares in Egyptian banks, while other foreign banks are registered as branches of the parent bank rather than as subsidiaries (see also the reports in CMA, 2008).

The *Doing Business 2008* report has rated Egypt the top reformer across 178 countries. The 2007 *FSAP Update* and the 2007 *Access to Finance and Economic Growth* in Egypt report substantial progress in the Financial Sector Reform Programme since its launch in 2004, including implementation of most of the recommendations of the 2002 FSAP and the fulfilment of the performance indicators established under DPL (see World Bank Report, 2008). The period also involved comprehensive financial sector restructuring comprising bank mergers, privatization of state-owned banks, recapitalization of banks, resolution of non-performing loans, modernizing the payments system, enhancing and monitoring corporate governance in all banks, and improving the overall legal and regulatory framework for financial activities.

Anecdotal evidence seems to suggest reasonable success for the financial sector reforms in Egypt in the sense that the sector has been experiencing a revival since the introduction of the main reforms in the 1990s. Financial consolidation appears to have brought about tremendous transformation in the Egyptian financial sector (see Table 3A.2 in the Appendix for detailed bank performance). The size of the banking sector, measured by total assets, fully reflects all positive developments on the economic, banking and business climate fronts, reporting a remarkable growth of 23.2 per cent year on year in 2007, outperforming its already high 12 per cent average growth per annum over the previous five years, to reach a record high of LE937.9 billion (see Bank Audi, Egypt Economic Report, 2008). The results reported in Table 3A.2 specifically show that the main banks in Egypt achieved high returns on average equity (ROAE) for 2005–2007. Also, most banks increased their total assets, which reflects the loan creation process of the banks. However, there were some state banks that appear to have recorded weak performances during the period (Table 3A.2).

Overall, Egypt has not suffered a major banking or currency crisis during the reform period. Since 2005, privatization has been placing about half of the banking sector into private hands and the government has restructured public banks, paying off non-performing loans owed by state enterprises, while fostering the resolution of private sector NPLs. Complementary regulatory and judicial reforms (such as setting up specialized economic courts, promoting out-of-court arbitrage and enhancing the role of credit bureaux led by the private sector) are helping to improve contract enforcement and creditor protection, thereby addressing key obstacles for bank lending to SMEs (see World Bank Report, 2008). Also, recent reforms have enabled most banks to expand their provision of non-traditional services such as brokerage, investment consultations, asset valuation and sales and mutual fund operations, which also helped improve capital market services. Furthermore, improvements have been recorded in the payments system. The emphasis has been on upgrading and modernizing the institutional framework of the payments system at the central bank, including introducing the real time gross settlement system (RTGS) and the Automatic Clearing House (ACH) to reduce the total processing time of cheques issued by different banks.

3.3.4 Banking and financial sector reforms in Alg

Considered against the background of South Africa,
Algeria presents a special case. Before 1980, Alge
strategies which emphasized the key role of the st

The financial services sector was regulated very tightly. Resource allocation was assured via central credit allocation, preferential interest rates and exchange controls. The banking system was segmented, with little competition and no foreign bank participation. Bond and equity markets were virtually non-existent in the early 1980s, due to the predominant role of state ownership and lack of a legal basis for capital market activity. Specifically, banking sector reforms were introduced and implemented during 1986–1996.

The main elements of the financial reforms in Algeria were fivefold. First, the initial steps in the reform of the financial sector involved raising interest rates in order to achieve positive real interest rates, and by 1990 deposit interest rates were fully liberalized. The ceilings on lending rates were lifted and limits on banking spreads were abolished in December 1995. The second element was to relax the policy of directed credit. This was initiated in 1987 and by 1994 banks were operating on the basis of market-based credit allocations to firms and households.

The third element involved prudential regulation and banking supervision. New banking laws were introduced which emphasized liberalization and deregulation of financial activities. By 1999, all banks were aiming to meet the risk-weighted capital adequacy ratios recommended by the Basel committee. The fourth element was to enhance competition among banks. The key measures included opening the sector to foreign bank entry, allowing banks to pursue market-based lending decisions, and creating opportunities for many types of financial intermediaries. The fifth element was capital account liberalization. In April 1994 foreign exchange controls were removed and foreign investors were allowed to repatriate earnings.

It would appear that by 2005 the positive outcomes of these banking sector reforms were becoming visible. As shown in Table 3A.3, the main banks in Algeria exhibited stable performances during 2005–2007. In general, the banks achieved positive and reasonably high returns on average equity as well as returns on average assets.

3.4 Competitiveness of banking sector in African economies

Each African economy has its own challenges in assessing the competitiveness of its banking sector. This section looks at the performance of banks within a given regulatory environment and how this impacts on competitiveness. Banking regulation is not without cost for banks and affects their risk-taking behaviour.

Below, we report the results of recent research by Kasekende et al. (2009) that measures the competitiveness of banking in South Africa, Algeria, Nigeria and Egypt. The research follows the work of Panzar and Rosse (1987), and that of Bresnahan (1982, 1989) and Lau (1982) (see Kasekende et al., 2009). This line of work focuses on testing statistically for three forms of market structure: monopoly or short-run conjectural variation oligopoly, monopolistic competition and perfect competition. From the Panzar–Rosse approach, we obtain the so-called H-statistic, which is calculated from reduced-form bank revenue equations and measures the sum of the elasticities of the total revenue of the bank with respect to the bank's input prices. The H-statistic allows us to distinguish between oligopolistic, monopolistic and competitive markets, where non-positive values of H (i.e. $H \leq 0$) imply monopoly power or short-run conjectural variation oligopoly, while $0 < H < 1$ supports the case for monopolistic competition and $H = 1$ for perfect competition.

The second approach follows the Bresnahan-Lau model for measuring the market structure of the banking industry in each of the four countries. The metric obtained, often referred to as the *θ-statistic* in the literature, measures the industry average of bank competition, and is composed of three basic ingredients: the behaviour of banks in terms of how they set the prices of inputs and outputs; the behaviour of banks in terms of how they manage costs; and the interdependence among the banks (or collusive behaviour). As such, the *θ-statistic* expresses the degree of market power exerted by banks, where a value of zero denotes perfect competition and a value of one indicates monopolistic competition.

3.4.1 Competition in South African banking industry

The evidence for South Africa for the theta (θ) and H measures of competitiveness for the period 1992–2007 is reported in Figures 3.1 and 3.2. Figure 3.1 shows annual estimates of the theta (θ) measure, the industry average of competition in the South African banking market and their 95 per cent confidence intervals. Except for the first year, 1992, the results reject $\theta = 1$, or pure monopoly conditions. Moreover, the Cournot benchmark lies within the 95% confidence interval of θs. As a result, the overall competitiveness condition in the bank loan market in South African commercial banking appears to be more competitive than under Cournot oligopoly conditions. Furthermore, except for years 1997, 1999 and 2007, the results for other sample periods fail to reject

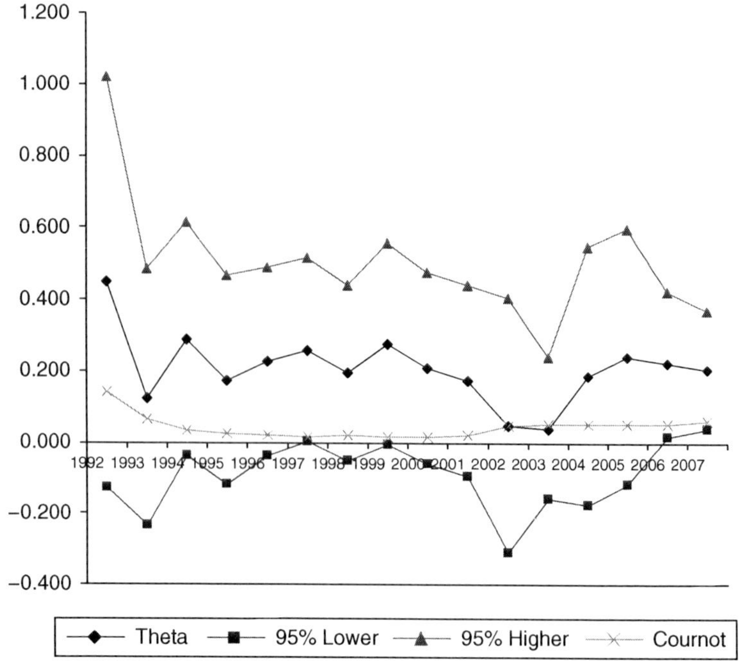

Figure 3.1 Industry average of bank competition in South Africa, 1992–2007

$\theta = 0$, perfect competition conditions, and the lower confidence band suggests the possibility of the presence of super competition. Looking at the movement pattern of the point estimates of θs, despite several temporary setbacks it shows a downward trend, and registers a sustainable decrease for the period 1999–2003. Thereafter, it rises in 2004 and 2005, and declines again in 2006 and 2007. In summary, competition seems to be intensified until 2003. The short-term fluctuation of θs before 1999 and the rebound of θs after 2003 would result from the presence of super competition. Hence, the South African banking market has been characterized by fairly intense competition during the period under study.

Figure 3.2 gives the results derived from *H*-statistics, and the comparison between the conjectural variations parameters and the *H*-statistics for South African banks. The limitations of *H*-statistics entail the caution of viewing the results. First, it requires the long-run equilibrium for the identification of perfect and monopolistic competition. In the case of South African banks, our test for the presence of the long-run

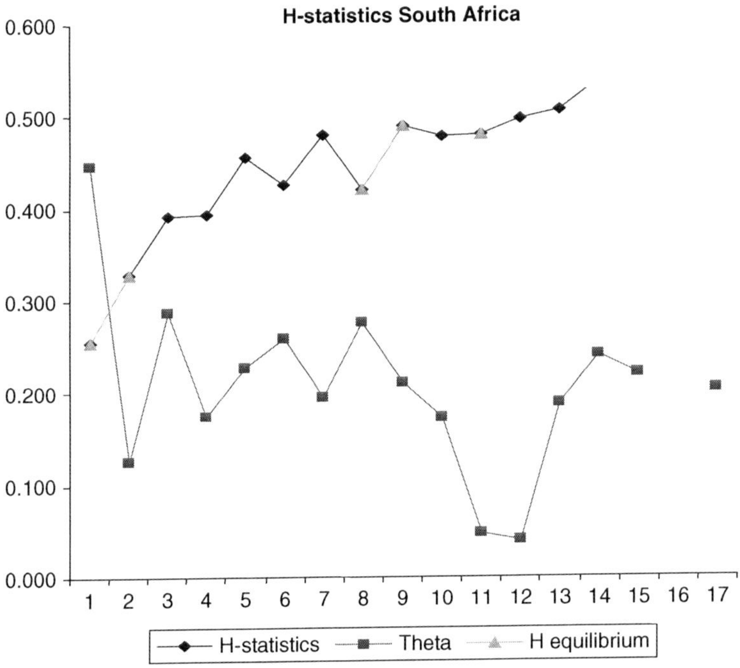

Figure 3.2 Theta parameters and *H*-statistics for South Africa

equilibrium indicates that only half of our sample period satisfies this requirement.[8] Second, the economic interpretation of the magnitude of the derived *H*-statistic (apart from the long-run competitive equilibrium value of 1) is ambiguous. This is because the *H*-statistic does not map directly into any static or dynamic oligopoly equilibrium concept. Overall, for the periods that passed the test for long-run equilibrium, the evidence suggests that the South African banking market is generally characterized by monopolistic competition. Furthermore, the change in *H*-statistics in 10 out of 16 data points appears to be opposite to that of θs, which gives a roughly similar picture of the change in the degree of competition to that of θs.

3.4.2 Competition in Algerian banking industry

In Figures 3.3 and 3.4 we report the evidence for Algeria from the two main approaches, which generate the θ and H metrics, respectively, for the period 1993–2008. For the entire period under study, the results reject pure monopoly conditions ($\theta = 1$) and perfect competition

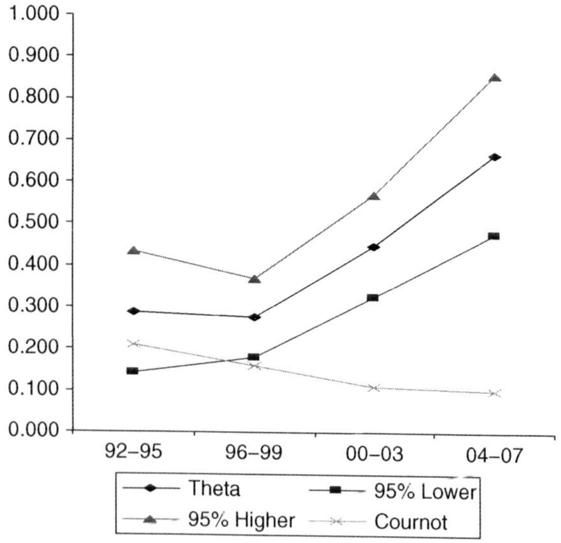

Figure 3.3 Industry average of bank competition in Algeria, 1992–2007

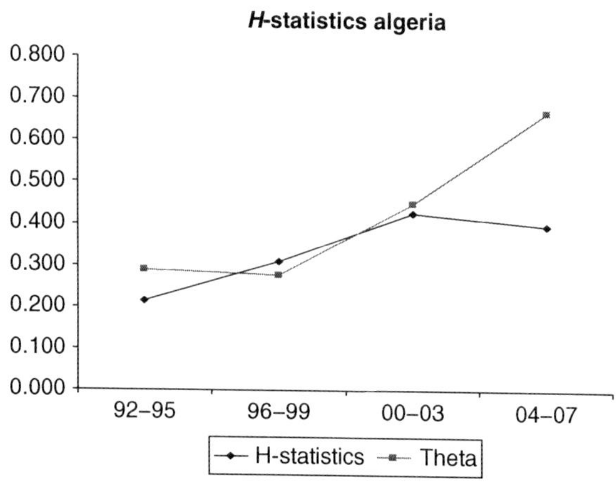

Figure 3.4 Theta parameters and *H*-statistics for Algeria

conditions ($\theta = 0$). The results also reject the Cournot oligopoly, except for the period 1992–1995. In general, therefore, the overall structure of the lending market in Algerian commercial banking is characterized by a higher level of oligopoly than Cournot, although there is a higher level of competition than with joint profit maximization. The change in the degree of competition appears to decrease over time.

Table 3.4 shows that the main results of the change in the degree of competition in Algeria holds when we look at the results derived from the *H*-statistics. The sum of elasticity of input prices with respect to profitability suggests that all four estimates pass the long-run equilibrium test.

3.4.3 Competition in Nigerian banking industry

As previously noted, recent Nigerian banking reforms followed a big bang approach. Figures 3.5 and 3.6 indicate the impact of these reforms on the competitiveness of the banking industry in Nigeria for the period 1993–2008, where the data for 2006–2008 covers the recent reforms. Figure 3.5 reports the estimates of annual θ, the industry average of competition, and their 95 per cent confidence interval.

The results show that over the entire sample period, the evidence rejects $\theta = 1$, or the pure monopoly hypothesis. The Cournot oligopoly is also rejected, except in 1997. Moreover, except for years 1996 and 2008, where the market exhibited a super competition situation, the results reject $\theta = 0$, or perfect competition. This implies that the

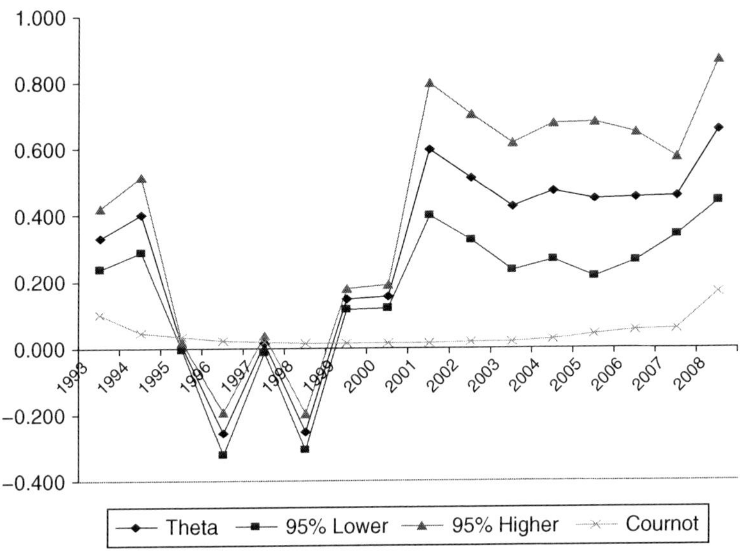

Figure 3.5 Industry average of bank competition in Nigeria, 1993–2008

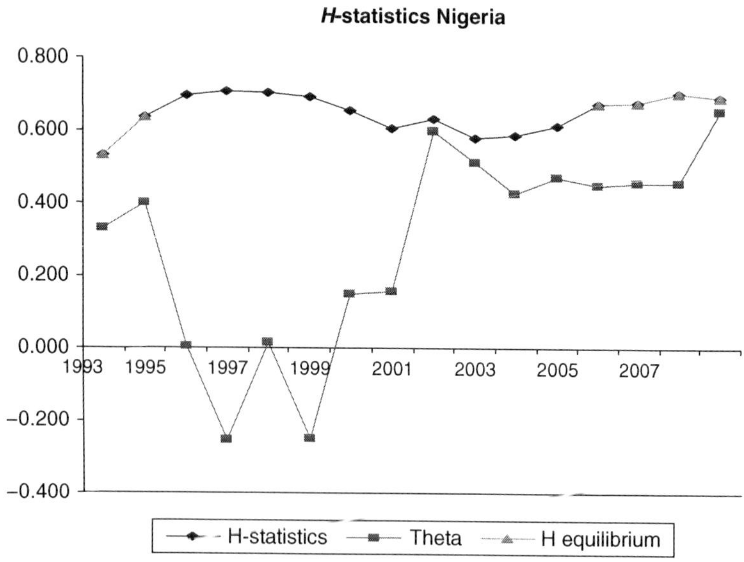

Figure 3.6 Comparing theta parameters and *H*-statistics for Nigeria, 1993–2008

degree of competition in Nigerian commercial banking is characterized by a certain level of oligopoly and was less competitive than Cournot.

Regarding the change in the degree of competition during the period under study, after 1994 competition seems to have improved and resulted in a super competition situation. The downward trend was reversed up to 2001, followed by a new round of improvements during 2001–2007. Overall, the degree of competition seems to have improved after the reform period in 2005. Figure 3.6 shows that the *H*-statistics results are generally consistent with the results derived from the conjectural variations approach.

3.4.4 Competition in Egyptian banking industry

As stated above, in the 1990s Egypt began undertaking significant banking reforms with a view to introducing more competition and improving efficiency. In Figures 3.7 and 3.8 we assess the impact of these reforms on the structure of the banking industry in Egypt for the period 1993–2007. Figure 3.7 plots the estimates of annual theta, the industry average of competition for the period 1993–2007, and their 95 per cent confidence. As shown, over the entire sample period the results reject

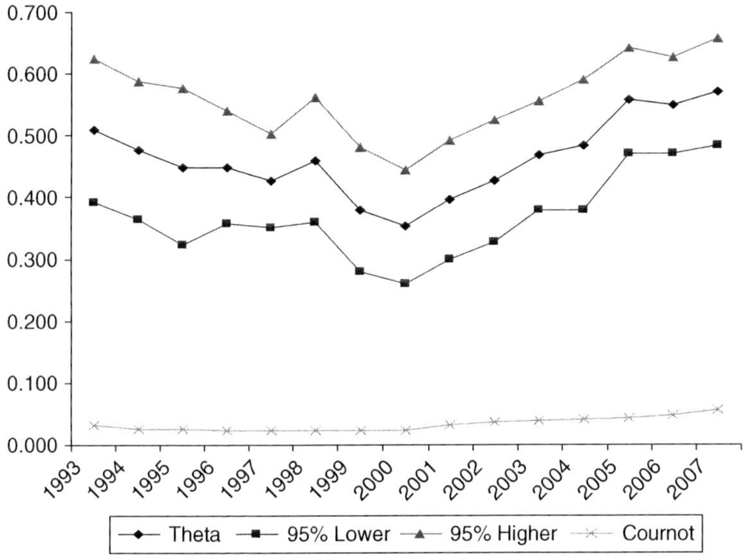

Figure 3.7 Industry average of bank competition in Egypt, 1993–2007

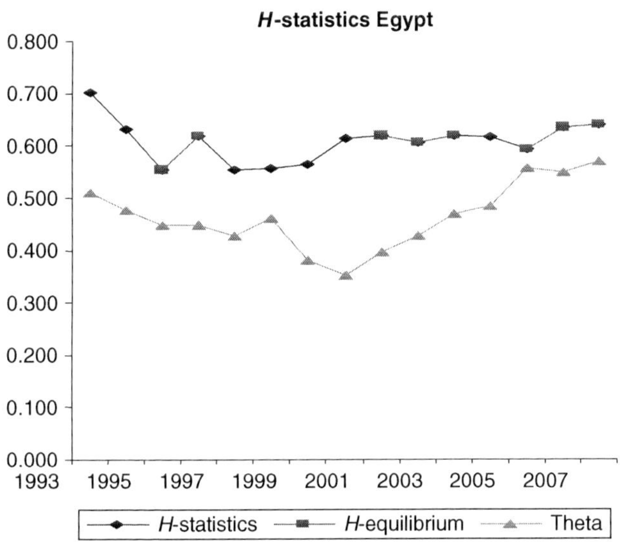

Figure 3.8 Theta parameters and *H*-statistics for Egypt, 1993–2007

the equation $\theta = 1$ or pure monopoly, the Cournot oligopoly and the equation $\theta = 0$, or perfect competition. Therefore, the degree of competition in Egyptian commercial banking is characterized by a higher level of oligopoly than Cournot, although there is a higher level of competition than joint profit maximization. The change in the degree of competition during 1993–2007 indicates the shift from an improvement to a deterioration of competition, with 2000 as the watershed year.

Figure 3.8 also confirms that, notwithstanding the general limitation of *H*-statistics, as far as the change in the degree of competition is concerned, the two approaches give similar results.

3.5 Policy implications and recommendations

This chapter provided a comparative overview of bank regulatory experiences and their impact on bank competition and intermediation efficiency in selected African economies. The chapter offers two 'big ideas' for policymakers: first, African economies that have been implementing banking sector reforms since the early 1990s are likely to recover faster from the global financial crisis; second, African countries should note that, while banking reforms are needed, they do not have to be the same for all countries; each country must determine the approach that is most appropriate.

The first 'big idea' is derived from the observation that the current financial meltdown has important implications for financial reforms and bank competitiveness in Africa. The nature of the current global crisis is such that the vulnerability of African economies is non-uniform, although all economies currently seem to be characterized by distortions in external sector indicators. The global financial crisis has even hit countries, such as South Africa and Nigeria, which have implemented financial sector reforms and displayed evidence of bank competitiveness through their financial links with other world regions. Countries with relatively more developed and integrated financial sectors have suffered from considerable pressure on exchange rates, a decline in capital flows, a fall in equity markets and scarcity of foreign finance for companies and banks. Hence, the current global financial crisis has the potential to derail many of the reforms in the financial services sector, especially because banks and capital markets are vulnerable as a result of globalization and contagion effects. However, the message from this chapter is that it is African economies that have undertaken key financial reforms and have competitive banking sectors which are likely to recover from the crisis much faster than those countries that have not done so. Hence, the immediate policy action lies in strengthening domestic banks and consolidating regional financial networks. Such action requires not only changes in legal infrastructure and trading of currencies but, more importantly, the political will to survive the global financial crisis.

The second 'big idea' is based on the observed differences in pace and approach of banking sector reforms undertaken in selected African economies, in order to enhance the competitive conditions in financial services. South Africa's approach is one of gradualist restructuring, which led to South African banks spawning the financial services sector in the rest of Africa; Nigeria has adopted a shock-treatment type of banking sector reform, which amounts to a big bang; Egypt presents mixed signals in terms of effort and success, which seem to suggest that the country should take it one step further; and Algeria, which has been a slow reformer, seems to be embracing full financial restructuring.

South Africa's gradualist approach offers some interesting lessons for other African countries. We trace the process of gradual financial restructuring in South Africa since the end of apartheid in the early 1990s, when the financial sector was restructured to become internationally competitive and play a leading role in Africa. What is particularly illustrative for other African economies is that in 2003, along with Botswana, Lesotho, Namibia and Swaziland, South Africa agreed on a free trade agreement (FTA) designed to lower trade barriers and open markets. South Africa's commitments resulted in increased access to its market in all areas, including banking, securities and insurance. This is a model that many other large well-endowed countries may wish to consider; especially in view of the evidence that the South African banking sector represents stable, competitive conditions.

Also, important lessons can be learned from Nigeria's adoption of a big bang approach to banking sector reforms in 2005, although broadly the reforms also involved the capital market, insurance and pension services. Anecdotal evaluation seems to indicate that the reforms have created new developments and opportunities. We have noted that the banking sector has benefitted from the consolidation and recapitalization programme that was initiated in 2006. It is fostering growth in the services sector as well as the broader private sector through increased financial intermediation, including stability in the financial sector, with stronger and larger banks having a larger capital base. Consolidation has also enhanced the ability of the financial sector to finance key growth sectors and has improved corporate governance.

The research findings show that the reforms in Nigeria have engendered more competitiveness in the financial services sector. Overall, banks have been strengthened by the reforms and are now exploring new opportunities in markets beyond Nigeria into other parts of Africa. Raising the domestic banking market to international standards, where domestic banks have transparent corporate governance practices to enable them to compete favourably with any new foreign banks in the market, is a policy objective that many African countries should emulate, especially in view of the global financial crisis.

In the case of Egypt's experience with banking reforms, there are three main lessons for the rest of Africa. First, banking reform has led to the promotion of transparency and the use of adequate accounting and supervision standards. In Egypt this led to a friendlier investment climate that, in turn, yielded a strong private sector supply response, according to the World Bank. Second, there has been an increase in banks' deposit and lending rates to compensate for losses attributable to loan defaults; however, high real interest rates failed to increase savings or boost investment. Third, the quality of the legal system is important. Egypt has been committed to strengthening the legal, regulatory and supervisory framework of the financial sector as a whole, including forensic finance procedures. However, the financial sector continues to face important challenges because of the sector's low levels of competition, relatively high intermediation costs, limited innovation and dominance of state ownership. The banking system is burdened by high levels of NPLs, while the non-bank segment is characterized by underdeveloped bond, insurance and mortgage markets; thin trading in equities; weak corporate governance; and weak infrastructure for effective payment systems. The reform process continues.

In Algeria, although progress has not been at the same level as in other large African economies, reforms have played an important role in ensuring effective intermediation of the country's large savings as well as improving bank governance. The development of the local capital market has yielded a number of benefits, and there is evidence of positive spillover effects from the financial services sector to the rest of the economy. Algeria has also made progress toward both global and regional economic integration, which compares well with earlier lessons from South Africa and Nigeria.

Competitiveness and efficiency are central to these economies as they become more service-oriented. Even in South Africa, which has the most sophisticated and relatively well-developed financial system, only four big banks (out of a total of 22 local banks and 15 branches of foreign banks) control almost 84 per cent of banking sector assets. These numbers do not necessarily imply greater competition unless the market structure is changed. Further, despite their domination of the financial system, local banks remain small in terms of assets and capital compared with emerging and international banks. Hence, an immediate policy question relates to reforming and restructuring the financial system, especially the banking sector. As previously noted, in Nigeria the recent restructuring and consolidation of the banking sector has made the sector stronger and safer, and contributed to the growth of the Nigerian Stock Exchange. Overall – and within the context of the WTO and specifically GATS, which requires countries to open their banking sectors to international competition – the banking sectors in African economies, such as South Africa or Egypt, are to varying degrees competitive enough to withstand foreign bank entry.

Appendix

Table 3A.1 Performance indicators for main banks in Nigeria, 2005–2007

Name of the bank	Year	ROE	Capital strength ('000 US$)	Asset size ('000 US$)	Soundness capital/asset ratio
Access Bank PLC	2005	0.035	110,986.07	527,788.58	21.03
	2006	0.025	227,887.73	1,376,716.35	16.55
	2007	0.214	223,873.26	2,591,806.87	8.64
Afribank Nigeria PLC	2006	0.092	213,419.28	1,035,335.92	20.61
	2007	0.122	223,172.35	1,441,135.44	15.49
Diamond Bank PLC	2005	0.122	163,422.71	987,321.93	16.55
	2006	0.11	276,220.93	1,761,831.00	15.68
	2007	0.128	425,685.44	2,466,427.49	17.26
Ecobank Nigeria PLC	2005	0.229	221,547.00	2,199,230.00	10.07
	2006	0.226	382,088.00	3,503,739.00	10.91
	2007	0.27	513,548.00	6,550,224.00	7.84
Fidelity Bank PLC	2005	0.136	71,065.50	349,359.12	20.34
	2006	0.123	201,272.31	1,188,857.43	16.93
First Bank PLC	2005	0.272	352,330.62	2,977,332.59	11.83
	2006	0.263	480,952.75	4,260,028.39	11.29
	2007	0.237	610,071.72	6,016,886.19	10.14
First City Monument Bank PLC	2005	0.11	57,000.12	405,357.56	14.06
	2006	0.107	208,517.55	842,111.29	24.76
	2007	0.187	244,619.77	2,075,875.90	11.78

Table 3A.1 (Continued)

Name of the bank	**Year**	**ROE**	**Capital strength ('000 US$)**	**Asset size ('000 US$)**	**Soundness capital/asset ratio**
Guaranty Trust Bank PLC	2005	0.147	284,765.26	1,321,925.00	21.54
	2006	0.213	320,018.43	2,402,020.00	13.32
	2007	0.274	373,460.26	3,766,389.00	9.92
Oceanic Bank PLC	2005	0.189	249,933.13	1,751,235.69	14.27
	2006	0.253	302,814.75	2,987,347.62	10.14
	2007	0.077	1,788,387.34	8,283,286.87	21.59
Platinum Habib Bank PLC	2005	0.055	101,771.43	415,360.75	24.50
	2006	0.084	229,023.16	1,245,029.76	18.39
	2007	0.211	290,414.35	3,046,216.31	9.53
Standard Chartered Bank	2004	0.267	38,451.37	269,179.30	14.28
	2005	0.091	206,611.15	531,285.17	38.89
Sterling Bank PLC	2006	0.04	211,570.16	881,546.84	24.00
	2007	0.072	215,437.25	1,173,429.85	18.36
Union Bank of Nigeria PLC	2005	0.239	308,612.66	3,141,186.21	9.82
	2006	0.104	754,673.08	4,082,056.94	18.49
	2007	0.125	762,126.35	4,888,398.13	15.59
United Bank for Africa PLC	2005	0.262	142,299.03	2,001,028.93	7.11
	2006	0.24	382,805.46	6,842,773.31	5.59
	2007	0.12	1,324,927.65	8,861,318.32	14.95
Unity Bank	2006	0.148	21,889.28	263,223.93	8.32
	2007	0.12	244,091.90	908,352.05	26.87
Wema Bank PLC	2005	0.034	191,331.10	772,214.37	24.78
	2006	−0.321	162,000.16	947,307.09	17.10
	2007	0.101	198,617.43	1,302,007.50	15.25
Zenith Bank PLC	2005	0.189	299,798.98	2,640,897.23	11.35
	2006	0.114	796,514.59	4,845,444.66	16.44
	2007	0.155	895,147.34	7,012,621.38	12.76
Intercontinental Bank PLC	2005	0.154	256,483.74	1,293,976.85	19.82
	2006	0.159	424,462.64	2,841,532.16	14.94
	2007	0.095	1,227,297.06	5,224,376.03	23.49

Note: ROE is return on equity; capital strength is measured by tier 1 capital.
Source: Compiled by authors from BankScope.

Table 3A.2 Performance indicators for main banks in Egypt, 2005–2007

Name of the bank	Year	Total assets (US$ mil)	Equity (US$ mil)	Return on average equity (ROAE)	Deposit & short-term funding (USD mil)
National Bank of Egypt	2007	37425	1259	4.37	32850
	2006	32175	1193	4.57	27941
	2005	27707	1135	4.89	24667
Banque Misr S.A.E .	2007	24209	941	3.42	22239
	2006	19175	626	4.08	17724
	2005	18490	609	4.03	16566
Banque du Caire S.A.E.	2007	8876	455	1.99	7803
	2007	8876	455	1.99	7803
	2006	7943	510	1.12	7079
	2005	7840	506	1.9	6799
Commercial International Bank (Egypt)	2007	8634	755	29.51	7611
	2007	8634	755	29.51	7611
	2006	6561	567	24.09	5753
	2005	5302	464	21.57	4464
National Société Generale Bank S.A.E.	2007	8590	642	20.19	7427
	2007	8590	642	20.19	7427
	2006	6914	445	5.93	6010
	2005	2913	231	43.77	2563
Arab African International Bank	2007	8015	386	39.47	7424
	2007	8015	386	39.47	7424
	2006	4918	259	31.77	4543
	2005	3312	207	27.6	3011
Bank of Alexandria	2007	5953	361	19.6	5270
	2007	5953	361	19.6	5270
	2006	5764	322	123.33	4806
	2005	6657	292	6.19	5735
HSBC Bank Egypt S.A.E.	2007	4986	427	42.45	4467
	2007	4986	427	42.45	4467
	2006	3110	336	41.15	2700
	2005	2342	178	44.81	2109
Arab International Bank	2007	4200	534	9.02	3634
	2007	4200	534	9.02	3634
	2006	3833	497	4.54	3297
	2005	3654	487	6.84	3141
Faisal Islamic Bank of Egypt	2007	4004	122	0	3684
	2007	4004	122	0	3684
	2006	3372	119	17.4	3075
	2005	2864	119	15.32	2591
Crédit Agricole Egypt	2007	3906	286	35.16	3456
	2006	2763	247	1.48	2427
	2005	2430	242	44.77	2058

Table 3A.2 (Continued)

Name of the bank	Year	Total assets (US$ mil)	Equity (US$ mil)	Return on average equity (ROAE)	Deposit & short-term funding (USD mil)
Barclays Bank – Egypt S.A.E.	2007	3242	241	41.02	2908
	2006	2374	129	34.38	2156
	2005	1222	134	38.82	1036
EFG – Hermes Holding Company	2007	2439	1715	15.97	596
	2006	1630	1404	16.21	282
	2005	420	154	43.03	247
Al Watany Bank of Egypt	2007	2255	233	20.99	1958
	2006	1765	182	11.6	1524
	2005	1632	103	11.62	1490
Housing and Development Bank	2007	1932	137	26.52	891
	2006	1599	109	21.29	859
	2005	1638	72	15.81	1039
National Bank for Development	2007	1710	131	−62.83	1532
	2006	1537	55	−38.27	1445
	2005	1503	81	−0.13	1342
Export Development Bank of Egypt	2007	1544	152	0.99	1033
	2006	1276	113	−21.72	884
	2005	1332	140	7.51	855
Société Arabe Internationale de Banque	2007	1487	167	11.72	1251
	2006	868	149	10.67	663
	2005	734	146	9.64	546
Bank Audi S.A.E.	2007	1474	197	−5.13	1244
	2006	1000	100	0.53	890
	2005	55	0	−199.9	49
MISR Iran Development Bank	2007	1359	162	23.64	1170
	2006	1058	123	16.21	898
	2005	935	116	16.05	784
Arab Banking Corporation – Egypt	2007	1101	111	7.06	854
	2006	444	100	6.2	328
	2005	405	94	7.5	297
Ahli United Bank (Egypt) S.A.E.	2007	1049	148	19.75	845
	2006	706	117	0.03	518
	2005	644	100	24.42	497
Egyptian Gulf Bank	2007	933	127	10.64	782
	2006	804	110	14.18	670
	2005	648	102	16.63	528
African Export-Import Bank	2007	812	346	11.43	442
	2006	623	293	11.35	312
	2005	587	264	8.97	305
Union National Bank – Egypt S.A.E.	2007	571	114	38.87	436
	2006	332	−42	263.95	358
	2005	351	30	0	313

Source: Compiled by authors from BankScope.

Table 3A.3 Performance indicators for main banks in Algeria, 2005–2007

Name of the bank	Year	Total assets (US$ mil)	Net loans/ total assets (%)	Equity (US$ mil)	Net income (US$ mil)	Return on average equity (ROAE)	Return on average assets (ROAA)	Deposits and short-term funding (US$ mil)
Banque d'Algérie	2005	61,607	2.42	1,014	n.a.	n.a.	n.a.	40,722
Banque Extérieure d'Algérie	2005	13,968	21.95	464	17	3.71	0.13	12,005
	2006	20,940	14.86	566	87	16.7	0.49	18,253
	2007	31,861	12.96	1,183	n.a.	n.a.	n.a.	28,940
Banque Nationale d'Algérie	2005	8,300	47.78	277	−40	−15.3	−0.47	6,249
	2006	10,076	49.28	351	61	19.26	0.66	7,879
Crédit Populaire d'Algérie	2005	5,844	31.51	450	37	8.52	0.64	4,990
	2006	6,857	28.22	653	111	19.87	1.72	5,731
Banque de Développement Local	2005	2,795	35.07	75	2	2.52	0.07	1,874
	2006	3,155	36.82	83	3	4.12	0.11	2,153
Banque Algérienne de Développement	2005	1,532	72.31	82	25	35.66	1.52	372
BNP Paribas El Djazaïr	2005	500	41.4	55	6	14.01	1.5	269
	2006	832	38.35	74	14	22.06	2.14	428
	2007	1,146	47.53	109	23	24.46	2.25	669
Société Générale Algérie	2005	520	46.17	43	7	20.16	1.69	375
	2006	909	52.39	50	9	18.69	1.23	665
Banque Al Baraka d'Algérie-Albaraka of Algeria	2005	564	66.23	46	9	21.29	1.64	299
	2006	646	64.65	68	15	25.09	2.36	388
	2007	842	67.02	90	20	24.4	2.59	667

Table 3A.3 (Continued)

Name of the bank	Year	Total assets (US$ mil)	Net loans/ total assets (%)	Equity (US$ mil)	Net income (US$ mil)	Return on average equity (ROAE)	Return on average assets (ROAA)	Deposits and short-term funding (US$ mil)
Natixis Algérie	2005	256	24.97	38	4	14.04	1.86	194
	2006	518	51.26	59	3	5.31	0.67	311
Arab Banking Corporation – Algeria	2005	429	20.47	45	8	17.89	1.98	245
	2006	418	24.68	38	−9	−20.87	−2.06	242
Algeria Gulf Bank	2005	70	50.77	21	1	4.99	1.97	48
	2006	142	57.48	42	5	14.82	4.38	100
	2007	218	61.06	47	8	17.07	4.25	170
Banque du Maghreb Arabe pour l'Investissement et le Commerce	2005	195	9.51	68	2	2.96	1.08	125
	2006	210	4.3	73	3	4.68	1.63	135
Trust Bank Algeria	2005	107	44.18	22	4	26.45	5.26	67
	2006	172	59.02	46	0	1.15	0.28	102
Housing Bank for Trade and Finance – Algeria	2006	119	39.22	39	n.a.	n.a.	n.a.	49

Source: Compiled by authors from BankScope.

Notes

1. Aghion et al. (2001) develop and highlight the theoretical and empirical link between financial reforms, productive efficiency, spillovers and competitive conditions.
2. Bear in mind that most African economies exhibited symptoms of financial repression during the 1970–1980 period, although by the end of the 1990s most had embarked on financial reforms. See also the evidence in Kasekende and Atingi-Ego (1999) and Reinikka and Svensson (1999) on Uganda, as well as Senbet and Otchere (2006) and World Bank (2008) on financial sector reforms in some African countries.
3. A recent Gallup poll covering 18 African countries shows that only 19 per cent of residents have personal bank accounts. There is wide variation between countries: in South Africa 49 per cent of citizens have personal bank accounts, followed by Kenya (29 per cent) and Zimbabwe (28 per cent), while in the Democratic Republic of Congo and Niger, only 1 per cent of citizens have personal bank accounts (see http://gallup.com/poll/127901 accessed 12 May 2010.
4. See Kasekende et al. (2009) chapter in the *Africa Competitiveness Report*, 2009.
5. According to the Central Bank of Nigeria's 2008 *Annual Report*, the main objectives of these reforms include removing controls on interest rates to increase the level of savings and improve allocative efficiency; eliminating non-price rationing of credit to reduce misdirected credit and increase competition; adopting indirect monetary management in place of the imposition of a credit ceiling on individual banks; enhancing institutional structures and supervision; strengthening the money and capital markets through policy changes and distress resolution measures; and improving the linkages between the formal and informal financial sectors.
6. See speech by Governor Sanusi at the University of Kano, 26 February 2010.
7. In June 2010 the central bank reported that margin lending and loans backed by stocks stood at ₦1.2 trillion.
8. The equilibrium test is performed by replacing the dependent variable with an indicator of bank return, such as ROA, in the estimation equation. In equilibrium, the rates of return should be uncorrelated with input prices, such that $H = 0$ implies the data are in equilibrium.

References

Aghion, P., C. Harris, P. Howitt, and J. Vickers. 2001. 'Competition, imitation and growth with step-by-step innovation'. *Review of Economic Studies*, 68(3): 467–92.

Bank Audi. 2008. Egypt Economic Report. Cairo: Bank Audi.

Bresnahan, T.F. 1982. 'The Oligopoly solution concept is identified'. *Economic Letters*, 10: 87–92.

Bresnahan, T.F. 1989. 'Empirical studies of industries with market power'. In R. Schmalensee and R. D. Willig (eds.), *Handbook of Industrial Organization*, vol. 2. Amsterdam: North Holland.

Capital Market Authority. 2008. *Capital Market Authority for Egypt*, Annual Report. Cairo: CMA.

Central Bank of Nigeria. 2008. *Annual Report*. Abuja: Central Bank of Nigeria.
Claessens, S. and L. Laeven. 2004. 'What drives bank competition? Some international evidence'. *Journal of Money, Credit, and Banking*, 36(2): 563–84.
Evans, A.D., C.J. Green, and V. Murinde. 2002. 'Human capital and financial development in economic growth: New evidence using the translog production function'. *International Journal of Finance and Economics*, 7(2): 123–40.
Green, C.J., C.H. Kirkpatrick, and V. Murinde. 2005. *Finance and Development: Surveys of Theory, Evidence and Policy*. Cheltenham: Edward Elgar.
IMF. 2009. *World Economic Outlook*. Washington D.C.: IMF.
Kasekende, L.A. and M. Atingi-Ego. 1999. 'Uganda's experience with aid'. *Journal of African Economies*, 8: 617–49.
Kasekende, L., K. Mlambo, V. Murinde, and T. Zhao. 2009. 'Restructuring for competitiveness: The financial services sector in Africa's largest economies'. In World Economic Forum ed., *Africa Competitiveness Report 2009*, Chapter 3, pp. 49–81. Washington, D.C.: The World Bank.
Kirkpatrick, C.H., V. Murinde, and M. Tefula. 2008. 'The measurement and determinants of X-inefficiency in commercial banks in sub-Saharan Africa'. *European Journal of Finance*, 14(7): 625–39.
Lau, L. 1982. 'On identifying the degree of competitiveness from industry price and output data'. *Economic Letters*, 10: 93–9.
Levine, R. and A. Demirgüç-Kunt. 2009. 'Finance and economic opportunity'. Proceedings of the Annual World Bank Conference on Development Economics 2008. Washington, D.C.: World Bank.
Matthews, K., V. Murinde, and T. Zhao. 2007. 'Competitive conditions among the major British banks'. *Journal of Banking and Finance*, 31(7): 2025–42.
Mboweni, T.T. 2004. *The South African Banking Sector: An Overview of the Past 10 Years*. Basel: Bank for International Settlements.
Murinde, V. 2009. *Bank Performance Indicators*. University of Birmingham, UK: Mimeo.
Panzar, J. and J. Rosse. 1987. 'Testing for Monopoly Equilibrium'. *Journal of Industrial Economics*, 35: 443–56.
Reinikka, R. and J. Svensson. 1999. 'Confronting competition: Investment response and constraints in Uganda'. Unpublished Working Paper. Washington, D.C.: World Bank.
Senbet, L. and I. Otchere. 2006. 'Financial sector reforms in Africa: Perspectives on issues and policies.' Annual Bank Conference on Development Economics, pp. 81–119. Washington, D.C.: World Bank.
World Bank. Various years. *Doing Business* Annual Reports, 2005–2008. Washington, D.C.: World Bank.
World Bank. 2008. *World Bank Report 2008*. Washington, D.C.: World Bank.
World Bank. 2010. *World Development Indicators 2010*. Washington, D.C.: World Bank.

4
Regulatory Reforms and Their Impact on the Competitiveness and Efficiency of the Banking Sector: A Case Study of Kenya

Francis M. Mwega

4.1 Introduction

Increased competition and efficiency of the financial sector can contribute to greater financial stability, product innovation and access by households and firms to financial services, which in turn can improve the prospects for economic growth (Hauner and Peiris, 2005). It is therefore important to identify the kind of reforms and environments that may help to promote competition and efficiency in the financial systems of African countries. Kenya makes a useful case study for an evaluation of the success of financial sector reforms in a low-income country as it has a well-developed financial system for a country of its income level (Beck and Fuchs, 2004). In this respect, this is one of few studies that systematically analyses the impact of regulatory reforms on the level of banking competition and efficiency in Africa. However, there is concern that the recent reforms, particularly the consolidation within the banking system, may have resulted in a sound but uncompetitive system that could fail to deliver on greater access and financial deepening, even though increasing the sector's profitability.[1] The objective of this chapter is therefore to analyse these issues by tracing the reform steps and by empirically examining the development of financial sector competition and efficiency.

Financial sector reforms have mainly been motivated by the financial repression paradigm promulgated by McKinnon (1973) and Shaw (1973) who emphasized the role of government failures in the sector. Accordingly, the objective of financial reforms is to reduce or reverse this 'repression'. According to the McKinnon–Shaw hypothesis, financial repression arises mainly when a country imposes ceilings on nominal deposit and lending interest rates at a low level relative to inflation. The resulting low or negative real interest rates discourage savings mobilization and the channelling of the mobilized savings through the financial system. While the low and negative interest rates facilitate government borrowing, they discourage saving and financial intermediation, leading to credit rationing by the banking system with negative impacts on the quantity and quality of investment and hence on economic growth.

Advocates of this hypothesis postulate that many financial systems in Africa were until recently subjected to financial repression characterized by low or negative real interest rates; high reserve requirements which led to high spreads thereby imposing an implicit tax on financial intermediation; mandatory credit ceilings; directed credit allocation to priority sectors which undermined allocative efficiency; and heavy government ownership and management of financial institutions.

An important component of financial sector reforms was interest rates liberalization. It was argued that this would raise real interest rates, and increase saving and the supply of investable resources in the economy. The productivity of investment would also rise as these resources were channelled to projects that had higher rates of return than hitherto. Liberalization of interest rates would also discourage capital flight and help to stabilize the economy. Financial sector reforms also included (a) reducing direct and indirect taxation of financial institutions through reserve requirements, mandatory credit ceilings and credit allocation guidelines; (b) reducing barriers to competition in the financial sector by scaling down government ownership through privatization; (c) facilitating entry into the sector by domestic and foreign firms; and (d) restructuring and liquidation of solvent banks (Inanga, 1995).

The pertinent issue addressed in this chapter is the extent to which Kenya's banking sector has improved its competitiveness and efficiency with financial sector reforms and liberalization. The rest of the chapter is organized as follows. Section 4.2 describes financial sector reforms in Kenya; while Section 4.3 investigates their impact on competitiveness; and Section 4.4 looks at the efficiency of Kenya's banking system. Section 4.5 concludes the chapter.

4.2 Financial sector reforms and developments in the banking sector in Kenya

Up to the early 1980s, Kenya's financial sector was highly repressed. Its financial system was characterized by interest rate restrictions, domestic credit controls, high reserve requirements, segmented financial markets, underdeveloped money and capital markets, and exchange rate and international capital controls (Kamau, 2009). Kenya undertook financial sector reforms from the late 1980s. The financial reforms were aimed at liberalizing interest rates, reducing controls on credit, enhancing competition and efficiency and productivity gains in the financial system. Furthermore, the reforms were directed towards strengthening the central bank's supervisory framework and improving the effectiveness of monetary policy through greater reliance on market forces (Brownbridge and Harvey, 1998).

Kenya's financial sector has therefore undergone reforms for about the last two decades. The country formally adopted financial sector forms in 1989, supported by a US$170 million World Bank adjustment credit. Financial reform proposals were first incorporated in the 1986–1990 structural adjustment programme. The main feature of the programme was full interest rate liberalization which was achieved in July 1991 after a gradual increase in nominal rates in the 1980s. In the first half of the 1980s, for example, nominal deposit rates were increased by about 100 per cent and lending rates by about 50 per cent, from relatively low levels. Before the reforms, the government followed a low interest rate policy whose main objective was to promote investment. For about a decade and a half, from the time the Central Bank of Kenya (CBK) was established in 1966 until 1980, interest rates were only adjusted upwards once, in 1974, by 1 to 2 percentage points. Liberalization gave more freedom to market forces to determine interest rates by removing preferential credit schemes and by establishing a market for government debt instruments.

A major component of reforms has been the restructuring of financial institutions, usually undertaken after a banking crisis. The country experienced a banking crisis in 1986 when a number of 'specified' non-bank financial institutions (NBFIs) and a small commercial bank collapsed. Consequently, eight financial institutions were taken over and merged into a state bank in 1989 (Consolidated Bank of Kenya). The CBK also strengthened the supervision and the inspection of financial institutions and introduced a Deposit Protection Fund which guarantees deposits up to Ksh. 100,000 to protect small depositors. The initial capital requirements for setting up financial institutions were increased for both commercial banks and 'specified' NBFIs. In addition, the cash ratio was reintroduced to moderate excess liquidity within commercial banks.

The second banking crisis occurred in 1998, when five banking institutions were placed under statutory management (Kamau, 2009). The bank failures were attributed to a high burden of non-performing loans. Following this crisis, the CBK put in several measures to foster a sound and stable banking system. First, the CBK in consultation with the Ministry of Finance raised further the minimum paid up capital requirements for banks to enhance their capitalization while the government was encouraged to divest progressively from the banking system. It was also recommended that efforts be made to improve the judiciary in order to improve the efficiency of courts in handling disputes involving the financial sector. The CBK also encouraged small banks to merge so as to ensure adequate capitalization and bank regulations were tightened. The Banking Act was also amended to give the CBK more powers to enforce banking laws and regulations, including the power to levy monetary penalties for non-compliance.

4.2.1 Mergers and acquisitions in Kenya's financial sector

A substantial number of mergers and acquisitions have taken place in the banking sector in Kenya, partly occasioned by the need to meet the increasing minimum core capital requirements and to enhance the market share of institutions in the local banking industry (Kamau, 2009). Between 1994 and 2005 there were 20 successful mergers, with the number increasing to 26 by 2007, with one merger in 2008.

In addition to mergers, some banks have expanded their branch networks in the region. For instance, Kenya Commercial Bank has expanded regionally and opened branches in Juba and Rumbek in Southern Sudan and has announced plans to open several additional branches in Rwanda, Uganda and Burundi. This is in addition to their existing operations in Tanzania.

4.2.2 Movement towards universal banking in Kenya

Narrowly defined, universal banking combines commercial banking activity (collections of deposits and making loans) and investment banking (issuing, underwriting, placing and trading company shares). Defined broadly, financial institutions are permitted under universal banking to perform an array of functions and services. It allows a bank to decide its own portfolio of businesses, and appropriate service delivery channels and infrastructure, yet within an applicable regulatory framework. According to Saunders and Walter (1994), universal banking involves 'the conduct of a range of financial services comprising deposit-taking and lending, trading of financial instruments and foreign exchanges (and other derivatives), underwriting of new debt and equity issues, brokerage, investment management and insurance'.[2]

Kenya has increasingly moved into universal banking. This is reflected in the elimination of NBFIs, which converted to become commercial banks, merged with the parent banks or closed.[3] Kenya therefore issues full banking licences without functional delineation between merchant and commercial banking. There is now reduced segmentation of banking into deposit-taking, lending, funds management, and so on, with a growing reliance on products and processes like securitization. Movement towards universal banking is also reflected in an increasing share of net commissions and fees in the banks' total income which increased from 10 per cent in 1998 to 21 per cent in 2007 as shown in Table 4.1.[4]

The country now has banks that own insurance companies and some have set up insurance agencies to push forward their concept of bank assurance; others own stock brokerage firms (e.g. Cooperative Bank of Kenya) or are in the process of acquiring or establishing one inhouse (e.g. Equity Bank). Hence there have been increased synergies between the banking, insurance and securities sectors with removal of regulatory barriers between the different segments of the financial sector. Given the convergence and consolidation of the financial services, some players have called for the establishment of an overall services regulatory authority (Mutuku, 2008).

According to the CBK, the convergence of financial services is a global phenomenon, with among its key drivers being the customer demands for 'one stop financial services super markets' and competition.[5] This poses regulatory challenges as different financial sector entities are subject to different regulatory regimes. Some countries such as Britain have addressed the situation by the formation of an overall financial services regulatory authority. The CBK has adopted a consolidated supervision approach, which takes a holistic view of the risks facing banks including those emanating from domestic and foreign banks as well as their non-bank subsidiaries. This requires information sharing and coordination amongst the various regulators in the financial sector. The CBK and the various regulatory agencies across the capital market, insurance

Table 4.1 Percentage share of fees and commissions (net) in banks' total income

1998	1999	2000	2001	2002	2003	2004	2005	2006	2007	2008
10	15	17	21	22	24	26	21	22	22	21

and pensions recently signed a memorandum of understanding (MoU) for collaboration among themselves in the supervision of financial institutions and other matters of mutual interest.[6]

Financial sector reforms have undoubtedly strengthened Kenya's banking sector in the last decade or so, in terms of product offerings and service quality, stability and profitability (Kamau, 2009). Some microfinance institutions like K-Rep Bank and Equity Bank have emerged, targeting the small-scale borrowers. Equity Bank, which converted to a commercial bank in 2004, had over two million customers by 2008, more than 35 per cent of the entire industry. During this period, only two banks have been put under CBK statutory management (Prudential Bank and Charterhouse Bank), in comparison to the 1980s and early 1990s when a large number of banks collapsed.[7]

A 2007 CBK banking survey provides the following summary of the developments and stylized facts of the Kenya banking sector in the last decade or so.

- There had been a shift of focus to the consumer with the introduction of some new retail products. There had been major expansion of lending to individuals in salaried employment through mortgages and consumer loans.
- There had been an aggressive expansion into the retail banking sector by several banks not previously active, such as Kenya Commercial Bank, Cooperative Bank of Kenya and Equity Bank. Banks were expanding their branch networks to capture lower cost retail deposits.
- Several banks (including foreign banks) were now favourably looking at public sector lending because of improved governance. The establishment of commercial courts had improved the lending environment and reduced the time taken to resolve default cases.
- There was a concentration of banks in the urban areas and the rural areas were under-served. Despite a proliferation of financial institutions, the survey results indicated that 38 per cent of Kenyans had no access to financial services and products, hence classified as 'unbanked' or financially excluded. This indicates a big gap in access to financial services and products by Kenyans. In view of this, there were enormous opportunities in the economy to expand banking services to parts of the population that do not hold bank accounts, particularly in the rural areas including mobile telephone money transfer services such as MPESA and ZAP.

- Industry fragmentation was high, with banks neither working together nor being fully open with each other. There had been an over-emphasis on the use of collateral. Historically, banks had placed a major emphasis on physical security. On the corporate side, they had often overlooked cash flows and the viability of projects. This was changing with a growth in unsecured lending.
- Banks have not provided transparent pricing, making comparisons difficult. Also, the big banks (13 in 2007) compete for about 80 per cent of the market, while the remaining banks share 20 per cent of the market. The market segments that were highly competitive to the banking sector included the corporate and retail sectors; and merchant and investment banking. The market sectors that were least competitive included internet banking, home loans and vehicle financing.
- Islamic banking was rapidly taking root in the Kenyan market. Some banks had launched strictly Islamic products and this was likely to increase competition in the banking sector. Four banks so far – Barclays Bank of Kenya, Kenya Commercial Bank, K-Rep Bank and Dubai Bank – had introduced Islamic banking products in the market.
- The banking sector had witnessed re-packaging of banking and financial services to satisfy the changing needs of customers. This had resulted in the rapid growth of consumer banking products including Unsecured Personal Loans, Auto Loans, Unsecured Professional Loans, Safari Savings Accounts, Jumbo Junior Accounts and SME Business Model Accounts. An increased number of institutions were offering e-banking to their customers.

4.3 Impact of regulatory reforms on the competitiveness of Kenya's banking system

This section investigates whether the financial sector reforms, particularly the consolidation in the banking system in the last decade, has enhanced competition in the sector. It also analyses the role of bank size and foreign ownership in the competitive condition and performance of the banking system. While some of the relationships among competition, stability and banking system performance have been analysed in the theoretical literature, empirical research on the issue of banking competition, particularly in Africa, is still at a very early stage.

The analysis is based on the premise that competition is one of the most important and fundamental issues in the financial services sector, especially at this point of financial globalization and a global financial crisis, with competition hypothesized to stimulate productivity growth either by general technical progress or by efficiency improvement, or both (Kasekende et al., 2009). It however exacerbates the moral hazard problem of financial institutions, especially banks, so that the issue of competition in the financial services sector carries very important implications for productive efficiency, financial stability and for the effective regulation and supervision of the financial services sector.

4.3.1 The structure-conduct-performance model

One way to analyse the competitiveness of the banking system is through the Herfindahl–Hirschmann Index (HHI) and other concentration measures.[8] These measures tend to associate the market structure with the pricing conduct of market participants. Hence, the approach is based on the premise that higher market concentration leads to higher prices and excess returns for example through collusion. This justifies regulations that remove entry restrictions and hence reduce market concentration.

Estimates of the HHI and the concentration ratio of assets of the four top banks (CR4) reveal that the Kenyan banking sector has experienced reduced concentration and presumably more competition in the sector over 1998–2007 for all categories of banks, with a slight increase in 2008 (Table 4.2).[9] The data however show that the share of the 13 largest banks (with assets of more than Ksh. 20 billion) slightly increased over 1998–2008 at the expense of 21 medium-size (Ksh. 4–20 billion) and 9 small banks (less than Ksh. 4 billion), so that the picture is not clear-cut. The share of foreign banks increased to a peak of 0.484 in 2002–2003, but declined thereafter to a low of 0.359 in 2008.

The results also suggest that small banks are the least competitive (most concentrated) followed by large banks and then medium-sized banks. This pattern seems to reflect the number of banks in each component. In 2008, for example, the country had 9 small banks (typically accounting for 2–5 per cent of total assets in the previous decade); 13 large banks (accounting for 78–81 per cent in the previous decade); and 21 medium-sized banks (accounting for 16–18 per cent in the previous decade). Similarly, foreign banks (11 in 2008, for example and accounting for 36–48 per cent in the previous decade) are less competitive (more concentrated) than local banks (32 in 2008, and accounting for 51–64 per cent in the previous decade).

The structure-conduct-performance model that underpins the HHI and other concentration measures has various limitations. The theory of industrial organization for example suggests that the competitiveness

Table 4.2 HHI and other concentration indices

	HHI (Bank assets)						CR4	Market share			
	Large banks	Medium banks	Small banks	Foreign banks	Local banks	All banks	All banks	Large banks	Medium banks	Small banks	Foreign banks
1998	0.167	0.084	0.194	0.304	0.165	0.108	0.567	0.793	0.164	0.043	0.402
1999	0.159	0.080	0.194	0.287	0.152	0.101	0.560	0.785	0.172	0.043	0.414
2000	0.153	0.078	0.151	0.270	0.142	0.096	0.545	0.784	0.172	0.044	0.434
2001	0.144	0.068	0.145	0.264	0.124	0.092	0.527	0.785	0.173	0.042	0.457
2002	0.145	0.062	0.143	0.266	0.112	0.092	0.532	0.79	0.172	0.038	0.484
2003	0.140	0.061	0.144	0.262	0.104	0.089	0.520	0.788	0.178	0.034	0.484
2004	0.129	0.061	0.142	0.272	0.101	0.085	0.512	0.803	0.165	0.032	0.445
2005	0.114	0.059	0.140	0.240	0.096	0.075	0.478	0.8	0.172	0.028	0.424
2006	0.107	0.059	0.129	0.221	0.096	0.072	0.457	0.807	0.165	0.028	0.425
2007	0.106	0.055	0.127	0.221	0.094	0.071	0.445	0.811	0.165	0.024	0.426
2008	0.111	0.061	0.130	0.236	0.111	0.085	0.447	0.812	0.149	0.039	0.359

of an industry cannot be measured by market structure indicators alone, such as the number of institutions, or the Herfindahl–Hirschman and other market concentration indices (Baumol et al., 1982). The threat of entry can be a more important determinant of the behaviour of market participants.

Testing for the degree of effective competition therefore requires a structural, contestability approach, along the lines pursued in much of the industrial organization literature. The basic idea of market contestability is that, on the one hand, there are several sets of conditions that can yield competitive outcomes, with a competitive outcome possible even in concentrated systems. As in other sectors, the degree of competition in the banking system should be measured with respect to the actual behaviour of (marginal) bank conduct. To date, however, few studies have applied this approach to African countries, with the exception of Buchs and Mathisen (2005) and Claessens and Leaven (2003). These considerations suggest some advantages of using a more structural approach to assess the degree of competition in the banking sector in Kenya.

4.3.2 The Panzar-Rosse model

A frequently utilized approach is the one suggested by Panzar and Rosse (1987), which uses bank-level data to investigate the extent to which changes in factor input prices are reflected in (equilibrium) revenues earned by a specific bank. Under perfect competition, an increase in input prices raises both marginal costs and total revenues by the same amount as the rise in costs. Under monopoly, an increase in input prices will increase marginal costs, reduce equilibrium output, and consequently reduce total revenues. The P-R model therefore provides a measure ('H-statistic') of the degree of competitiveness of the system, with $H \leq 0$ being a collusive (joint monopoly) competition, $0. > .H. < 1$ being monopolistic competition, and $H = 1$ being perfect competition.

The advantage of the P-R methodology is that it uses bank-level data and allows for bank-specific differences in the production function. It also allows one to study differences between types of banks (e.g. large versus small, foreign versus local banks). Its drawback is that it assumes that the banking industry is in equilibrium, but we can test whether this condition is satisfied.

The P-R model has been extensively used to analyse the nature of competition in mature banking systems, but only more recently in emerging markets' banking systems. We estimated the P-R model using a reduced form revenue equation proposed by Hauner and Peiris (2005). We utilize an annual panel dataset of 43 banks over 1998–2007 compiled by Oloo (2008):

$$\text{Ln INTYAS}_{it} = \beta_0 + \beta_1 \text{Ln ADMEAS}_{it} + \beta_2 \text{Ln INTEDEP}_{it},$$
$$+ \beta_3 \text{Ln OTHEREAS}_i + \dots$$

where

- INTYAS is the ratio of gross interest revenue to total assets (proxy for output price of loans). Gross interest revenue is given by the sum on interest income from loans and advances as well as government securities.
- ADMEAS is the ratio of administrative expenses (which mainly comprises staff costs) to total assets (proxy for input price of labour).
- INTEDEP is the ratio of interest expenses to total deposits (proxy for input price of deposits); and
- OTHEREAS is the ratio of other operating and administrative expenses to total assets (proxy for input price of equipment/fixed capital). This was derived by deducting the interest and administrative expenses from a bank's total expenditures.

This model is similar to models used previously in the literature to estimate *H*-statistics for banking industries. The *H*-statistic test is defined as the sum of the elasticities of the above equation with respect to input prices (that is, the linear combination of the coefficients of $\beta_1 + \beta_2 + \beta_3$). The panel was estimated by a random effects estimator. The results reported in Table 4.3 are plausible and suggest that the we can use this model to generate H-statistics.

With a combined value of about 0.38, the *H*-statistic for Kenya suggested that monopolistic competition is the best description of the degree of competition in the country with the statistic in the range between zero and one. All the three factor prices significantly drive the *H*-statistic in Kenya's banking system. These results are supported by an earlier study by Claessens and Laeven (2003) which found an *H*-statistic of 0.58 for Kenya banking system over 1994–2001. The results are also consistent with those found for other countries in the region (see Table 4.4).

Disaggregating the data (Table 4.5), the results suggest that, as with HHI results, small banks are the least competitive followed by large

Table 4.3 Random effects regression results: dependent variable Ln INTYAS*

	Coeff	*Z*	*P* > *Z*
Ln ADMEAS	0.153	3.37	0.001
Ln INTEDEP	0.130	5.39	0.000
Ln OTHEREAS	0.084	2.48	0.013
CONST	0.228	0.67	0.502
Number of obs = 349			
R-sq: overall = 0.5111			
Wald Chi^2 (12) = 469.28			
Prob > Chi^2 = 0.0000			

*Other independent variables and equation diagnostics are not shown.

Table 4.4 Banking sector market structure in selected SSA countries

Country	Sample period	*H*-statistic	No. of banks	No. of observations
Ghana	1998–2003	0.56	13	65
Kenya	1994–2001	0.58	34	106
Nigeria	1994–2001	0.67	42	186
South Africa	1994–2001	0.85	45	186
Uganda	1999Q1–2002Q3	0.30	15	196
Uganda	2002Q4–2004Q2	0.49	15	97

Source: Hauner and Peiris (2005); Buchs and Mathisen (2005); Claessens and Laeven (2003).

Table 4.5 *H*-statistics from disaggregated data

	H-statistics	No. of observations	Wald tests
Foreign banks	0.199	91	$Chi^2(3) = 3.56$, with Prob > $Chi^2 = 0.31$
Local banks	0.525	258	$Chi^2(3) = 64.33$, with Prob > $Chi^2 = 0.00$
Small banks	0.138	74	$Chi^2(3) = 1.84$, with Prob > $Chi^2 = 0.61$
Medium banks	0.315	171	$Chi^2(3) = 29.71$, with Prob > $Chi^2 = 0.00$
Large banks	0.298	104	$Chi^2(3) = 19.22$, with Prob > $Chi^2 = 0.00$

banks and then medium-sized banks reflecting the size of the sample (banks) in the various segments of the market. Similarly, foreign banks are less competitive when compared to local banks.[10]

Despite the advantages, the P-R method has several limitations (Kasekende et al., 2009). First, the method assumes that market participants are price-takers in the input market, so that factor prices are exogenous. Second, the P-R method assumes long-run equilibrium for the identification of the models of perfect and monopolistic competition. Third, the economic interpretation of the *H*-statistic is not without problems. Although the sign of *H* is informative, the specific value of *H* carries an ambiguous economic interpretation under existing theoretical analysis as it does not map monotonically into any static or dynamic oligopolistic behaviour.

The empirical test for long-run equilibrium as explained by Shaffer (2004) stipulates that competitive capital markets will equalize risk-adjusted rates of return across banks such that, in equilibrium, rates of return should not be correlated statistically with input prices. The idea behind this test is that, in equilibrium, returns on bank assets should be unrelated to input prices. Since the P-R model is only valid if the market is in equilibrium, we therefore tested this hypothesis by estimating the following equation:

$$\begin{aligned}\text{Ln ROA}_{\text{it}} = \beta_0 + \beta_1 \text{ Ln ADMEAS}_{\text{it}} + \beta_2 \text{ Ln INTEDEP}_{\text{it}} \\ + \beta_3 \text{ Ln OTHEREAS}_{\text{it}} + \cdots\end{aligned}$$

where ROA is the pre-tax rate of return on assets given by a bank's pre-tax profits divided by assets. We define the equilibrium *E*-statistic as $\beta_1 + \beta_2 + \beta_3$. We tested whether $E = 0$ again using a Chi^2-Test. If rejected, the market is assumed not to be in equilibrium. The results are given in Table 4.6 and suggest that the Kenya banking system was in some equilibrium during the period under investigation. The joint *E*-statistic is non-significant at least at the 10% level, with the estimated $\text{Chi}^2(3) = 2.61$ with $\text{Prob} > \text{Chi}^2 = 0.4558$.

4.3.3 The persistence of profitability (POP) model

This model captures the competitive dynamics by examining the persistence of rate of return and is therefore consistent with the test for market equilibrium discussed above. The basic argument is that high excess profits would attract new entrants into the market thereby reducing the

Table 4.6 Random-effects GLS regression results: dependent variable ROA*

	Coeff	*Z*-value	*P* > *Z*	Coeff	*Z*-value	*P* > *Z*
Ln ADMEAS	0.002	0.03	0.973			
Ln INTEDEP	−0.067	−1.56	0.120	−0.064	−1.63	0.104
Ln OTHEREAS	0.017	0.29	0.771			
CONST	0.893	1.45	0.147	1.258	11.63	0.000
Number of obs = 316				Number of obs = 355		
R-sq: overall = 0.1955				R-sq: overall = 0.1740		
Wald $Chi^2(12) = 40.26$				Wald $Chi^2(4) = 33.99$		
Prob > $Chi^2 = 0.0001$				Prob > $Chi^2 = 0.0000$		

*Other independent variables and equation diagnostics are not shown.

excess returns. Therefore, if excess profits tend to persist from year to year, then there might be barriers to entry or banks might be exploiting monopoly power. Due to the difficulty of formulating a structural model brought about by the unobservable threat of entry, the standard POP study is typically based on an auto-regressive model for bank profitability.

As suggested by Kasekende et al. (2009), we estimate the following POP model:

$$\text{Ln MK}_{it} = \beta_0 + \beta_1 \text{ Ln MK}_{it-1} + \beta_2 \text{ MK}_{it-1}{}^{*}\text{D2003} + \cdots$$

where MK_{it} is the mark-up on performing loans at time t, defined as the ratio of their price over their marginal cost, MK_{it-1} is the mark-up at time $t-1$.

The coefficient β_1 measures the persistence of MK_{it-1} into MK_{it}. A significantly negative value for β_2 would suggest a reduction in the persistence of the mark-up in the period 1998–2002 compared to 2003–2007, which in turn could indicate an increase in the intensity of competition. In the chapter, we proxy MK by the ratio of banks' total income to total expenditure.[11] Since the lagged dependent variable might be endogenous to the error term through e_{it-1}, the model was estimated by the Allerano and Bond dynamic panel estimator. The results are given in Table 4.7.

The results show evidence of profit persistence, with the dependent variable significant at the 1% level. The mark-up has however reduced in the study period, perhaps to indicate an increase in the intensity of competition.

Table 4.7 Dynamic panel regression results: dependent variable Ln MK_i

	Coeff	Z-value	P > Z	Coeff	Z-value	P > Z
Ln MK_{it-1}	0.508	3.17	0.001	0.762	4.23	0.000
MK_{it-1}*D2003	−1.031	−5.64	0.000	−1.270	−6.33	0.000
CONS	−0.007	−0.43	0.669	−0.0001	−0.01	0.992
Number of obs = 239				Number of obs = 239		
Wald $Chi^2(8) = 45.97$				Wald $Chi^2(3) = 47.54$		

*Other independent variables and equation diagnostics are not shown.

4.3.4 The conjectural variation model

In this section, we investigate how financial reforms affected the degree of competition in the Kenya banking sector using the more sophisticated conjectural variation approach, based on the method devised by Bresnahan (1989). Based on microeconomic foundations, this method allows the derivation of an index of the firm's market power that is calculated as the deviation of the market price from the marginal cost. By estimating parameters of a market power index interacted with a post-2003 dummy variable, we evaluate whether competition increased or not.

As in Kubo (2006), we consider a loan market in which banks face a demand function with both labour and deposits as factor inputs, and loans as banks' sole output. From Bank i's profits maximization, we derive the Lerner index of market power:

$$\frac{p - MC_i}{p} = \frac{\theta_i}{\eta}, \tag{1}$$

where MC_i isthe marginal cost, and η is the elasticity of loan demand to the lending interest rate; and θ_i is Bank *i*'s conjectural elasticity of total loans of the banking industry with respect to its own loans, that is, Bank *i*'s expectation on how other banks react to its output change. This term indicates the bank's market power – that is, the extent to which the bank can manipulate the loan supply and the lending interest rate by collusion with other banks. When the market is in perfect competition, θ_i, takes the value of zero for all banks. In a monopoly, θ_i equals one. The estimated Lerner index, L ε [0,1], measures the mark-up of price over marginal cost, indicating the market power of a bank. We estimate a cross-sectional average of θ_i/η interacted with a post-2003 dummy to see how it has evolved over time.

Rearranging Equation (1) yields

$$R_i = q_i\, MC_i + \frac{\theta}{\eta} . q_i \tag{1'}$$

where R_i refers to Bank *i*'s interest income.

As an empirical strategy, we estimated the bank's supply function (1′) simultaneously with the cost function on the assumption that this will improve the precision of the estimation results.

The results showed that the Lerner index of market power ($= \frac{\theta}{\eta}$) was significant at the 1 per cent level and that it declined in the post-2003 period, consistent with the Persistence of Profitability (POP) model results. The decline is however only significant at 12–13 per cent level. The Lerner index is also quite low, consistent with our earlier finding from the Panzar-Ross model results that the Kenya banking system can be characterized by monopolistic competition.

The results showed a highly significant demand elasticity of loans, which was quite stable in the post-2003 period, suggesting a decline in the conjectural variation coefficient (θ) post-2003. The results are therefore consistent with an increase in the banking competition post-2003 as found under the POP methodology.

4.4 Impact of financial reforms on the efficiency of Kenya's banking system

In this section, we briefly discuss the efficiency of Kenya'ss banking system based on recent literature on the subject. There are two typical ways to estimate the efficiency of the banking sector: through the non-parametric Data Envelope Analysis (DEA); and through the parametric stochastic frontier approach (SFA).

The DEA is a linear programming procedure for a frontier analysis of inputs and outputs (Trick, 1996). It assigns a score of one to a unit only when comparisons with other relevant units do not provide evidence of inefficiency in the use of any input or output. As well, it assigns an efficiency score less than one to (relatively) inefficient units. A score less than one means that a linear combination of other units from the sample could produce the same vector of outputs using a smaller vector of inputs. The score reflects the radial distance from the estimated production frontier to the decision making unit (DMU) under consideration.

The advantages of the DEA is that it can handle multiple input and multiple output models; it does not require an assumption of a functional form relating inputs to outputs; DMUs are directly compared with a peer or combination of peers; and inputs and outputs can have very different units. On the other hand, DEA has a number of limitations. First, since it is an extreme point technique, noise such as measurement error can cause significant problems. Second, DEA is good at estimating the 'relative' efficiency of a DMU but it converges very slowly to 'absolute' efficiency. In other words, it can tell you how well one is doing compared with peers but not compared with a 'theoretical maximum.' Third, since DEA is a non-parametric technique, statistical hypothesis tests may not be available or are difficult to find. Fourth, since a standard formulation of DEA creates a separate linear programme for each DMU, large problems can be computationally intensive.

The SFA, on the other hand, utilizes econometrics whereby a regression model includes both a normally distributed random error term and an efficiency component assumed to follow a one-sided distribution. SFA is therefore stochastic, but requires the choice of a functional form and an ad hoc assumption about the distribution of the efficiency component. The SFA, for example, may entail a regression of the total costs faced by a bank against input prices and output variables. In this case, a standard multi-product transcendental logarithmic (translog) cost function is typically specified and deviations from the cost frontier are estimated based on this function.

Kamau (2009) provides DEA score estimates (based on three inputs and two outputs discussed below); and stochastic frontier efficiency scores over 1996–2006, roughly corresponding to our study period. The DEA technical efficiency scores were estimated from both constant returns to scale (CRS) and variable returns to scale (VRS).

Table 4.8 presents the results of efficiency scores for the banking sector in Kenya. The results show the following. First, the different measures of technical efficiency give different efficiency scores (lowest for DEA constant returns, highest for SFA scores), so that the focus should be on the pattern over time and across different types of banks. The average efficiency score in the banking sector was 0.58 (DEA constant returns), 0.65 (DEA variable returns) and 0.84 (SFA). This implies that the commercial banks in Kenya could have increased outputs by between 15.9 per cent and 41.8 per cent over the study period if they operated efficiently. The results also show a general increase in efficiency score over time, especially after 2001. This is consistent with our earlier findings of increased competitiveness of the Kenya banking system post-2003.

Table 4.8 Technical efficiency of Kenya's banking system

Year	DEA technical efficiency		SFA technical efficiency
	Constant returns	Variable returns	
1997	0.487	0.576	0.825
1998	0.447	0.536	0.691
1999	0.478	0.573	0.857
2000	0.451	0.53	0.849
2001	0.490	0.577	0.863
2002	0.650	0.752	0.860
2003	0.689	0.776	0.863
2004	0.652	0.731	0.868
2005	0.650	0.733	0.866
2006	0.633	0.718	0.871
Mean	0.582	0.650	0.841

Source: Kamau (2009).

The DEA and SFA efficiency results agree that large banks are least efficient with the results disagreeing on the relative efficiency of small and medium banks.[12] These results seem to reflect the market shares of the components of the banking system. Large banks typically account for 78–81 per cent of the assets of the banking system (hence have more market power).The gap between small and medium banks is much narrower, with small banks accounting for 2–5 per cent of the assets of the banking system and medium-sized banks accounting for 16–18 per cent, respectively; hence they have relatively less much power.

In terms of bank ownership structure based on DEA results, foreign banks seem to be most efficient (unlike the competitiveness results) followed by local private banks, then local public banks as expected.[13] This is confirmed by diagnostic analysis (based on the Mann-Whitney test) which shows a significant difference between foreign and local public banks but a non-significant difference between foreign and local private banks. Surprisingly, the gap between local public and local private banks is not significant (see Table 4.9 and 4.10).

Kenya has historically encouraged foreign banks to enter and expand banking operations in the country. The difference between foreign and local banks may be due to technology and ease of technology transfer as well as better managerial skills since foreign banks are generally multinational companies. Kamau (2009) also attributes the relative efficiency of foreign banks to the fact that these banks mainly concentrate in major towns and target corporate customers, whereas large local

Table 4.9 Technical efficiency score by bank size

	No. of banks	DEA technical efficiency		SF technical efficiency
		Constant returns	Variables returns	
Small banks	15	0.537	0.639	0.841
Medium bank	13	0.537	0.591	0.877
Large banks	12	0.524	0.588	0.828
	No. of banks	**Mann-Whitney test results**		
		Constant returns	**Variables returns**	
Small vs. large	15	573 (–322**)	544 (–3.58**)	
Medium vs. large	13	462 (–4.47)**	979 (–0.74)	
Small vs. medium	12	1264 (–0.7)	764 (4.02)**	

Source: Kamau (2009). The Mann-Whitney test results were not reported for SFA estimations.
**Significant at 5%.

Table 4.10 DEA technical efficiency score by ownership

	No. of banks	Constant returns	Variable returns
Foreign	9	0.640	0.727
Local private banks	24	0.547	0.653
Local public banks	7	0.496	0.564
		Mann-Whitney test scores	
		Constant returns	**Variable returns**
Foreign vs local public	9	182.5 (–5.84)**	525.5 (–5.93)**
Foreign vs local private	24	858 (–1.59)	824 (–1.85)
Local public vs local private	7	981.5 (–1.79)	1204 (–0.5)

Source: Kamau (2009). The SFA results were not reported.
**Significant at 5%.

banks spread their activities more widely across the country. Foreign banks therefore refrain from retail banking to specialize in corporate products while large domestic banks are less discriminatory in their business strategy. These different operational modalities affect efficiency and profitability.

4.5 Conclusions

First, the Kenya financial sector has strengthened in the last decade or so, in terms of product offerings and service quality, stability and profitability. Second, estimates of the HHI and the concentration ratio of assets and deposits (CR4) reveal that the sector has experienced reduced concentration and presumably more competition over 1998–2007 with a slight increase in 2008. The data however shows that the share of the 13 largest banks (with assets of more than Ksh. 20 billion) slightly increased at the expense of 21 medium-size (Ksh. 4–20 billion) and 9 small banks (less than Ksh. 4 billion), so that the picture is not clear-cut. The share of foreign banks increased to a peak of 0.484 in 2002–2003, but declined thereafter to a low of 0.359 in 2008.

The HHI results also suggest that small banks are the least competitive (most concentrated) followed by large banks and then medium-sized banks. This pattern seems to reflect the number of banks in each component. In 2008, for example, the country had 9 small banks (typically accounting for 2–5 per cent of total assets in the previous decade); 13 large banks (accounting for 78–81 per cent in the previous decade); and 21 medium-sized banks (accounting for 16–18 per cent in the previous decade). Similarly, foreign banks (11 in 2008 and accounting for 36–48 per cent of assets in the previous decade) are less competitive (more concentrated) than local banks (32 in 2008, and accounting for 51–64 per cent of assets in the previous decade).

Third, the Panzar-Rosse model results show that, with a combined value of about 0.38 based on 43 Kenyan banks over 1998–2007, the *H*-statistic suggests that it is monopolistic competition that best characterizes banks' market behaviour with the statistic in the range between zero and one. These results are supported by an earlier study by Claessens and Laeven (2003) which found an *H*-statistic of 0.58 for the Kenya banking system over 1994–2001. Evidence further shows that the Kenya banking system was in some equilibrium during the study period, with the joint *E*-statistic from a counterpart ROA equation non-significant at least at the 10 per cent level.

There is also further evidence of banking market segmentation with the Panzar-Rosse results showing that, as with HHI results, small banks are the least competitive followed by large banks and then medium-sized banks, reflecting the size of the sample (banks) in the various segments of the market. Similarly, the results suggest that foreign banks are less competitive than local banks.

Fourth, estimation of a POP model show evidence of profit persistence, with the lagged mark-up (proxied by the banks' income–expenditure ratio) significant at the 1% level. The mark-up has however significantly declined over the study period, to indicate an increase in the intensity of competition, consistent with the HHI and CR4 results.

The above findings are further supported by the results of a conjectural variation model. The results show that the Lerner index ($= \frac{\theta}{\eta}$) was significant at the 1% level and that it declined in the post-2003 period. The Lerner index is also quite low consistent with the findings from the Panzar-Rosse model that the Kenya banking system can be characterized by monopolistic competition. The results further show a highly significant demand elasticity of loans (η), which was quite stable in the post-2003 period, suggesting a decline in the conjectural variation coefficient (θ) post-2003. The results are therefore consistent with an increase in the banking competition post-2003 as found by various models in the study.

Lastly, we cite results from Kamau (2009) who provides DEA and SFA scores over 1996–2006, roughly corresponding to our study period. The results show that the average efficiency score in the banking sector was 0.58 (DEA constant returns), 0.65 (DEA variable returns) and 0.84 (SFA). This implies that the commercial banks in Kenya could have increased outputs by between 15.9% and 41.8% over the study period if they operated efficiently. The results however show a general increase in efficiency score over time, especially after 2001. This is consistent with our earlier findings of increased competitiveness of the Kenya banking system post-2003.

The DEA and SFA efficiency results agree that large banks are least efficient with the results disagreeing on the relative efficiency of small and medium banks. These results seem to reflect the market shares of the components of the banking system, with large banks typically accounting for 78–81 per cent of the assets of the banking system (hence having more market power) while the gap between small and medium banks is much narrower: small banks account for 2–5 per cent of the assets of the banking system and medium-sized banks account for 16–18%, and hence have relatively less much power.

In terms of bank ownership structure based on DEA results, foreign banks seem to be most efficient (unlike the competitiveness results) followed by local private banks, then local public banks as expected. This is confirmed by diagnostic analysis (based on the Mann-Whitney test) which shows a significant difference between foreign and local public banks but a non-significant difference between foreign and local private banks. Surprisingly, the gap between local public and local private banks is not significant.

Notes

1. Kamau (2009) for example finds a significant negative correlation between profits and efficiency in Kenya banking system over 1996–2006. Profits in turn were positively correlated with relative bank sizes (0.62). The number of commercial banks in Kenya declined from a peak of 67 in 1999 to 44 in 2009 as a result of mergers, acquisitions and closures.
2. The study and the quote are cited in an article on the 'Age of Universal Banking (Nigeria)' in *African Business*, 1 June 2001, available on the Internet.
3. In June 1994, the CBK instructed NBFIs to convert and operate as commercial banks. Consequently by May 2007, 19 NBFIs had converted to commercial banks, 7 had merged with their parent commercial banks and others had closed, hence substantially reducing their numbers, explaining the rapid expansion of commercial banks (their number peaked in 1999), and making this the largest component of Kenya's financial sector. By December 2007, there was only 1 NBFI in the country, with this NBFI converting to a commercial bank in 2008.
4. This compares unfavourably to Germany's 46 per cent and Switzerland's 47 per cent (Mbaru, 2005).
5. See the interview with the CBK Governor in Oloo (2008).
6. See *Daily Nation*, 8 September 2009.
7. By 1998, 37 banks had collapsed following the banking crises of 1986–1989, 1993–1994 and 1998 which led to a tightening of the regulatory framework.
8. The Herfindahl–Hirschmann index is measured by $\sum(Yi/\sum Yi)^2)$, where Yi is bank i's assets (or deposits). It ranges between zero in the case of perfect competition and one in the case of a monopoly.
9. Use of deposits instead of assets did not change the pattern.
10. Following Gelos and Roldos (2002), we also estimated a reduced-form unscaled revenue equation because the specification above could provide a price equation (see Buchs and Mathisen, 2005). Estimating the reduced-form revenue equations with unscaled interest revenue however did not substantially change the above results. The H-statistic remains 0.37 and is significantly different from zero, as judged from the Wald test.
11. Use of the ratio of interest income to total expenditure (to be consistent with in the empirical P-R model) did not change the above conclusions.
12. In econometric results, Kamau (2009) found that the SFA efficiency declined with the core capital ratio but increased with relative bank size, with

the latter two variables negatively correlated. Efficiency also declined with profits, themselves positively correlated with relative bank size and HHI.

13. Econometric results by Kamau (2009) show that the extent of foreign ownership was the most significant factor driving banks' SFA efficiency. Local public banks, on the other hand, are the most afflicted by non-performing loans which reduce bank efficiency.

References

Baumol, W., J. Panzar and R. Willig. 1982. *Contestable Markets and the Theory of Industry Structure*. San Diego, CA: Harcourt Brace Jovanovich.

Beck, T. and M. Fuchs. 2004. 'Structural issues in the Kenyan financial system', World Bank Policy Research Working Paper 3363, July 2004. Washington D.C.: World Bank.

Bresnahan, T.F. 1989. 'Empirical studies of industries with market power'. In R. Schmalensee and R. Willig (eds.), *Handbook of Industrial Organization*, vol. 2. North-Holland: Amsterdam, pp. 1011–57.

Brownbridge, M. and C. Harvey. 1998. *Banking in Africa*. Trenton: Africa World Press.

Buchs, T. and J. Mathisen. 2005. 'Competition and efficiency in banking: behavioral evidence from Ghana', IMF Working Paper No. 05/17. Washington D.C.: International Monetary Fund.

Claessens, S. and L. Laeven. 2003. 'What drives bank competition? Some international evidence', *Journal of Money, Credit, and Banking*, 36 (2): 563–84.

Gelos, R. Gaston and Jorge E. Roldos. 2002. 'Consolidation and market structure in emerging Market Banking Systems', IMF Working Paper No. 02/186. Washington D.C.: International Monetary Fund.

Hauner, D. and Shanaka J. Peiris. 2005. 'Bank efficiency and competition in low-income countries: the case of Uganda', IMF Working Papers WP/05/240. Washington D.C.: International Monetary Fund.

Inanga, E.L. 1995. 'Financial sector reforms in Sub-Sahara Africa'. Paper Presented at the XI World Congress of the International Economic Association in Tunis on 18–22 December.

Kamau, Anne W. 2009. *Efficiency in the Banking Sector: An Empirical Investigation of Commercial Banks in Kenya*. PhD Thesis, University of Nairobi.

Kasekende, L., K. Mlambo, V. Murinde and T. Zhao. 2009. 'Measuring the competitiveness of the financial services sector: what are the lessons for African economies?' Tunis: African Development Bank.

Kubo, K. 2006. 'The degree of competition in the Thai banking industry before and after the East Asian crisis'. Institute of Developing Economies. Discussion Paper No. 56.

Mbaru, J. 2005. 'Mobilizing resources through the bond market'. Paper Presented at Africa Growth Research Mid-Year Conference, Johannesburg, South Africa.

McKinnon, Ronald I. 1973. *Money and Capital in Economic Development*. Washington D.C.: Brookings Institution.

Mutuku, N. 2008. The Case for Consolidated Financial Sector Regulation in Kenya. See http://papers.ssm.com/sol3/papers?cfm?abstract_id=1837354 accessed 21 January 2011.

Oloo, M. 2008. The Banking Survey, Kenya. Nairobi: Think Business Ltd.
Panzar, J. and Rosse, J. (1987), 'Testing for monopoly equilibrium', *Journal of Industrial Economics*, 35: 443–56.
Saunders, A. and I. Walter. 1994. *Universal Banking in the United States*. New York: Oxford University Press.
Shaffer, S. 2004. 'Comment on "what drives bank competition? Some international evidence" by Stijin Claessens and Luc Laeven', *Journal of Money, Credit, and Banking*, 36: 585–92.
Shaw, Edward S. 1973. *Financial Deepening in Economic Development*. New York: Oxford University Press.Trick, M. 1996. Data Envelope Analysis for Consultants. Available at http://mat.gsia.cmu.edu/classes/mstc/dea/dea.html.

5

Bank Competition, Risk Taking and Productive Efficiency: A Case Study of Banking Reforms in Nigeria

Tianshu Zhao

5.1 Introduction

One of the important repercussions of the global financial crisis is that countries were forced to re-examine their bank regulatory frameworks. Some critics argue that the entire international regulatory system is 'not fit for purpose'. But the pendulum of bank regulations has been swinging back and forth for quite some time. For example, it is well known that the public policy paradigm on banking regulation has shifted from 'economic regulation' to deregulation and prudential re-regulation (Padoa-Schioppa, 2001).[1] On the one hand, the economic justification of financial deregulation is based on the presumption that deregulation fosters bank competition which, in turn, may engender bank productivity efficiency. Bank competition is seen as a stimulus to exert downward pressure on costs, reduce managerial slack and even incentivize innovation (Nickell, 1996). On the other hand, concern about the adverse impact of increased competition on bank risk taking behaviour has motivated the adoption of prudential re-regulation alongside deregulation. Although prudential re-regulation is designed to mitigate excessive risk taking and foster stability, it may impose higher regulatory costs and hamper competition. Overall, therefore, such a mixed process of deregulation and prudential re-regulation may have opposite effects on bank behaviour with respect to competition, risk taking and productivity efficiency, at least in theory.

It is curious that there is hardly any clear-cut evidence on what, in theory, are the opposite effects of policy reforms on these key aspects of bank behaviour. While there are numerous chapters which evaluate the impact of financial reforms on bank efficiency and productivity, or the impact of reforms on competition, or the relationship between competition and banks' risk taking, the evidence is inconclusive (as shown in Section 5.2). Moreover, the literature tends to look at each of the three aspects of bank performance in isolation. The inextricably intertwined relation among the 'trinity' of bank performance (i.e. bank competition, risk taking and production efficiency) has not been investigated empirically. In addition, there is little understanding of the role played by the implementation of prudential re-regulation in the financial reform processes.

This chapter investigates the interrelationships among bank competition, risk taking and productivity efficiency in the context of banking reforms in Nigeria during 1993–2008. The main contributions of the chapter are twofold. First, the study of Nigeria's commercial banking reforms in an important period of recent economic history complements a large, mostly qualitative, literature on banking sector development in Africa. Allowing for the mixed process of reforms, we divide the reforms into three phases: the introduction of deregulation during 1986–1993; the introduction of universal banking and associated reforms during 1993–2004; and the 'big bang' during 2004–2008, which is still current. Second, we find new evidence that deregulation and prudential re-regulation influence bank risk taking and bank productivity efficiency directly (direct impact) and via competition (indirect impact). The evidence also suggests that as competition increases, excessive risk taking decreases and efficiency increases. Additionally, the implementation of 'big bang' appears to bring about a trade-off between efficiency and risk taking, which is independent of its impact on competition.

The rest of the chapter is structured as follows. Section 5.2 discusses previous research on the effects of financial reforms on bank production efficiency and competition, and on the relationship between competition and risk taking behaviour. Section 5.3 briefly reviews the banking sector reforms implemented in Nigeria during 1993–2008, while Section 5.4 explains the main findings of the case study. Section 5.5 concludes with policy implications.

5.2 Literature review

A considerable proportion of the body of empirical literature has examined the impact of financial reforms on bank performance, measured by either efficiency or productivity, without accounting for the effects of competition and risk taking. The evidence appears to be mixed; some studies report improvements in productivity while others suggest little, no, or even negative productivity growth (Zhao et al., 2008). There is controversy over not only whether deregulation stimulates productivity growth, but also the sources of productivity growth. While some studies show that productivity growth is due to technological progress (e.g. Tortosa-Ausina et al., 2008), others attribute it to improved efficiency (e.g. Isik and Hassan, 2003).

In addition, there is no conclusive evidence of how regulatory changes in the late 1990s affected bank competition, according to the structure-conduct-performance (SCP) literature (Allen and Gale, 2004). The evidence derived from the new empirical industrial organization (NEIO) approach, as an alternative to SCP, is also inconclusive. While some studies document a positive link between deregulation and competition (e.g. Angelini and Cetorelli, 2003; Claessens and Laeven, 2004), there is no evidence of an increase in competition following the rapid deregulation in the EU (Fernandez De Guevara et al., 2005; Maudos and Fernandez De Guevara, 2004), nor in the UK banking market (Matthews et al., 2007). The reasons for the conflicting evidence are not clear. Among other reasons, the oligopolistic banking market structure could be a contributory element; in a highly concentrated oligopolistic market, deregulation of interest rates and credit allocation may give more scope for collusive behaviour by banks to maximize profits. For example, in Korea a bank cartel stepped in to fix interest rates whenever the authorities relaxed their control over lending or deposit rates (Demetriades and Luintel, 2001). Moreover, the impact on competition of implementing prudential re-regulation alongside deregulation is not well understood (Carletti et al., 2007; Matthews et al., 2007).

Parallel research on the effect of financial reforms and increased competition on banks' risk taking behaviour also yields contentious results. Deregulation and more competition may induce banks to take on greater risk, especially if banks' monitoring function in the provision of loans is weak (Allen and Gale, 2004; Boyd and De Nicolo, 2005), suggesting a negative relationship between competition and stability. Yet, deregulation and increased competition may also reduce the risks banks are taking, by increasing the scope for diversification and removing barriers for cost saving and revenue generating (Gonzalez, 2005). In addition, while it may erode the bank charter value by squeezing out abnormal returns associated with anti-competitive conduct, increased competition speeds up the reallocation of the charter value across banks, fuelling the incentives of banks to reduce asymmetric information (Boot and Thakor, 2000). Hence, in general, while deregulation and competition enhance banks' risk taking and destabilize the banking system (Dick, 2006; Keeley, 1990; Rhoades and Rutz, 1982), banks tend to behave more prudentially in a more competitive environment (Boyd and De Nicolo, 2005; Yeyati and Micco, 2007).

Overall, therefore, the evidence in the banking literature is inconclusive on the question of the relationship among deregulation, competition and production performance, as well as the issue of the relationship among deregulation, competition and risk taking. Moreover, a systematic examination of the interaction among banking reforms, competition, risk taking and production performance does not exist. This chapter seeks to fill the gap in the literature and to shed further light on the inconclusive evidence in the context of the deregulation and prudential re-regulation experience of banking in Nigeria during 1993–2008.

5.3 Key reforms in Nigeria's banking sector

Nigeria has the second largest financial sector in Africa in terms of bank assets, market capitalization and the number of listed companies on the stock market. The banking sector is the main source of financing in the Nigerian financial sector.

Nigeria embarked on a Structural Adjustment Programme (SAP) in 1986, in which deregulation of the banking sector was an integral element. The objective was to enhance bank efficiency in savings mobilization and financial intermediation through increased competition. However, the reforms of 1986–1993, in general, were not sustainable and underwent several reversals. It appears that the new banks focused on liberalized foreign exchange trading rather than financial intermediation, as evidenced by the co-existence of more market participants and increased disintermediation (Beck et al., 2005). The combination of weak skills (e.g. credit scoring, risk assessment) and ethical issues (e.g. corruption, insider lending) contributed to the deterioration of banks' loan portfolios (Brownbridge, 1998). There was a dramatic increase in the number of banks that over-stretched the capacity of regulation, but this problem was only brought to light during the 1990–1991 prudential regulation and financial reporting guidelines (Lewis and Stein, 1997). Economic recession and political instability hastened the decline; by mid-1993, half of the licensed banks were distressed or insolvent, placing at risk two-thirds of bank assets and close to 75 per cent of bank deposits.

Further new reforms were introduced during 1993–2004, including aggressive deregulation in 1998–2004. The mandatory capital level was increased to ₦500 million, while the statutory minimum risk-weighted capital ratio remained at 8 per cent in 1997. Universal banking was adopted in 2001 when banks were allowed to undertake various financial service activities, which encompassed money and capital markets, as well as insurance business. There was no geographical restriction either. The Central Bank of Nigeria (CBN) strengthened the regulatory and supervisory framework and increased the required capital level to ₦2 billion in 2002, while the risk-weighted capital ratio was raised to 10 per cent.

A new phase, the big bang, took effect in July 2004, when the CBN announced a new 13-point reform agenda. Based on the assumption that capital and business size are essential for a well-functioning banking system, the new reform agenda aims at promoting integration, stability and efficiency of the Nigerian banking system and enhancing its competitiveness. All banks were required to raise the minimum capital base to ₦25 billion within 18 months and to maintain the statutory minimum risk-weighted capital ratio at 10 per cent. The attempt to meet the minimum capital base triggered bank mergers and acquisitions;[2] the number of banks fell from 89 to 25, comprising 21 private publicly quoted banks, 4 foreign banks, and no government-owned bank (14 banks, accounting for 6.5 per cent of deposits, failed to meet the recapitalization criteria and had their licences revoked in 2005).

The key banking indicators, namely total savings (i.e, savings plus time deposits), bank credit to the private sector and total bank assets, trended downward during 1993–1997, but started to increase from 1997 when deregulation was reintroduced (Figure 5.1). However, the difference between total assets and credit to the private sector increased (Figure 5.1). Similarly, the difference between credit to the private sector and saving also increased, mainly after 2001, suggesting weaker intermediation, perhaps due to the increase of the required capital base.

In terms of bank market structure, Table 5.1 shows that, although the number of banks dramatically decreased after 2005, the number of branches remained stable because of consolidation and exit. Hence, the 25 banks represented the hub of financial intermediation post-big bang. It also suggests that the strength of the branch network to mobilize deposits was not negatively affected by the big bang, concurring with the statistics that bank saving and credit to the private sector

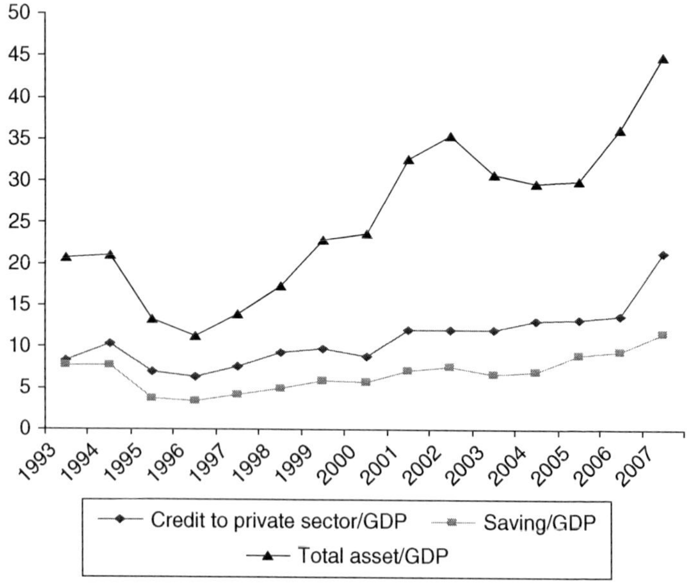

Figure 5.1 Time paths of key banking indicators, 1993–2007

Table 5.1 Selected bank market structure and performance indicators, 1993–2007

Year	Number of banks[a]	Number of branches[b]	CR3[a]	ROE[a]	Net interest margin[a]	Overhead cost/ total assets[a]
1993	66	2358	0.892	0.269	0.088	0.089
1994	65	2403	0.794	0.313	0.061	0.076
1995	64	2368	0.647	0.291	0.079	0.098
1996	64	2407	0.478	0.315	0.073	0.095
1997	64	2330	0.451	0.445	0.105	0.091
1998	51	2107	0.386	0.307	0.100	0.085
1999	57	2234	0.408	0.25	0.079	0.075
2000	90	2234	0.414	0.325	0.085	0.082
2001	90	3247	0.388	0.225	0.107	0.092
2002	90	3247	0.391	0.091	0.103	0.09
2003	90	3010	0.387	0.207	0.092	0.091
2004	89	3247	0.388	0.204	0.085	0.078
2005	25	3492	0.445	0.154	0.064	0.054
2006	25	3004	0.511	0.191	0.055	0.048
2007	24	3897	0.399	0.183	0.054	0.044

Data source: [a]Collected from A New Database on Financial Development and Structure, World Bank (2010).
[b]Collected from CBN (2010).

Table 5.2 Profile of non-performing loans (NPLs) in Nigerian commercial banking, 1993–2007

Year	NPL ratio (%)	NPL	Total credit
1993	38.7	18597.67	48056
1994	38.1	35289.74	92624
1995	29.5	41638.07	141146
1996	32.7	55342.13	169242
1997	24.9	57419.4	230600
1998	20.3	55397.69	272895
1999	26.4	93213.38	353081
2000	21.5	109284.9	508302
2001	16.9	134551.7	796164
2002	21.3	203335.8	954628
2003	20.45	247451.7	1210033
2004	21.6	328156.3	1519242
2005	24.1	479866.2	1991146
2006	8.77	221380.8	2524297
2007	8.44	406258.4	4813488

Data source: CBN.

increased during the same period, as shown in Figure 5.1. The three-bank concentration ratio (CR3) shows that the decrease of the number of banks from 89 to 25 was accompanied by a decrease in concentration.

In terms of the quality of loan portfolios (Table 5.2), non-performing loans (NPLs) as a percentage of total credit consistently decreased over time, suggesting that the quality of loan portfolios, in relative terms, had improved. The increase in the absolute amount of NPLs implies that the increase of NPLs was higher than the recovery of NPLs, suggesting some banks were involved in 'window dressing': banks brought down their NPLs ratio not through recovery of NPLs but rather through inflating their loan portfolios. Indeed, the correlation coefficient of the natural logarithm of total credit and that of NPLs is 0.969. The correlation coefficient of the natural logarithm of NPL ratio and that of NPL is –0.682. The results depict an interesting interrelationship among these three factors, in which the increase of the amount of loans dilutes NPLs in percentage terms.

Finally, in terms of the risk-weighted capital adequacy ratio (CRAR), it is shown in Table 5.3 that there was a marked increase after the big bang, although the big bang only applied to a minimum capital base while the 10 per cent statutory CRAR was unchanged. However, given the fact that the required minimum capital base was increased from ₦2 billion in 2004 to ₦25 billion in 2005 (i.e. 12.5 times), the increase of CRAR

Table 5.3 Risk-weighted capital adequacy, 2004–2007

	CRAR (%)	Qualifying capital base	Risk-weighted assets
2004	14.17	351021	2477212
2005	17.86	554520	3104815
2006	22.6	1041000	4606195
2007	20.9	1711000	8186603

Data source: Central Bank of Nigeria.

from 14.17 per cent to 22.6 per cent may not be as impressive as it looks. The data in Table 5.3 suggest that the increase of the capital base was accompanied by an increase of risk-weighted assets.

5.4 Analysis and findings

In terms of productivity efficiency, we study the impact of financial reforms and competition in Nigeria's banking sector on the ability of banks to raise deposits and intermediate them into loans and other earning assets. We develop a simple model of the bank production process to comprise three inputs (interest expense, non-interest expense and financial capital), and three outputs (loans, other earning assets and deposits) as shown in Table 5.4.[3] As reforms are characterized by changes in incentives and constraints, their impact on banks' production performance includes efficiency change and technology change, and our production performance indicators encompass those two components.

We then examine the impact of deregulation and prudential re-regulation on the degree of competition, controlling for other factors. We focus on three important regulatory initiatives. First, the reimplementation of interest rate deregulation in 1997 is measured using a dummy variable, *deinterest*. It takes the value of one for the period 1993–1996, and zero otherwise. The second initiative, the removal of the regulatory barrier between merchant and commercial banking in 2001 is captured using a dummy variable, *universal*. The dummy takes the

Table 5.4 Inputs and outputs of Nigerian banks

Inputs	Outputs
X1: Interest expense	Y1: Loans
X2: Non-interest expense	Y2: Other earning assets
X3: Financial capital	Y3: Deposits

Table 5.5 Basis of analysis of degree of competition

Variables	Description
Translog cost function (2)	
• Total non-interest expense (C_{it})	= total cost – total interest expense
• The quantity of loans (q_{it})	= the book value of loans
• Total loanable fund (d_{it})	= total deposits + total money market funding
• Total non-interest expense price (w_{it})	= total non-interest expense/(loans + total loanable fund)
Revenue equation (3)	
• Total interest income (R_{it})	= total interest income received
• Total interest expense (E_{it})	= total interest expenditure
• The ratio of total loans to total loanable fund (q_{it}/d_{it})	= total loans/total loanable fund
Inverse demand equation (4)	
• Implicit interest rate of loans (p_{it})	= total interest income/total loans
• Real GDP growth rate (gdp)	= real GDP growth rate
• Size effect (total assets)	= total assets
• Capitalization (cap)	= financial capital/total assets

value of zero up to 2001 and one thereafter. The third element relates to the big bang measures, which were announced in July 2004. The reforms included a dramatic increase of minimum capital base requirement from ₦2 billion to ₦25 billion, with the requirement that banks had to comply fully before December 2005 otherwise they would be delicensed, which led to a remarkable reduction of the number of banks from 89 in 2004 to 25 in 2005. The dummy, *bigbang,* is used to capture the measures; it takes the value of zero up to 2004 and one thereafter.

Further, we take into account the impact of market structure, which is measured using a three-bank concentration ratio (CR3) on the degree of competition. The traditional SCP paradigm indicates that the presence of a few larger banks restricts competition; it predicts a negative relation between concentration and competition. In contrast, the efficiency structure hypothesis predicts that concentration is induced by the increase of market share gained by more efficient banks, which suggests that concentration is not a reliable indicator of the degree of competition. Also, we introduce real GDP growth rate (*gdp*). The motivation to control for economic growth differs from the present case, it is intended to capture the impact of the change in economic fundamentals on the dynamics of competition. The change in economic fundamentals affects expectations of market participants about the future level of demand,

Table 5.6 Impacts of reforms on degree of competition at industry level

Variables	Description
Dependent variable	
Competition (θ_t)	The conjectural variations (CV) parameters
Explanatory variables	
• *Deinterest*	Set equal to 1 for 1997–2008, 0 otherwise
• *Bigbang*	Set equal to 1 for 2005–2008, 0 otherwise
• *Universal*	Set equal to 1 for 2001–2008, 0 otherwise
• CR3	Three-bank concentration ratio
• Gdp	Real GDP growth rate

which may change the competitive interactions between market participants. Moreover, it is useful to distinguish between fundamentals-driven and conduct-driven components of competitive interactions. Furthermore, Kandori (1991) indicates that these oligopolistic dynamics crucially depend on whether market participants' competitive strategy is long-term forward looking. If future demand is expected to grow (fall), the cooperation between market participants is easier (more difficult) because their competitive strategy has a long-term outlook. On the other hand, if the market participants' competitive strategy is myopic, the opposite is true. Table 5.5 presents the basis of the analysis of the degree of competition, while Table 5.6 presents our conception of the reforms.

Finally, we also investigate the impact of financial reforms on bank risk taking and bank productive efficiency, taking into account both the direct effect of policy actions and the indirect impact through competition. The basis of our analysis is presented in Table 5.7.

BankScope annual balance sheets and income statement data on Nigerian commercial banks are obtained for 1993–2008. We start with the universe of all commercial banks and, after checking the data for completeness, we obtain a final unbalanced panel sample of 91 banks with a total of 630 observations. Real GDP growth rate over 1993–2008 is collected from IMF International Financial Statistics Database. All variables used in our analysis are either expressed as ratios or measured in real terms, using a GDP deflator with 2000 as the base year. Table 5.8 provides summary statistics for the variables.

Our first set of results regarding the changes in the degree of competition at the industry level are reported in Figure 5.2. These results show the estimated values of θ_t together with their 95 per cent confidence intervals. It is found that, over the period, the results reject $\theta = 1$, pure monopoly, except for 2008. The competitive conditions in years

Table 5.7 Bank productive efficiency and bank risk taking

Variables	Description
Dependent variable	
• Bank-specific productive efficiency	Derived from the first-stage using DEA
• Bank-specific credit risk	= loan loss provisions/total loans
Independent variable shared by both equations	
Industry-wide variables: competition, reforms and economic condition	
• Competition	The conjectural variations (CV) parameters
• Reforms	A vector of three dummy variables: (1) Deinterest: set equal to 1 for 1997–2008, 0 otherwise; (2) Universal: set equal to 1 for 2001–2008, 0 otherwise; (3) Bigbang: set equal to 1 for 2005–2008, 0 otherwise
• Economic condition	Real GDP growth rate
Bank-specific characteristics	
• Size effect	= total assets
• Capitalization	= financial capital/total assets
Independent variable specific for bank risk taking equation	
• Degree of specification	$SP = \sum_{i=1}^{2} S_i^2,\ S_i = y_i / \sum_{i=1}^{I} 2y_i,$ y_1 : interest-income; y_2: non-interest income
• Net interest margin	= (total interest income − total interest expense)/(loans + other earning assets)
Independent variable specific for productive efficiency equation	
• Credit risk	= loan loss provisions/total loans

1996 and 1998 are characterized by a super competition situation, while the conditions in 1995 and 1997 reflect perfect competition; for the rest of the sample period, Nigerian commercial banking demonstrates a certain level of oligopoly. Overall, the estimated CV parameters suggest that the change in the degree of competition in Nigerian commercial banking can be divided into three sub-periods: an increase in the degree of competition during 1993–1998; a decrease in the degree of competition during 1998–2001; and an increase in the degree of competition during 2001–2008.

The results regarding the impact of financial reforms on the degree of competition are reported in Table 5.9. The results show that *deinterest*, the proxy for the reimplementation of interest rate deregulation, is positive and statistically significant at the 7 per cent level. *Universal*, the proxy for the adaptation of universal banking, is also positive and significant (1 per cent level). This evidence suggests that the

Table 5.8 Descriptive statistics of main variables

Variables	Obs	Mean	Std dev.	Min	Max	Median
Loans	630	29.442	148.741	0.001	1893.004	5.498
Other earning assets	630	64.601	431.621	0.118	7085.522	8.925
Deposits	630	49.278	172.682	0.014	2203.300	12.748
Interest expense	630	4.595	25.038	0.001	378.499	0.907
Non-interest expense	630	7.065	34.166	0.073	406.958	1.327
Financial capital	630	14.813	81.363	0.013	989.079	1.892
Loan loss provisions to total loan ratio	630	0.059	0.114	0.000	1.677	0.034
Capitalization	630	0.152	0.276	0.017	5.586	0.116
Net interest margin	630	0.076	0.053	−0.159	0.347	0.076
The degree of specification	630	0.598	0.096	0.500	0.980	0.568
Total loanable fund	630	49.241	173.147	0.014	2203.300	12.079
Non-interest expense price	630	0.088	0.077	0.005	1.688	0.080
Total interest income	630	11.024	63.619	0.001	880.380	2.080
Total assets	630	104.503	574.986	0.170	8354.947	17.200
Implicit interest rate on loans	630	0.477	0.562	0.002	8.582	0.370
CR3	16	0.487	0.155	0.386	0.892	0.412
Real GDP growth rate (%)	16	6.019	5.285	−0.307	21.180	5.356

Note: Data, if not expressed in ratio, is measured in Naira million and is deflated by GDP deflator using 2000 as the base year.
Data source: BankScope and IMF International Financial Statistics Database.

deregulation of the interest rate and the expansion opportunities into universal banking do not promote competition but rather nurture collusion. This result is in line with the view that deregulation of both interest rates and banking business lines essentially give more scope for collusive behaviour of banks in an oligopolistic market. In addition, the coefficient of *bigbang* is negative. However, the result is not statistically significant. Therefore, the expected increase in the integration of the market and its subsequent positive effect on the degree of competition through consolidation does not seem to be materialized in our sample period. This result concurs with the statistics on the movement of interest rates on loans. As indicated by Somoye (2008), although the interest rate on loans witnessed a sharp decline immediately following the implementation of the big bang, it later rose to surpass the level of the pre-consolidation period. Among others, the 'bricks and mortar' delivery channel of financial intermediation predominately employed

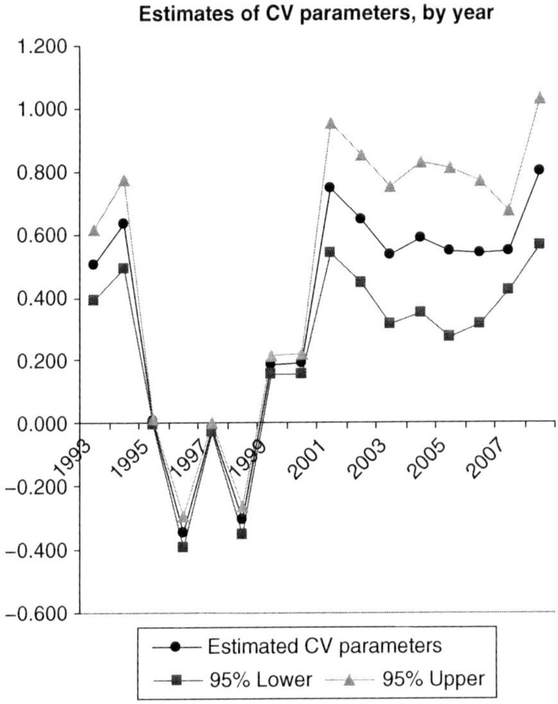

Figure 5.2 Estimated conjectural variation parameters, 1993–2008

Table 5.9 Effects on degree of competition

	Result
Deinterest	Positive and significant
Bigbang	Negative but not significant
Universal	Positive and significant
CR3	Positive and significant
Gdp	Positive but not significant

by the Nigerian banks could act as the main barrier for the reduction of market segmentation. Given this, the impact of big bang recapitalization, taking the form of consolidation on the integration of the market, may need significant time to become adequate.

The market share occupied by the largest three banks, *CR3*, has a statistically significant positive coefficient, suggesting that increased concentration increases the degree of collusion in the market place, in line with the prediction of the traditional SCP paradigm. Further, the estimated coefficient of *gdp* is not statistically significant; indicating the difficulty for market participants to formulate representative expectations about future demand, given the overall unstable macroeconomic conditions during the sample period.

We investigate the impact of financial reforms on bank risk taking and bank productivity efficiency. First, we focus on results for the bank risk taking equation. Regarding the direct impact of financial reforms on bank risk taking, the evidence reported in Table 5.10 shows that interest rate deregulation and the adaptation of universal banking both negatively and significantly affect bank risk taking. The negative relation between interest rate deregulation and bank risk taking suggests that deregulating the interest rate opens up opportunities for banks to use pricing as a risk management tool: banks are able to price risk according to the expected default risk. The negative impact of the adaptation of universal banking on bank risk taking reflects the risk diversification benefit across different business lines. In contrast, the results show a positive and statistically significant coefficient of *big bang*, indicating that the dramatic increase of the minimum capital base requirement

Table 5.10 Results of bank productivity efficiency and bank risk taking

Dependent variable: bank risk taking (loan loss provision /total loans)	
	Result
Deinterest	Negative and significant
Universal	Negative and significant
Bigbang	Positive and significant
Conjectural variations (CV) parameters	Positive and significant
Gdp	Negative but not significant
Capitalization (financial capital/total assets)	Negative and significant
Size (ln[total assets])	Negative but not significant
Net interest margin	Positive and significant
The degree of specification	Negative but not significant
Dependent variable: bank productive efficiency	
Deinterest	Positive and significant
Universal	Positive and significant
Bigbang	Positive and significant
Conjectural variations (CV) parameters	Negative and significant
Gdp	Negative and significant
Risk (loan loss provision/total loans)	Negative and significant
Capitalization (financial capital/total assets)	Negative and significant
Size (ln[total assets])	Positive and significant

is positively related to bank risk taking. These results seem to suggest that the increase of the minimum regulatory capital base may have induced a proportionate increase of risk taking at the industry level. It would result from attempts by banks to maintain shareholder return on a 'higher capital'. Indeed, the 18-month time frame to achieve the dramatic increase in the required capital base resulted in a race among banks to compete for capital to beat the CBN deadline; banks would be under pressure to generate higher returns from the additional capital, thereby forcing them to expand the balance sheet and take on greater risks (Adedipe, 2006). In addition, the destruction of financial intermediation due to the loss of soft information and the harmony of credit culture in the process of policy-induced organizational rationalization would also be a contributor. Arguably, the cooperation problem among partners and the likelihood of creating an ill-fit risk management team for the merged banking entity would be more significant when the consolidations were to be imposed by the regulator rather than a development warranted by identified business opportunities (Somoye, 2008). Further, with respect to the impact of competition, the estimated coefficient is statistically significant and positive, which implies that an increase in competition yields lower risk taking, as proposed by the 'competition-stability' view.

Regarding bank-specific characteristics, the results indicate that banks with higher capitalization have lower risk taking, confirming our previous argument that well-capitalized banks are more risk averse. This result does not necessarily conflict with our results of a positive relation between the 'big bang' on bank capital requirement and bank risk taking, as the latter is a policy on the level of capital, not on the ratio of capital to total assets. Moreover, the estimated coefficient of the 'big bang' refers to the average impact on the industry, without accounting for the heterogeneity of banks. Our results also show that higher net interest margins are associated with higher risk taking, implying that banks that charge higher risk premiums (associated with higher expected probability of default) face higher ex-post credit risk. In addition, the estimated coefficient of the degree of diversification is negative, which agrees with the view that diversification by jointly producing different types of bank outputs may lead to a decrease of risk. Finally, the size effect, measured by total assets, indicates the risk benefit of economies of scale, although it is not statistically significant.

Second, we consider the regression results for the bank productivity efficiency model. In terms of the direct impact of reform initiatives, our results indicate a substantial gain in bank productivity efficiency following the reimplementation of interest rate deregulation, the adaptation of universal banking and the significant tightening of capital requirement, as the coefficients on three reforms dummies are all positive and statistically significant. Although these three important events in the Nigerian banking reforms all appear to stimulate productivity efficiency, there are three further interpretations of the propagation mechanisms of these reforms. First, with respect to interest rate deregulation, it may be the case that the freedom of banks to raise interest rates on deposits and loans enhances banks' operational flexibility in providing financial services. Banks are able to carry out financial intermediation that might not have been profitable under the regime of regulated interest rate. Second, regarding the adaptation of universal banking, the evidence may be interpreted to reflect the cross-selling behaviour of banks, that is banks sell existing and new products to additional consumers brought about by the expansion of business lines, which enables banks to produce more outputs from a given level of inputs. Third, the positive outcome of the big bang suggests an increase in the capacity of financial intermediation, resulting in increased outputs for the existing market participants. The results may also reflect banks' eagerness to expand their balance sheets to generate higher returns for the shareholders.

Regarding the impact of competition on bank productivity efficiency, the significant and negative coefficient confirms that an increase of competition may enhance bank production performance, as predicted by microeconomic theory. Macroeconomic conditions, measured by the real GDP growth rate, appear to be negatively associated with bank productivity efficiency, suggesting that banks' production performance decreases in a more favourable economic environment. This result suggests that more favourable macroeconomic conditions may induce an increase in the demand for financial services on the one hand, and an increase of banks' ability to charge higher interest rates, on the other hand. Indeed, the estimated results suggest that a higher GDP growth rate is associated with higher implicit interest rates. As banks operate in an imperfectly competitive market, the two effects on banks production performance may offset each other. The negative relationship between real GDP growth rate and bank productivity efficiency seems to suggest that the expected improvement in productivity efficiency induced by the increase of demand is outweighed by the decrease in the quantity of production due to the increase of interest rates.

Regarding the influence of bank risk taking on bank productivity efficiency, our results indicate that the increase in bank risk taking is inversely related to bank productivity efficiency, as expected. In terms of other bank-specific characteristics, the results show a positive and statistically significant coefficient for total assets, which suggests that banks enjoy economies of scale. The negative estimated coefficient of capitalization indicates that well-capitalized banks have a lower bank productivity efficiency, which probably reflects a more conservative attitude by well-capitalized banks towards expansion of production.

The results regarding the impact of reforms on bank risk taking and bank productivity efficiency presented above are based on the separate estimations of risk taking and productive efficiency equations. Taking into account the possibility that bank productivity efficiency and bank risk taking are subject to common shocks which we did not fully consider in the separate estimation,[4] we also estimate the risk taking and productivity efficiency equations simultaneously using a full-information maximum likelihood (FIML) estimator as a check for robustness. The results are reported in Table 5.11.

As shown in Table 5.11, the deregulation of interest rates and the adaptation of universal banking are still positively related to bank risk

Table 5.11 Simultaneous bank risk taking and bank productivity efficiency

Dependent variable: risk (loan loss provision/total loans)	
Deinterest	Negative and significant
Universal	Negative and significant
Bigbang	Positive and significant
Conjectural variations (CV) parameters	Positive and significant
Gdp	Negative but not significant
Capitalization (financial capital/total assets)	Negative and significant
Size (ln[total assets])	Negative but not significant
Net interest margin	Positive and significant
The degree of specification	Negative and significant
Dependent variable: productive efficiency	
Deinterest	Positive and significant
Universal	Positive but not significant
Bigbang	Positive and significant
Conjectural variations (CV) parameters	Negative and significant
Gdp	Negative and significant
Risk (loan loss provision/total loans)	Negative but not significant
Capitalization (financial capital/total assets)	Negative and significant
Size (ln[total assets])	Positive and significant

taking while the opposite is true for the imposition of the big bang. Moreover, the increase of competition seems to enhance the safety of the loan portfolio. The magnitudes of the estimated coefficients are similar to the ones in Table 5.10, and the results are significant as well. With respect to productivity efficiency, all three important reforms appear to promote productive efficiency, although the result for adaptation of universal banking is not significant. The increase of competition, again, positively contributes to the increase of productivity efficiency. Finally, the result also suggests that banks with higher risk taking have lower productivity efficiency.

As a whole, we find that financial reforms influence bank competition, which affects bank risk taking and bank productivity efficiency, which is the indirect effect. In addition, financial reforms have a direct impact on bank risk taking and bank productivity efficiency. The relationship between competition and bank risk taking is negative, suggesting that banks behave more prudently in an increasingly competitive environment. The relationship between competition and bank productivity efficiency, however, is positive, implying that banks make an effort to catch up with the best practices in view of an increase in competition. We also find evidence suggesting a negative association between bank risk taking and bank productive efficiency.

Additionally, our results suggest that deregulation and prudential re-regulation affect bank risk taking and bank productivity efficiency in different ways in terms of both direct impact and indirect impact through competition. Deregulation initiatives offer banks the opportunity to price risk and to diversify their business lines, hence promoting both productivity efficiency of banks and the safety of banks' loan portfolios. The decrease of risk taking tends to further reinforce the increase of productivity efficiency. However, the positive outcome of deregulation on both bank risk taking and bank productivity efficiency may be offset by the negative impact on the degree of competition. By contrast, the tightening of the minimum capital base increases bank risk taking and productivity efficiency. Moreover, there is concern that the increase of risk taking may counterbalance the increase of bank productivity efficiency. Unlike the impact of deregulation initiatives, the impact of tightening the minimum capital base on bank risk taking and bank productivity efficiency seems to be exclusively associated with its direct impact. Its impact on the degree of competition is insignificant.

5.5 Conclusion

Despite the fact that the recent process of deregulation and the concomitant prudential re-regulation have been dominant features in financial sector reforms, the empirical work on the impact of such policy reforms on bank competition and performance is limited and inconclusive. To explore this issue further, we develop a three-stage procedure and perform a systematic investigation of the interaction among variables that proxy financial reforms, bank competition, bank risk taking and bank production efficiency. We argue that the change in the regulatory policy on banks' financial intermediation behaviour has far-reaching implications for further policy development to achieve a stable and efficient banking system. To contribute to the understanding of banking sector development in Africa, we apply this three-stage analysis to the reform experience of the Nigerian commercial banking sector during 1993–2008.

The Nigerian banking system has undergone remarkable regulatory changes since 1986. Among other factors, these changes have been initiated by deregulation of the interest rate and business lines at the national level, and the opening of countries to international competition. Particularly noticeable is the big bang, which involved the recapitalization of banks and had the immediate effect of reducing the number of banks, resulting in some mega banks in the sector.

Our empirical results suggest that the deregulation of the interest rate, the adaptation of universal banking and the implementation of a big bang influence bank risk taking and bank productivity efficiency directly (direct impact) as well as through their impact on bank competitive conditions (indirect impact). The investigation shows the multiple dimensions of the issue of regulation and its effect on competition, productivity efficiency and financial stability. We recommend that future research on banking reforms should carefully account for all the factors in order to enhance the empirical relevance for policy implications.

In addition, the analysis suggests that the increase in bank competition is beneficial for a well-functioning banking sector, because increased competition is associated with a reduction in bank risk taking and the enhancement of bank productivity efficiency. Hence, our findings lend support to policy initiatives that foster bank competition. However, we argue that the question of whether the policy shift really induced competition in the market place has to be empirically examined using an appropriate approach. Indeed, our results indicate an increase in the degree of competition at the industry level brought about by the deregulation of interest rates and the expansion of business lines and an insignificant relationship between the big bang and the degree of competition. While we contribute the former to the oligopolistic market structure in Nigerian banking, we believe that the latter would be a reflection of the difficulty to integrate a segmented banking market which has been relying on its physical presence to engage in financial intermediation. As a whole, our results highlight the importance of the market and the operational characteristics for the apprehension of the effectiveness of public policy in promoting competition in the banking industry.

Our empirical analysis further reveals that the direct effect of the implementation of big bang on the risks that banks are taking appears to be different from that of the deregulation of the interest rate and the adaptation of universal banking at the industry level. While the removal of the administrative interest rate regime and the restriction on business lines would bring in new risk management tools and positive diversification effects, the increase in the mandatory capital base seems to be associated with an increase in bank risk taking. Despite the difficulty in pinpointing the true source to drive such a result, the bottom line implies deterioration in the soundness of balance sheets accompanied by the expansion of the balance sheet, jointly allowing for the positive association between bank productivity efficiency and the implementation of a big bang. Moreover, such trade-off seems to be induced by the direct effect of the implementation of a big bang rather than the indirect impact through competition. This finding suggests that a higher capital base does not automatically result in low risk taking incentives, better risk management practice and proper and fit corporate governance. The implication for regulation and supervision of Nigerian banks is to encourage banks to maintain a good balance between growth and improved corporate governance in the post-big bang period, given the rising financial resources at the disposal of Nigerian banks and the increased organizational complexity of business lines of Nigerian banks.

Notes

1. Economic regulation uses structural measures and may limit competition; the regulators prescribe prices and take responsibility for potential prudential problems. In contrast, prudential re-regulation focuses on market efficiency by relaxing structural rules and encouraging incentive-based prudential behaviour by banks.

2. According to CBN guidelines, mergers and outright acquisitions are the only legal modes of consolidation.
3. To measure the productive efficiency of banks (to transform inputs into outputs), we use non-parametric grand Data Envelopment Analysis (DEA) with an output-maximization orientation. Our specification of inputs and outputs and our choice of output-maximization orientation are heavily motivated by the central objectives of this research as well as the existing literature. Regarding inputs, we specify interest expense, non-interest operating expense and equity. Therefore, the selection of inputs encompasses the overall economic costs of financial intermediation. Specifically, interest expense and non-interest operating cost are associated with loanable funds, and labour and physical cost, respectively. Equity is associated with the opportunity cost of financial capital. The introduction of equity into the input side is relevant in our case as one of the important regulatory measures during our sample period is capital requirement. On the output side, we consider loans, other earning assets and deposits, in line with Bhattacharyya et al. (1997). Such choice corresponds to the argument that deposits are one of the services provided by banks. It is also due to our intention to control for the financial disintermediation incentive appearing during our sample period. Constructing the measure of output-oriented productive efficiency reflects the extent to which outputs can be improved from the given level of inputs, while the remaining output mix remains unchanged. As mentioned earlier, one of the major objectives of the reforms in the Nigerian banking sector is promoting deposit mobilization. As a whole, the measurement derived from our specification assesses the performance of banks to intermediate deposits from a given level of economic cost, and keeping the asset structure and credit-deposit ratio unchanged. The evaluation of the impact of financial reforms and competition on the ability of banks to raise deposits and intermediate them into loans and other earning assets from the given interest expense, operating expense and financial capital are all relevant for our study. In addition, the grand DEA frontier provides a single benchmark over the pooled sample against which to assess production performance. The productivity efficiency scores derived contain the information on the change in production performance over time, and are comparable in both time-series and cross-sectional dimensions.
4. Indeed, risk taking and risk management are central to banks' production process, and are governed by banks' overall operational philosophy, analysis and control.

References

Adedipe, B. 2006. 'Bank consolidation: Breasting the tape, facing new challenges'. *Zenith Economic Quarterly*, 1(5): 38–48.

Allen, F. and D. Gale. 2004. 'Competition and financial stability'. *Journal of Money, Credit and Banking*, 36: 453–80.

Angelini, P. and N. Cetorelli. 2003. 'The effects of regulatory reform on competition in the banking industry'. *Journal of Money, Credit and Banking*, 35: 663–84.

Beck, T., R. Cull and A. Jerome. 2005. 'Bank privatization and performance: Empirical evidence from Nigeria'. *Journal of Banking and Finance*, 29: 2355–79.

Bhattacharyya, A., C.A.K. Lovell and P. Sahay. 1997. 'The impact of liberalization on the productive efficiency of Indian commercial banks'. *European Journal of Operational Research*, 98: 332–45.

Boot, A.W. and A.V. Thakor. 2000. 'Can relationship banking survive competition?'. *Journal of Finance*, 55: 679–713.

Boyd, J.H. and G. De Nicolo. 2005. 'The theory of bank risk taking and competition revisited'. *Journal of Finance*, 60: 1329–43.

Brownbridge, M. 1998. 'Financial distress in local banks in Kenya, Nigeria, Uganda and Zambia: Causes and implications for regulatory policy'. *Development Policy Review*, 16: 173–88.

Carletti, E., P. Hartmann and G. Spagnolo. 2007. 'Bank mergers, competition and liquidity'. *Journal of Money, Credit and Banking*, 39: 1067–105.

Claessens, S. and L. Laeven. 2004. 'What drives bank competition? Some international evidence', *Journal of Money, Credit, and Banking*, 36: 563–84.

Demetriades P. and K. Luintel. 2001. 'Financial restraint in the South Korean miracle'. *Journal of Development Economics*, 64: 459–76.

Dick, A.A. 2006. 'Nationwide branching and its impact on market structure, quality and bank performance'. *Journal of Business*, 79: 567–92.

Fernandez De Guevara, J., J. Maudos and F. Perez. 2005. 'Market power in European banking sectors'. *Journal of Financial Services Research*, 27: 109–37.

Gonzalez, F. 2005. 'Bank regulation and risk-taking incentives: An international comparison of bank risk'. *Journal of Banking and Finance*, 29: 1153–84.

Isik, I. and M.K. Hassan. 2003. 'Financial deregulation and total factor productivity change: An empirical study of Turkish commercial banks'. *Journal of Banking and Finance*, 27: 1455–85.

Kandori, M. 1991. 'Correlated demand shocks and price wars during booms'. *Review of Economic Studies*, 58: 171–80.

Keeley, M. 1990. 'Deposit insurance, risk and market power in banking'. *American Economic Review*, 80: 1183–200.

Lewis, P. and H. Stein. 1997. 'Shifting fortunes: The political economy of financial liberalization in Nigeria'. *World Development*, 25: 5–22.

Matthews, K., V. Murinde and T. Zhao. 2007. 'Competitive conditions among the major British banks'. *Journal of Banking and Finance*, 31: 2025–42.

Maudos, J. and J. Fernandez de Guevara. 2004. 'Factors explaining the interest margin in the banking sectors of European Union'. *Journal of Banking and Finance*, 28: 2259–81.

Nickell, S. 1996. 'Competition and corporate performance'. *Journal of Political Economy*, 104: 724–46.

Padoa-Schioppa, T. 2001. 'Bank competition: A changing paradigm'. *European Finance Review*, 5: 13–20.

Rhoades, S. and R. Rutz. 1982. 'Market power and firm risk'. *Journal of Monetary Economics*, 9: 73– 85.

Somoye, R.O.C. 2008. 'The performance of commercial banks in post-consolidation period in Nigeria: An empirical review'. *European Journal of Economics, Finance and Administrative Sciences*, 14: 62–73.

Tortosa-Ausina, E., E. Grifell-Tatjé, C. Armero and D. Conesa. 2008. 'Sensitivity analysis of efficiency and Malmquist productivity indices: An application to Spanish savings banks'. *European Journal of Operational Research*, 184: 1062–84.
Yeyati, E.L. and A. Micco. 2007. 'Concentration and foreign penetration in Latin American banking sectors: Impact on competition and risk'. *Journal of Banking and Finance*, 31: 1633–47.
Zhao, T., B. Casu and A. Ferrari. 2008. 'Deregulation and productivity growth: A study of Indian commercial banking'. *International Journal of Business Performance Management*, 10: 318–43.

6
Financial Sector Reforms, Bank Competitiveness, Efficiency and Economic Growth: A Case Study of Zambia

Abraham Mwenda

6.1 Introduction

In 1992, Zambia was under new administration[1] and commenced implementation of radical market-based financial sector reforms as part of the programmes supported by the IMF and World Bank to promote economic stabilization and structural adjustment (see, for example, Martinez, 2006). The financial sector reforms were aimed at removing distortions (such as negative real interest rates, inefficient credit rationing, high bank concentration, inefficient state-owned banks and foreign exchange controls created by years of financial repression by the previous government) and promoting a more competitive, efficient, deep and sound financial system in general, and for the banking sector in particular. This was expected to improve financial savings mobilization and their efficient allocation, effectiveness of the payment and settlement system, risk management and business, all of which were considered crucial for accelerating private investment, economic growth and poverty alleviation in Zambia.

This chapter evaluates the effects of Zambia's financial sector reforms on commercial banking sector competitiveness and efficiency and economic growth. More specifically the chapter seeks to answers the following questions. Have financial sector reforms enhanced bank competition? Have the financial reforms improved the operational efficiency of banks? What are the significant factor determinants of bank operational efficiency? What has been the impact of financial sector reforms on economic growth? What lessons and policy implications can be drawn from Zambia's experience with market-based financial sector reforms? Hence, the chapter is expected to inform key policy debates that includes the role of finance in Africa (see, for example, Beck and Honohan, 2007; Gulde et al., 2006), the factors driving bank competition (for example, Claessen and Laeven, 2004; Kasekende et al., 2009) and the role of monetary policy and the growth of the credit market (see, among others, Mutoti, 2008; Mwenda, 1993).

The chapter is organized as follows. Section 6.2 reviews the evolution of financial sector policies and how the financial system has developed under these policies over the 1964–2008 period. Section 6.3 evaluates the effects of financial sector reforms on commercial bank competitiveness. Section 6.4 assesses the impact of financial reforms on bank cost-efficiency and the factor determinants of cost-efficiency. Section 6.5 evaluates the effect of financial sector reforms on economic growth, and Section 6.6 concludes.

6.2 Evolution of financial sector policies

Financial sector policies in post-independence Zambia evolved through two main stages. The first is the financial repression phase, which covers the 1964–1991 period. The second is the post-1991 financial liberalization phase. We review the main features of financial policies and how the commercial banking structure evolved in these two phases.

6.2.1 Financial repression policies: 1964–1991

The socialist-oriented United National Independence Party (UNIP) Government adopted financial repression as one of the strategic pillars of its national development plans.[2] Financial repression targeted two main objectives. The first was to counter the dominance of subsidiaries of foreign-owned banks. The second was to direct credit allocation towards supporting the government's import substitution industrialization and economic growth objectives. Financial controls were comprehensive as they encompassed the nationalization of non-bank financial institutions; creation of state-owned specialized development finance institutions (DFI) monopolies; control of savings and lending interest rates, foreign exchange rates and capital account flows, thereby directing credit supply and allocation; and using direct monetary policy instruments.

In the early 1970s, adverse terms of trade shocks (precipitated by the copper and oil price crises), which adversely impacted on the country's tax revenues and foreign reserves, led to the intensification of financial repression. The main feature of the financial repression was the adoption of administrative controls on interest rates[3] and credit allocation. Intensification of interest rates controls was motivated by the desire to provide low-cost investment funds. Credit controls included ceilings on the level and growth rates of bank credit, directed credit schemes (such as automatic access for state-run banks to subsidized central bank credit allocation to priority sectors such as agriculture and manufacturing) and the SME credit guarantee scheme managed by the Bank of Zambia (BoZ).

Domestic private equity first entered the commercial banking industry in 1984 with the establishment of the now defunct Meridien Bank. Four more private banks entered the market in the second half of the 1980s, and by 1991 there were 13 banks owned and operated by local private investors. The government later formed another commercial bank in partnership with the Indian government (1984), and an export-import bank in 1987 to provide trade finance.

The government also adopted various forms of foreign exchange controls, including a single fixed exchange rate system (1964–1970), dual exchange rates and a crawling peg (1985–1987), a flexible exchange rate system based on the Dutch auction system, and a single fixed exchange rate regime with periodic adjustments until 1992 when a market-based flexible exchange rate system was introduced by the new Government.

Financial infrastructure remained underdeveloped throughout the financial repression era: these included the regulatory and supervisory, payment and settlement, credit information bureaux; asset and collateral registry; and credit contract and bankruptcy legal systems. The supervisory and regulatory system was poorly developed as it focused narrowly on off-site monitoring of banks using limited monetary information. The payment and settlement system was composed of a manual clearing house, based at BoZ, where bank officials met on a daily basis to exchange cheques and determine net positions to be settled through banks' accounts held with BoZ. Credit information bureaux were non-existent, while asset and collateral registries and the legal system for enforcing creditor rights and facilitating company bankruptcy were ineffective, according to the 2002 Financial Sector Adjustment Project (FSAP) Report (IMF and World Bank, 2002).

6.2.2 Financial development under repression

6.2.2.1 Financial structure

Restrictions on entry into the banking sector created a highly concentrated commercial banking system dominated by a few foreign-owned banks. The entry of a few domestic private banks and a foreign public bank failed to dilute bank concentration as these banks' capital bases were very small compared to the multinational private banks. The creation of private insurance and pension funds through the nationalization of private entities, the formation of DFIs and restriction of private entry into these sectors created a few state-owned monopolies in the various sectors. However, the poor financial performance (in terms of capital adequacy and solvency, profitability, asset quality and liquidity of virtually all state-owned financial intermediaries) deteriorated substantially due to the combination of lack of competition and poor corporate governance practices in the face of worsening macroeconomic conditions. Subsequently, some of the intermediaries, particularly in the agricultural sector, were liquidated and replaced by others whose financial performance in time also deteriorated due to the same fundamental causes, which remained unsolved.

6.2.2.2 Financial depth

Financial depth indicators are presented in Table 6.1. The indicators show a similar trend pattern, characterized by increases until the middle-to-late 1980s, and fluctuation on a declining trend thereafter. The broad money supply to GDP ratio rose from 29.2 per cent in 1970 to

Table 6.1 Financial depth indicators

	M2/GDP	PC/GDP	SD/GDP
1970	29.2	11.3	20.3
1975	31.2	18.6	24.2
1980	29.6	16.6	24.3
1981	28.1	22.2	22.6
1982	36.4	25.6	30.4
1983	34.8	25.2	28.9
1984	34.6	24.7	28.7
1985	29.8	19.1	24.9
1986	31.0	16.1	28.6
1987	31.7	13.0	26.9
1988	33.7	20.1	37.2
1989	30.3	16.5	26.2
1990	21.9	12.7	17.4
1991	22.2	10.5	17.9

Note: M2 = broad money supply, PC = private credit supply, SD = savings deposits.
Source: Bank of Zambia.

a high of 36.4 per cent in 1982, before declining to 16.9 per cent in 1991. The ratio of savings deposits to GDP increased from 20.3 per cent in 1970 to 37 per cent in 1988, before falling sharply to 13.6 per cent in 1991. The private credit to GDP ratio increased from 11.3 per cent in 1970 to 25.6 per cent, before collapsing to 7.8 per cent in 1991. The fall in financial depth, as captured by all indicators, was largely attributed to rising negative real savings and lending interest rates as inflation accelerated and capital flight was triggered by political and macroeconomic uncertainty, which combined to discourage the mobilization of financial savings and their efficient allocation. Thus, the continued adoption of financial repression policies in an environment of deteriorating macroeconomic stability eventually reversed the earlier gains made in the development of the financial system.

6.2.3 Financial liberalization policies: 1992–2008

In a fundamental departure from the financial repression regime of its predecessor, the newly elected MMD Government embarked on a programme of radical market-based financial sector reforms, as part of the economic stabilization and structural adjustment policies supported by the IMF and World Bank to place Zambia's economy on the path to recovery and sustainable growth. The financial sector reforms can be classified into three broad stages, with each stage differentiated by the government's approach to the design, implementation and focus of the reforms.

6.2.3.1 Stage one financial sector reforms: 1992–1994

Phase one financial sector reforms were characterized by a 'shock treatment'. The government moved swiftly to implement bold financial liberalization, which was aimed at removing endemic financial system distortions created by years of financial repression. A rapid financial liberalization programme was expected to facilitate the creation of a robust market-based financial system, which government considered a vital prerequisite for promoting economic growth and development. The financial liberalization programme commenced in earnest in 1992 with the removal of interest rate controls and credit supply ceilings. In early 1993 a Dutch auction system for Treasury bills was introduced to facilitate bank liquidity control and to finance government needs without resorting to monetization of the fiscal deficit. The decontrol of interest rates and credit allocation was accompanied by the removal of exchange controls, elimination of multiple exchange rates and a shift to market-determined exchange rates.

The dual exchange rate system was also swiftly replaced by a unified market-based exchange system. In the same year, the bureau de change legislation was enacted to facilitate market-based exchange rates,[4] while non-metal exporters were allowed to retain 50 per cent of their foreign earnings. In 1994 the BoZ foreign exchange dealing system was introduced while the Zambia Consolidated Copper Mine (ZCCM), the country's major exporter, was permitted to retain 55 per cent of its earnings, and the Exchange Control Act was repealed and all capital controls abolished, making the kwacha fully convertible. Other significant financial reforms implemented in phase one were financial infrastructure and institutional reforms, including the enactment of a new Banking and Financial Services Act (BFSA) in 1994 to govern the banking sector, restructuring the state-owned bank, adopting indirect and market-based instruments of monetary policy and reducing the required reserve and core liquid asset ratios.

6.2.3.2 Stage two financial sector reforms: 1995–2002

The phase two financial sector reforms focused on establishing and strengthening key financial infrastructure needed to support a sound and well-functioning banking system. Monetary authorities concentrated on two financial infrastructure areas, namely, bank supervision and regulation, and payment and settlement systems. The BFSA, introduced in 1994, was further enhanced through several rounds of revision aimed at upgrading the act in line with best practices consistent with the 25 principles of sound bank supervision and regulation recommended in the Basel Capital Accord. Notable upgrades to the act included introduction of off-site and on-site supervision, strengthening bank management and governance by introducing fit and proper tests for senior management, restricting maximum shareholding of a single investor to 25 per cent, and increasing bank regulatory capital to address the challenges of a fragile banking system (as many as ten banks collapsed in the early part of phase two). The BFSA also contained measures to reduce obstacles to competition and market segmentation by allowing greater freedom of entry into the banking industry, expanding the scope of permissible business activities for different types of financial institutions and relaxing restrictions on the activities of foreign-owned banks.

In recognition of their importance for efficient indirect monetary policy conduct, banking system liquidity management and money market transactions, the payment and settlement system also underwent significant reforms in phase two. In 1997, the BoZ relinquished control of the clearing function to the Bankers Association of Zambia, which established the Transitional Zambia Clearing House and introduced best practice clearing rules. In 1999, the Zambia Electronic Clearing House was launched with an automated electronic clearing system. The main objectives of the payment and settlement reforms were to improve the processing of payments efficiency, reduce the risk and uncertainty associated with non-cash payments and facilitate the adoption of indirect monetary instruments, all of which were crucial for fostering money and capital market development.

In phase two, monetary authorities instituted additional foreign exchange policy reforms to promote a more robust market-based foreign exchange market. In 1995 commercial banks were allowed to hold foreign exchange deposits. In 1996 the foreign exchange market was liberalized further when the retention rate of export earnings was increased to 100 per cent.

6.2.3.3 Stage three financial sector reforms: 2003–2008

In phase three, the government adopted a more development-oriented and holistic approach to financial sector reforms. Drawing on recommendations of the joint IMF-WBG FSAP 2002 Report, government formulated the Financial Sector Development Plan (FSDP) I, which guided the financial sector reforms during the 2004–2008 period. The FSAP report identified the following financial and banking system issues to be addressed by the plan: low level of financial intermediation or access to finance, especially banking credit; the continued dominance of commercial banks in the financial sector; very high net interest margins and ratio of fee income to average assets in banks relative to banks in Africa; poor credit culture; high credit risks; and the scarcity of financial skills (see FinMark Trust, 2008).

The vision statement of the FSDP I was to develop the Zambian financial system to become a stable and market-based financial system that would support efficient mobilization and allocation of resources necessary for economic diversification, sustainable growth and poverty reduction. The vision was to be pursued through the achievement of several objectives: these included restoration of sustained economic growth and macroeconomic stability, and the deepening of financial markets to enable banks, companies and households to have the means for effective liquidity management. The other objectives were to create a more balanced financial structure to promote competition, strengthen the credit culture, raise investment levels and strengthen the role of private investors in the financial sector by facilitating efficient price discovery, reducing financial intermediation costs, enhancing capital formation and broadening the non-banking financial sector.

Since the launch of FSDP I in 2004, additional financial sector reforms have been implemented for realizing the plan's vision and objectives. Notable among these reforms are the establishment of a credit reference bureau to enhance credit information infrastructure to combat the poor borrowing culture and improve access to financial services; issuance of a directive to banks to publish their interest rates and fees in the public media to enhance consumer awareness; and implementation of a risk-based supervision system and guidelines on risk management systems consistent with best practice as recommended by the Basel II Accord. In 2008 a follow-up FSAP assessment was conducted and its recommendations informed the design of FSDP II, which will guide financial sector reforms during the 2010–2012 period. The main objective of FSDP II is to improve the business environment for private sector growth by reducing financial sector impediments in respect of limited and costly access to finance. This is mainly to be achieved through technical assistance from strategic partners. The assistance will focus on three strategic pillars, namely, financial market infrastructure, enhancement of competition and alignment of financial system products and services with real sector needs.

6.2.4 Financial development under liberalization

6.2.4.1 Financial structure

The financial system structure has changed very little despite the implementation of radical market-based financial sector reforms. As under financial repression, commercial banks have continued to dominate the financial system, controlling as much as 80 per cent of the market based on total assets under control. However, the internal structure of the commercial bank sector has undergone significant changes in terms of the number of banks, their relative market shares and balance sheet changes. Implementation of market-based financial reforms in Zambia created new investment opportunities, which attracted new players to the commercial banking industry. Consequently, the number of banks rose to 20 in 1995, from 12 in 1991. The new entrants included foreign-owned private banks, foreign state-owned banks and regional and domestic private banks. New entrants to the commercial banking business were attracted by easy entry requirements in respect of low capital requirements, initially less stringent fit-and-proper tests for senior management and board members, and the opportunity to make huge returns on many opportunities including Treasury bill investments and lending and foreign exchange trading.

However, as noted above, between 1995 and 1998 ten domestic private banks collapsed, which triggered significant structural changes in the banking sector. The bank failures were caused by a combination of weaknesses of the financial reforms. The main weaknesses were poor sequencing of the financial reforms,[5] theft of depositors' funds and the low skills (and in some cases corruption) of bank managers who implemented unsound banking practices (such as risky lending policies to attract more customers and overly ambitious business expansion programmes). Other causes were binding liquidity and capital constraints, which many banks eventually faced when the super profits they had made in the early stages of the reforms were reduced when macroeconomic stability improved and more players entered the industry.

The failure of domestic private banks precipitated deposit and asset shifts, which resulted in significant changes in the structure of the commercial banking sector. Seeking safety for their savings and investments, and in the absence of a deposit insurance scheme, both retail and corporate depositors and investors switched their savings and investments into foreign-owned private banks, which were considered safe havens. The deposit and investment shifts were accompanied by shifts of assets, loans and capital into the same foreign-owned private banks. These balance sheet shifts reinforced the market dominance of foreign-owned big banks. Table 6.2 indicates the structural shifts in assets, credit supplied, deposits and capital of commercial banks for the 1997–2008 period. All indicators confirm the shift of deposits, credit and assets

Table 6.2 Shifts in bank market shares

	Market share (percentage of GDP)							
	Total assets		Net loans		Deposits		Capital	
	1997	2001	1997	2001	1997	2001	1997	2001
Foreign private	49.1	63.7	50.7	76.5	55.5	75.9	53.8	77.5
Foreign public	3.8	7.7	2.4	2.2	3.0	2.2	7.0	9.8
Domestic private	10.9	9.3	10.3	4.4	9.8	4.4	14.6	14.1
Public	22.8	19.4	23.1	16.9	22.6	16.9	15.2	0.0

Source: IMF and World Bank, 2002.

Table 6.3 Commercial banking structure by ownership

		Commercial bank type			
	Total	Foreign private	Domestic private	Foreign public	Public
1990	12	5	5	1	1
1995	20	5	13	1	1
2000	16	6	8	1	1
2005	14	7	5	1	1
2008	15	9	4	2	0

Source: Bank of Zambia.

into foreign-owned public and private commercial banks, away from domestic public and private banks.

The collapse of several banks during the nineties reduced the number of banks to 16 in 2000. Following the amalgamation of two local banks, the number of banks was further reduced to 14 in 2005, before increasing to 15 when a new regional and continental private bank entered the Zambian commercial banking industry. Table 6.3 presents trend movements in the total number of banks and a breakdown by ownership for selected years in the 1990–2008 period. As at the end of 2008, the banking system comprised 15 banks with nine foreign private banks (of which four were subsidiaries of multinational banking corporations), four domestic private banks and two foreign public banks. In terms of capital, the banks still remain relatively small by global standards. As at the end of 2008, the largest four banks had capitalization levels of between US$20 ₦24 million, four had between US$3 ₦13 million, and the remaining six had less than US$2 million each (IMF and World Bank, 2008).

In the last few years, the banking sector has started to show some signs of improvement and transformation. There has been a generalized increase in bank physical infrastructure such as new branches, agencies and automated teller machines. The expansion of bank infrastructure, coupled with the lowering of minimum account balances and increased interest in new investments, has also improved commercial bank intermediation, particularly in consumer lending to salaried individuals. Notwithstanding these positive developments, banking system assets and deposits remain highly concentrated in a few large foreign-owned banks, which suggests that the degree of bank competition in Zambia still remains low. Moreover, the market dominance of foreign

Table 6.4 Market share by bank ownership, and bank assets and deposits

	Percentage of total assets				Percentage of total deposits			
	PFB	DPB	FPB	DPRB	PFB	DPB	FPB	DPRB
1998	65.0	25.3	3.4	6.3	66.0	25.6	2.2	6.2
2004	66.6	19.7	6.0	8.0	62.4	23.6	6.6	6.1
2008	74.6	–	15.9	9.5	67.0	–	24.3	8.7

Note: PFB = private foreign banks, DPB = domestic public banks, FPB = foreign public banks, DPRB = domestic private banks.
Source: Bank of Zambia.

private banks not only continues to be high, but is generally rising as indicated by their increasing share of banking system assets and deposits in Table 6.4.

6.2.4.2 Bank competitiveness

Two statistical measures of bank competitiveness and concentration, the market share of the largest four banks and the Herfindahl index (IMF and World Bank, 2005) are presented in Tables 6.5 and 6.6, respectively. Trend movements of the market shares of the four top banks, based on assets, deposits and loans managed, all show that the four biggest banks controlled the majority of the commercial bank market, with average market shares of 72.9 per cent, 71.2 per cent and 67.3 per cent, respectively. In addition, with the exception of 2006 when bank assets and deposits fell sharply due to a marked appreciation of the kwacha exchange rate against the US dollar, the asset and deposit-based indicators show a general increase in the combined market share of the four biggest banks over the 1998–2008 period. However, the market share indicator based on loans shows a declining trend in market share.

Table 6.5 Bank concentration ratios (four banks)

	Assets	Deposits	Loans
1998	72.8	73.6	76.3
2004	71.1	73.3	79.1
2005	77.4	72.9	59.7
2006	66.9	61.8	76.5
2007	73.4	70.3	57.9
2008	76.3	75.1	54.2

Source: Calculated by researcher from Bank of Zambia.

Table 6.6 Herfindahl index

	Assets	Deposits	Loans
1998	1462.4	1590.1	1786.1
2004	1506.2	1618.1	1967.6
2005	1853.3	1583.2	1354.4
2006	1320.8	1256.0	1710.8
2007	1647.0	1472.6	1351.8
2008	1888.8	1583.0	1324.5

Source: Bank of Zambia, calculated by researcher

The declining trend in the loans-based indicator can be attributed to the declining importance of loans relative to alternative investments (for example, government securities) and the emergence of non-bank lenders, such as commercial microfinance institutions.

The Herfindahl index is defined as the sum of the squares of the market shares of each individual firm. It measures the degree of banking industry concentration based on the firm's size in relation to the industry. A low value of the index indicates the existence of a large number of small banks, and a large value the existence of a few banks in the industry. Thus a low Herfindahl index generally indicates loss of pricing power and, therefore, increasing competition, while a high index implies the opposite. Table 6.6 presents the trend movements of the Herfindahl index based on assets, deposits and loans for selected years over the 1998–2008 period. The asset and deposit indices generally indicate increasing values of the indices, which also confirm that the banking system in Zambia is, and has over time become, more concentrated and, therefore, less competitive in spite of the financial sector reforms.

6.2.4.3 Financial depth

Further to Table 6.1, a recent study by Mutoti (2008) shows that the trend movements of three indicators of financial depth and access, namely, the M2 to GDP, private sector credit to GDP and savings deposits to GDP. All three indicators exhibit a broadly similar trend pattern of changes in financial system depth during the study period. Financial depth fell sharply in phase one before increasing slightly and then stabilizing during the first two stages of phase two (with the exception of the savings deposit to GDP ratio indicator, which increased and then fell sharply in 2000 and 2005, respectively). In the third stage of phase two, financial depth began to increase steadily. However, the degree of financial depth during phase two was still below the historical high levels reached during the 1982–1988 period of phase one. Furthermore, as noted in the 2002 FSAP Report and 2008 FSAP Assessment Report, the depth of Zambia's financial system remains lower than those of financial systems in the Sub-Saharan Africa (SSA) region and similar low-income countries. Confirming the low level of financial depth in Zambia, the FSAP reports note that low-income economic entities, including retail and micro, and small and medium enterprises, have very limited access to financial services, while the private credit to GDP ratio is one of the lowest in the SSA region. These findings are also supported by recent surveys of the demand for and supply of financial services in Zambia by the FinMark Trust (2007). The survey results measures access to finance at only about 24 per cent in Zambia compared to more than 60 per cent in the SSA subregion.

6.2.4.4 *Financial performance*

Selected financial performance indicators for the banking sector of eight previous years are presented in Table 6.7. The indicators present generally favourable financial performance results. The financial soundness of banks has remained strong as they have maintained regulatory capital levels that are higher than the minimum required (10%). The quality of loan portfolios has improved significantly since 2006, despite the initial volatility. Bank profitability, in terms of returns on assets and equity, has also improved as the initial decline in bank profit rates has

Table 6.7 Financial performance indicators

	CAR	NPLR	ROA	ROE	NIM	LR
2002	28.0	11.4	6.5	52.8	15.3	78.6
2003	23.0	5.3	5.4	48.5	13.2	74.7
2004	22.2	7.6	3.1	29.8	11.8	66.6
2005	28.4	8.9	19.5	46.4	11.8	41.0
2006	20.4	11.3	16.1	30.6	12.8	41.3
2007	18.4	8.8	16.1	34.9	11.5	37.6
2008	19.3	6.0	32.8	36.6	11.3	32.8

Note: CAR = capital adequacy ratio (percentage of regulatory capital to risk-weighted assets); NPLR = non-performing loans ratio (percentage of past due loans to total loans); ROA = return on assets (percentage of net profit to average total assets); ROE = return on equity; NIM = net interest margin (percentage of net interest income to revenue); LR = liquidity ratio (percentage of liquid assets to total assets).
Source: Bank of Zambia.

been significantly reversed in the last three years of the period considered. Consequently, as the 2008 FSAP Assessment Report notes, banking profits in Zambia, on average, still remain relatively higher than those of banking systems in the Southern Africa Development Co-operation (SADC) region (IMF and World Bank, 2008). However, banks performed poorly in the areas of net interest income margin and liquidity, all of which declined over the last three years of the period considered.

6.3 Financial sector reforms and bank competitiveness

Econometric measurements, based on the Panzar-Rosse model of bank competition, using quarterly panel banking data and the ordinary least squares estimation method, are used to assess whether Zambia's market-based financial reforms have promoted a more competitive commercial bank market. Empirical findings indicate that the commercial banking market is characterized by imperfect or oligopolistic competition. This result agrees with the market share and Herfindahl indices presented in Section 6.2, which indicate the highly concentrated nature of the banking system in Zambia. These results, therefore, suggest that the implementation of radical market-based financial reforms in Zambia has not succeeded in promoting a more competitive banking sector, as the sector continues to be dominated by a few foreign big banks.

6.4 Financial sector reforms and bank efficiency

A two-step procedure is used to evaluate the effects of financial sector reforms on bank cost-efficiency performance. In step one, the cost-efficiency performance of individual banks relative to best available practice during the financial reform period is measured using an econometric estimation of a grand trans-log cost-efficiency stochastic frontier function. In step two, a cost-efficiency regression equation is estimated by the panel OLS method to evaluate key factor determinants of bank cost-efficiency. See Ncube (2009) on these methods. Quarterly time series data compiled by BoZ for the 1999–2008 period are used to estimate the cost-efficiency equation. Copper production data for estimating per capita GDP and INF are obtained from the Central Statistical Office.

6.4.1 Banking system cost-efficiency scores

The empirical results of cost-efficiency performance are presented in Table 6.8. The statistics include annual quarterly average efficiency

Table 6.8 Efficiency scores for the eleven banks (in per cent)

Bank	1999	2000	2001	2002	2003	2004	2005	2006	2007	2008	Average
1	80.92	65.33	67.19	61.17	66.68	80.55	65.59	72.62	74.80	77.00	71.19
2	75.04	55.03	69.32	57.82	73.42	71.05	71.31	79.69	82.49	82.35	71.75
3	52.77	67.33	72.45	64.87	62.15	76.77	79.33	75.91	79.77	75.45	70.74
4	54.21	86.38	72.64	64.44	31.67	48.77	52.56	51.62	36.68	48.88	54.79
Average	65.74	68.52	70.28	62.08	58.48	69.29	67.20	69.96	68.44	70.92	–
5	45.41	63.52	70.28	68.72	74.20	72.17	79.66	87.00	87.87	85.58	73.44
6	70.95	88.88	73.03	59.65	45.49	60.36	77.23	82.69	85.58	83.83	72.77
Average	58.18	76.20	71.66	64.19	59.85	66.27	78.45	84.85	86.73	84.71	–
7	68.47	72.15	49.52	54.52	59.32	70.12	83.60	69.64	50.46	61.83	63.97
8	63.50	75.14	58.84	75.50	60.53	68.20	73.47	73.80	66.41	64.56	68.00
9	86.62	90.32	86.19	81.14	66.42	75.67	71.96	70.34	69.86	71.70	77.02
10	43.87	56.29	58.11	61.92	80.42	72.74	82.21	82.07	82.22	78.14	69.80
11	57.69	80.47	65.58	70.62	72.09	65.89	82.01	75.70	68.38	70.66	70.91
Average	62.92	75.56	67.18	72.30	69.87	70.63	77.41	75.48	71.72	71.27	–
Total average	63.59	72.81	67.56	65.49	62.94	69.30	74.45	74.65	71.32	72.73	–

Note: 1–4 = foreign private-owned multinational banks, 5–6 = public-private banks, 7 = foreign state-owned bank, 8–11 = domestic private banks.

scores of each bank, groups of banks (by bank ownership type) and at the aggregate level. The results indicate great variance in individual bank cost-efficiency scores, which range from 54.79 per cent to 77.02 per cent, in terms of period averages. Furthermore, the cost-efficiency performance of banks has not converged over time, as per theoretical expectation, but has instead been characterized by mixed results with some bank scores converging and others diverging. Some domestic private banks have outperformed foreign-owned multinational banks, and vice versa, while public banks have outperformed some private domestic and foreign-owned banks. Intra-bank group differences in cost-efficiency scores also abound. In the class of private foreign-owned multinational banks, the efficiency score of one bank is particularly very poor. In the domestic private bank category there are also marked differences in relative cost-efficiency performance. Notwithstanding the foregoing, at the aggregate level, banking system cost-efficiency performance has fluctuated on an upward-sloping trend increasing from 63.59 per cent in 1990 to 72.73 per cent in 2008.

6.4.2 Determinants of bank cost-efficiency performance

Regression estimation results indicate that significant determinants of bank cost-efficiency are phase two and phase three financial reforms and bank attributes in respect of bank liquidity, profits, size, loan portfolio quality and the nature of bank ownership (private or public ownership), while macroeconomic variables (per capita GDP and inflation) are insignificant determinants of bank cost-efficiency. With regard to financial sector variables, both phases two and three financial sector reforms have positive effects on bank cost-efficiency. This means that the strengthening of bank supervision and regulation, payment and settlement, and money and capital market mechanisms have contributed to enhancing the cost-efficiency of financial intermediation. In addition, the adoption of comprehensive financial sector development planning, to guide financial sector reforms in phase three, has also contributed to improving cost-efficiency through channels such as the setting up of an information credit bureau and the introduction of regulation requiring banks to disclose their charges and fees.

Regarding bank attributes, only bank size has a positive effect on cost-efficiency. Hence, big banks have been able to reduce costs by increasing the scale and scope of their operations and attracting better qualified and experienced bankers. Other bank characteristics, including liquidity, profit, loan portfolio quality and bank ownership type, have negative effects on cost-efficiency. Higher bank liquidity levels have an adverse impact on cost-efficiency by increasing the opportunity cost of unremunerated idle liquidity. The negative effects of profit can be attributed to the uncompetitive nature of the banking system, which makes it possible for inefficient banks to charge higher interest rates and fees to clients. Deterioration in the loan portfolio quality negatively affects cost-efficiency by increasing loan loss provisions. The negative effect of private ownership of a bank on cost-efficiency is unexpected. Precisely how public-private partnership-based banks are able to perform better in terms of cost-efficiency requires further investigation into the quality of the management in these banks.

The insignificant effect of per capita GDP on bank cost-efficiency can be attributed to the low level of access or penetration of banking services in Zambia. Another reason is that under conditions of highly skewed income distribution, per capita GDP is not a robust measure of economic prospects, as the effects of rising income are not broad based. The negative, but insignificant, effect of inflation is rather surprising. This may, however, be explained by the fact that the relative stabilization of inflation, at just above single-digit rates over a number of years, is no longer a significant driver of intermediation costs in Zambia. The low explanatory power of the regression model used suggests that the variables included in the equation are by no means the only ones that have influenced bank cost-efficiency. Potential determinants of cost-efficiency for which data are not available are non-financial costs of doing banking business and qualitative indicators of bank organization and management systems. In this regard, more work needs to be done to develop data on these variables and analyse their effects on bank efficiency.

6.4.3 Financial sector reforms and economic growth

An endogenous economic growth model is developed, in which industrial production is the dependent variable, while bank cost-efficiency and financial depth and some macroeconomic controls (external openness and inflation) are the dependent variables. Panel bank data for the sample period 1999–2008 and the panel Ordinary Least Squares (OLS) method are used to evaluate the impact of financial reforms on bank cost-efficiency. The time series data for the macroeconomic variables are obtained from BoZ quarterly monetary and financial statistics reports. Data for the BCE variable are derived from panel bank data for the same period.

6.5 Empirical findings

Regression estimation results confirm expectations: increases in bank cost-efficiency, financial depth and the introduction of holistic financial sector development planning have positive effects on economic growth. However, policy reforms to improve the financial infrastructure seem to have an adverse effect on economic growth. This result may be attributed to strong credit contraction effects of restrictive and over-reaching supervision and regulatory reforms that offset the positive effects of improved payment and settlement and money and capital market mechanisms.

Macroeconomic conditions regarding external openness and the rate of inflation also have the expected effects on growth. In the case of increases in the degree of external openness, the effects on economic growth are positive. Thus, the opening up of the Zambian economy through the liberalization of the current and capital accounts has contributed to increasing economic growth by significantly improving the availability of foreign exchange (the country's foreign exchange reserves have increased over the last ten years from fewer than 2 months of import cover to 5–6 months of import cover). Double-digit increases in consumer price inflation have negative effects on economic growth.

6.6 Policy implications of empirical results

Several key lessons on the relationship between financial sector reforms and bank competitiveness and cost-efficiency, and on economic growth and policy implications, emerge from Zambia's experience with market-based financial sector reforms. First, financial sector reforms based on advice from the IMF and World Bank, although necessary, are not a sufficient prerequisite for promoting competitive and cost-efficient commercial banking systems. Additional measures are needed to break the dominance and discourage the collusive behaviour of a few big banks; examples are consolidation of very small banks, anti-competitive practice regulations and laws, and the promotion of non-bank financial intermediaries and capital markets to compete with banks. Second, cost-efficient performance conduct is not the preserve of foreign-owned multinational or domestic private banks. Public-private partnership banks may be equally, if not more, efficient. Third, the poor sequencing of market-based financial reforms in which a radical financial liberalization programme is implemented before strengthening financial infrastructure (particularly bank regulation and the supervisory framework) is a recipe for costly bank failures and financial system instability, which is disruptive to economic growth. Fourth, market-based financial reforms must be well grounded in rigorous country-specific analyses and diagnoses of the impact on bank competition and the efficiency of previous financial policies. Such analysis and diagnosis should ideally aim to identify financial system constraints and structural deficiencies, which should then become the focus of the reforms. Fifth, to be effective, financial sector reforms must be designed and implemented in the context of a holistic financial sector development plan.

Appendix: Major financial sector reforms in Zambia (1992–2008)

Policy measure	Date
Liberalization of commercial bank interest rates	Sep-92
Introduction of foreign exchange bureau	Oct-92
Unification of the exchange rate system	Dec-92
Introduction of the primary Treasury bills auction	Jan-93
Introduction of the 28-day Treasury bill	Mar-93
Introduction of the 182-day Treasury bill	Aug-93
Introduction of the BoZ foreign exchange dealing system	Dec-93
The Foreign Exchange Control Act revoked	Jan-94
Introduction of foreign currency accounts	Mar-94
Enactment of the Banking and Financial Services Act (BFSA)	Jun-94
Introduction of Government bond auctions	Dec-94
Introduction of BoZ open market operations (OMO)	Mar-95
Enactment of the BoZ Act No. 43	Dec-96
Introduction of the book-entry trading system in Government securities	Aug-97
Listing of Government bonds on the Lusaka Stock Exchange	Mar-98
Introduction of 18-month Government bonds	Oct-98
Establishment of the Zambia Electronic Clearing House	Sep-99
Introduction of an enhanced early warning system for the financial system	Mar-00
Introduction of longer term Government securities (273-day TBs and 24-month bonds)	Oct-00
Introduction of BoZ guidelines for foreign exchange trading	Feb-01
Introduction of repurchase agreement transactions in the money market	Feb-02
Introduction of broad-based interbank foreign exchange market	Jul-03

Introduction of the Zambia interbank payment and settlement system	Jun-04
Introduction of amendments bills to Building Societies, DBZ, and Payments System Acts	Oct-05
Introduction of microfinance regulations	Dec-05
Establishment of the Credit Reference Bureau	Jan-07

Source: Bank of Zambia annual reports and circulars.

Notes

1. The Movement for Multiparty Democracy (MMD) Government was elected into office in 1991 with a mandate to transform the Zambian economy through adopting radical market-based economic reforms.
2. Five four-year development plans were implemented during the period.
3. Government imposed floors on savings rates and ceilings on lending rates.
4. Under the dual exchange rate system, the market rate was determined by the BoZ weekly auction while the official rate was a below-auction one used for allocating foreign exchange, by the Foreign Exchange Management Committee (FEMAC), for debt-servicing, medical and educational supplies, oil imports, as well as for ZCCM and Zambia Airways (ZA) import requirements.
5. Implementation of the BFSA followed financial liberalization instead of preceding it.

References

Beck, T. and P. Honohan. 2007. *Making Finance Work for Africa*. Washington D.C.: The World Bank.

Claessen, S. and L. Laeven. 2004. 'What drives bank competition? Some international evidence'. *Journal of Money, Credit and Banking*, 36(2): 563–84.

FinMark. 2007. Making Financial Markets Work for the Poor, Johannesburg: FinMark.

FinMark Trust. 2008. *Measuring Financial Access in Zambia, The Supply Side*. Lusaka, Zambia: FinMark Trust.

Gulde, A., C. Pattillo and J. Christensen. 2006. *Sub-Saharan Africa Financial Sector Challenges*. Washington D.C.: IMF.

IMF and World Bank. 2002. *2002 FSAP Report*. Washington, D.C: The World Bank.

IMF and World Bank. 2005. 'Financial sector assessment'. *A Handbook*, Chapter 4. Washington, D.C.: The World Bank.

IMF and World Bank. 2008. *2008 FSAP Assessment Report*. Washington, D.C.: The World Bank.

Kasekende, L., K. Mlambo, V. Murinde and T. Zhao. 2009. 'Restructuring for competitiveness: The financial services sector in Africa's four largest economies'. In World Economic Forum (ed.), *Africa Competitiveness Report* 2009, p. 49.

Martinez, J. L. 2006. *Access to Financial Services in Zambia*. World Bank Policy Research Paper No. 4061. Washington, D.C.: The World Bank.

Mutoti, N. 2008. '*Monetary Transmission in Zambia*', PhD Thesis, University of Kansas.
Mwenda, A. 1993. '*Credit Rationing and Investment Behaviour Under Market Imperfections: Evidence from Commercial Banking in Zambia*', PhD Thesis, University of Gothenburg, Gothenburg
Ncube, M. 2009. 'South African banking sector and its efficiency'. Competitiveness of Financial Services in South Africa, Johannesburg, Wits Business School, University of the Witwatersrand, pp. 58–103.

7

Regulatory Policy Lessons from Banking Sector Reforms in Egypt

Sunil S. Poshakwale and Binsheng Qian

7.1 Introduction

The relationship between financial sector development and growth is particularly relevant to developing African economies. Previous research has shown that financial sector development is positively related to economic growth. However, financial sector development without simultaneous regulatory reforms is unlikely to help increase investments, and thus economic growth. For these reasons, the economic liberalization and financial sector reforms have been actively promoted and, in some cases, supported by the International Monetary Fund and the World Bank.

In view of the financial crisis of 2008–2009, the importance of the financial sector in economic development cannot be overemphasized. Many economies around the world are still recovering from the crisis, which started with subprime mortgage defaults in the US in 2008. However, the events have shown that the private sector has become highly dependent on credit markets in which banks and financial institutions play a critical role. The financial sector mobilizes savings and allocates credit across markets over time. The economic liberalization programmes, followed by many countries with developing economies, and the increase in cross-border trade and investment flows have globalized financial markets. The globalization of financial markets has meant that credit has to flow smoothly between countries and continents to facilitate investment and growth. Further, there is a link between economic activity and development of financial institutions: as the broader financial sector grows, pensions and other forms of institutional asset management begin to develop which, in turn, facilitate further expansion of equity and capital markets. These linkages and current developments in the global economy provide an interesting background for conducting research on this topical issue.

Research has shown that, despite financial reforms and the active pursuance of deregulation by developing countries around the world, the banking sector in these countries is dominated by political expediencies which lead to inefficient use of banking resources which, in turn, impedes potential economic growth. Like the rest of the developing world, African countries have undergone a number of important structural and policy reforms in their financial sector. It is well acknowledged that the role of a competitive and efficient financial sector is crucial for economic development and growth in Africa (see Kirkpatrick et al., 2008). Further, Kasekende et al. (2009) argue that the competitiveness and efficiency of the financial sector in countries like Egypt is important as it is one of the largest service-oriented African economies. They further suggest that extensive research on different African economies, especially SANE (South Africa, Nigeria, Egypt) economies, is required as these countries have undergone a series of very advanced financial reforms. Policymakers need to be informed on the outcomes and relevance of these reforms, especially in the wake of the current global financial crisis. This is particularly relevant as, in a study of 79 countries over the period 1980–1997, Beck et al. (2002) have shown that crises are less likely in countries with fewer regulatory restrictions on banking activities and in countries with institutions that encourage more competition.

In summary, there are several empirical issues in understanding the link between finance development and economic growth for developing countries. First of all, the choice of a particular efficiency or competition indicator in empirical studies is of particular policy relevance since it can influence the interpretations of competitive behaviour and productive efficiency within a given country. Second, it is important to understand the impact of the different stages of financial reforms, since this can help policymakers to improve the efficiency of reforms over time. Finally, it is critical to examine the link between financial reforms, finance development and economic growth, which has policy implications for regulatory reforms.

This chapter's aim is to provide important regulatory lessons by analysing the effect of key banking sector reforms implemented in Egypt. The Egyptian banking sector experienced continuous financial reform between 1992 and 2007, and thus provides an excellent case to study the interaction between financial reforms, competition, efficiency and economic growth.

The rest of the chapter is organized as follows. Section 7.2 explains the background and major developments in Egypt's financial sector. Section 7.3 explains the data, sample and methodologies employed in the analysis of data. Section 7.4 presents and discusses empirical results and Section 7.5 concludes and summarizes the main policy implications of this research.

7.2 Developments in Egypt's financial sector

7.2.1 Financial sector in Egypt

Egypt's financial sector is one of the oldest and most vibrant in the Middle East and North Africa (MENA) region. Despite a number of privatizations, the financial sector in Egypt has huge potential in its financial services, ranging from commercial banking to insurance, mortgage lending and financial advisory services. The overwhelming majority of approximately 76 million people in Egypt have yet to use consumer banking and insurance services. Additionally, despite a growing market for residential and leisure properties, the mortgage market is still in its infancy. Thus there is a huge potential for growth in the financial services sector.

There are 21 insurance and reinsurance companies in Egypt and recent policy changes now allow foreign institutions to own a majority stake in an Egyptian insurance company. Although still much lower by international comparison, insurance premiums as a percentage of GDP reached 0.83 per cent in 2007, from 0.59 per cent in 2006. Regulatory reforms were initiated to restructure the insurance market and the Egyptian Insurance Supervisory Authority was formed, which will have the responsibility to monitor risk management and financial solvency in the insurance sector. Recently, the parliament has passed a bill for mandatory insurance, covering civil liability in automobile accidents. This is likely to give a huge boost to the insurance services.

The private equity sector is also growing and Cairo-based Citadel Capital has become a regional leader with US$8.3 billion of investments under its control. The mortgage market is also rapidly growing and more than LE2 billion (LE is Livre Egyptienne, or Egyptian Pound) worth of mortgages have been issued since the passing of the Mortgage Finance Law in 2002. Other than banks, there are five specialized mortgage companies, and with the establishment of the Egyptian Mortgage Refinance Company (EMRC) the mortgage market is likely to experience rapid growth. The reduction in property registration fees to a maximum of LE2000 will further improve the eligibility for mortgage finance.

By the end of 2004, there were 57 banks in Egypt: 28 commercial banks, of which 4 are state-owned; and 26 investment banks, of which 11 are joint venture banks and 15 are foreign-owned. The remaining three are specialized banks of which two are state-owned. However, privatization of state-owned banks and consolidation of smaller banks reduced the number of banks to 37 in 2007.

Although the Egyptian financial sector is not as well integrated as in developed countries, the banking sector in Egypt is very important and commands a significant share in terms of its contribution to overall economic growth. The banking sector performs a crucial role in Egypt's financial system and accounts for more than 60 per cent of financial assets in the economy. The total bank deposits are around 100 per cent of GDP.

Figure 7.1 provides an overview of the growth in bank deposits and loans. Both show a steady growth over time. Loans grew from LE58,249 million in 1992 to LE353,746 million, registering a fivefold increase. On the other hand, bank deposits grew from LE110,171 million in 1992 to LE649,953 million in 2007, registering a huge increase of 490 per cent.

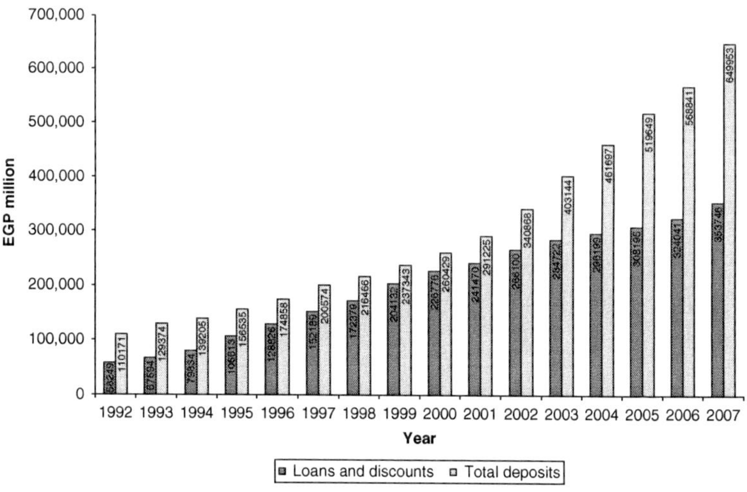

Figure 7.1 Banking sector loans and deposits (at the end of June)
Source: Central Bank of Egypt.

7.2.2 Structural reforms in Egypt's financial sector

The banking sector in Egypt is a cornerstone of its financial system and plays a critical role in the Egyptian economy. Before the introduction of the Economic Reform and Structural Adjustment Program (ERSAP), Egypt's banking performance was lacklustre and lagged the development in other sectors. The banking sector was dominated by the state and, as a consequence, it was uncompetitive and offered a low level of financial intermediation. The sector also lacked innovation and good quality governance. The decisions to offer credit were not taken with due commercial consideration and this distorted the incentive system and sound managerial practices. The inefficient management of banks led to the build up of large volumes of non-performing loans and poor asset quality on balance sheets (Central Bank of Egypt, 2007 report).

The banking reform process in Egypt started in 1990 with removing the banking sector monopoly through the liberalization of deposit and lending rates. This was followed by the elimination of ceilings on bank loans in 1992. More significantly, banks were allowed to set their own service charges and fees. In February 1991, the foreign exchange market was reformed and the central bank's control on exchange rates was lifted. In 1994, the Egyptian government actively embarked on the privatization process and, with an aim to reduce concentration and increase competition, four state-owned banks were directed to sell their holdings. In the second stage of reforms, the government of Egypt continued to pursue the economic liberalization programme. In 1996, the government amended the banking and credit legislation, which removed the 49 per cent ceiling on foreign ownership of Egyptian banks. In the third and most current phase of reforms starting in 2002, the government launched the Financial Sector Reform Programme aimed at divesting public sector ownership of banks, consolidating smaller banks and restructuring state-owned banks. The programme also aimed to privatize one of the four largest state-owned banks, namely Bank of Alexandria, which holds nearly 7 per cent of banking sector assets. Since 2005, the non-performing loans in Egyptian banks have been reduced or eliminated through restructuring. Between 2005 and 2007, 14 banks, including some state-owned banks, were either taken over by or merged with foreign banks (see Table 7.1 for details). Further, in the most recent phase of reforms, special courts have been set up to expedite the resolution of cases mainly involving financial disputes and contractual defaults. The central bank has upgraded and modernized its institutional framework for quicker processing of transactions

Table 7.1 Selected merger-and-acquisition activity in banking sector (2005–2007)

Buyer/investor	Acquired
National Bank of Kuwait	Al-Watany Bank of Egypt (2007)
Abu Dhabi Islamic Bank and Emirates International Investments Company	National Development Bank (2007)
Sanpaolo IMI	Bank of Alexandria (2006)
Ahli United Bank of Bahrain and consortium	Delta International Bank (2006)
Union National Bank	Alexandria Commercial and Maritime Bank (2006)
Banque Audi	Cairo Far East Bank (2006)
Crédit Agricole and Mansour-Maghrabi Investment and Development	Egyptian American Bank (2006)
Blom Bank	Misr Romanian Bank (2005)
National Société Générale Bank	Misr International Bank (MIBank) (2005)
Arab International Bank	Suez Canal Bank (2005)
Société Arabe Internationale de Banque (SAIB)	Port Said National Development Bank (2005)
Piraeus	Egyptian Commercial Bank (2005)
Arab African International Bank	Misr America International Bank (2005)
Société Générale	National Société Générale Bank (2005)

Source: Cairo and Alexandria Stock Exchanges.

between banks by introducing real-time settlement and establishing an automated clearing house.

7.2.3 Capital markets

The Cairo and Alexandria Stock Exchange (CASE) is one of the oldest and largest stock exchanges in Africa. It has been modernized over the last decade and is considered a very modern stock exchange. CASE was one of the best performing stock markets in 2007 when its index of 30 top stocks grew by 51 per cent compared with 2006. Market capitalization as a percentage of GDP reached 105 per cent, compared with 29 per cent in 2002. However, the CASE30 Index dropped sharply during 2008 recording an all-time single-year loss of 56.4 per cent following the global financial crisis, which hit the financial markets in September 2008 causing a global economic slowdown. Total market capitalization declined substantially in 2008 by 38.3 per cent to LE474 billion, down from LE768 billion in 2007. The decline is mainly attributable to the global financial crisis, which resulted in a selling frenzy in the last quarter of 2008. During 2008 the number of listed companies decreased by 15 per cent to 373, compared with 435 listed companies in 2007. The decrease in the number of listed companies may be attributed to the continuous implementation of strict listing and disclosure regulations. Although the number of traded companies declined by about 5 per cent in 2008 to 322, compared with 337 in 2007, the ratio of traded companies to total listed companies increased to 86.1 per cent in 2008, as opposed to 77.5 per cent in 2007. Despite its poor performance in 2008, the Egyptian stock market is considered one of the most attractive African emerging markets at its current prevailing market prices, relative to companies' earnings and dividends distribution.

Egypt's WTO financial services commitment in the securities sector provides for unrestricted market access and international investors are permitted to operate in the Egyptian stock market largely without restriction. Several foreign brokers, including US and European firms, have established or purchased stakes in brokerage companies. Participation of foreign investors in the Egyptian market has also been growing to around 30 per cent by 2007.

The mergers and acquisitions market has also been active. The total number of acquisitions amounted to LE105 billion in 2008, compared with LE37 billion in the previous year. The most notable of these was Lafarge's mega LE71 billion takeover of Orascom Building Materials Holding. The value of this deal alone represents around 67 per cent of the total value of all acquisitions in Egypt during 2008. In addition, Orascom Development Holding AG's deal to acquire 98 per cent of Orascom Hotels and Development in May was one of the major acquisitions of the year, valued at approximately LE16 billion (Cairo and Alexandria Stock Exchange, 2008 report).

Egypt's government bond market has developed rapidly during its short lifetime. The government has been issuing bonds in Egyptian Pounds since 2007, as well as in foreign currencies, including a series of Eurobonds from 2001. Currently, the value of listed bonds in the Egyptian market is LE20 billion, with LE14 billion in government bonds and bills, and LE6 billion in corporate bonds.

7.2.4 Developments in the financial sector

The developments in Egypt's financial sector can be seen from the figures provided in Table 7.2, which report selected indicators for the development of the Egyptian finance sector for the period 1992–2007. Furthermore, Figure 7.2 shows that domestic credit provided by banks in

Table 7.2 Development of financial sector in Egypt, 1992–2007

Year	Domestic credit provided by banks (% of GDP)	Domestic credit to private sector (% of GDP)	Money and quasi money (M2) as % of GDP	Market capitalization of listed companies (% of GDP)	Gross savings (% of GDP)
1992	82.981	26.194	77.663	7.789	26.646
1993	79.918	27.864	80.788	8.180	27.289
1994	80.613	32.146	80.366	8.208	21.880
1995	80.632	37.040	76.195	13.444	21.778
1996	82.033	41.484	74.797	20.957	18.099
1997	82.136	44.889	71.501	26.556	17.322
1998	90.588	52.681	73.279	28.741	18.568
1999	95.830	58.717	74.005	36.201	20.072
2000	96.401	58.682	72.759	28.788	18.716
2001	102.434	62.104	77.570	24.925	18.439
2002	109.565	61.943	82.912	29.702	19.998
2003	112.422	61.146	88.197	32.648	19.457
2004	111.616	60.401	89.902	48.850	20.490
2005	104.649	57.372	92.091	88.835	21.299
2006	99.258	55.278	90.996	86.969	22.029
2007	89.512	50.642	88.454	106.755	22.530

Source: World Development Indicators of World Bank.

the economy and credit provided to the private sector in relation to GDP significantly increased over time. Although figures for 2006 and 2007 show a decline in credit provided by banks, this may have been due to the onset of the credit crisis. However, compared with 1992, the levels of credit are still substantially higher. The rapid expansion of banking activities has resulted in more than 100 per cent growth in the banking sector's assets over time. The broad money (M2/GDP) ratio has shown a significant increase over time and reached 92 per cent in 2006, compared with 77 per cent in 1992. However, the ratio of gross savings to GDP shows a decline from 26 per cent in 1992 to 22 per cent in 2007. Most notable is the striking increase in the value of equity stocks traded in the Egyptian stock market. Market capitalization as a percentage of GDP reached 106.75 by 2007, which, although comparable with many other large developing markets, is still lower than those reported for developed markets.

Figure 7.3 provides a pattern of bank lending and deposit rates as well as interest rates and inflation from 1992 to 2007. Bank lending rates declined from 20 per cent in 1992 to 13 per cent in 2007. Not

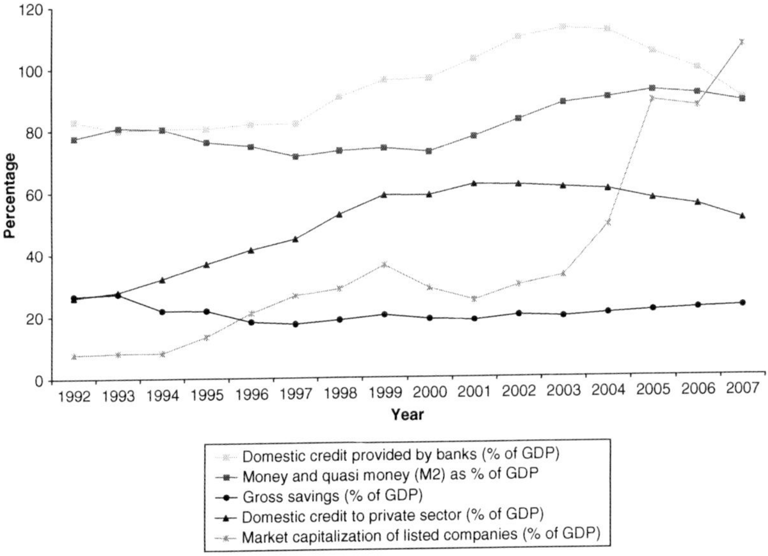

Figure 7.2 Development of financial sector in Egypt, 1992–2007

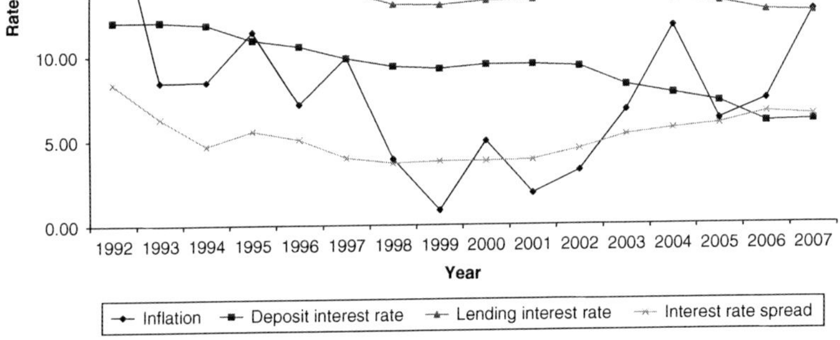

Figure 7.3 Interest and inflation rates in Egypt, 1992–2007

surprisingly, deposit rates also declined, from 12 per cent in 1992 to 7 per cent in 2007. Consequently, the interest rate spread for banks fell from around 8 per cent in 1992 to around 5.5 per cent in 2007. The interest rate decline has kept pace with the declining inflation, which fell sharply to around 1 per cent in 1999 from around 20 per cent in 1992. In 2007, the inflation rate was around 13 per cent. Deposit rates remained above inflation before 2002. However, since the middle of 2002, they have been lower than the inflation rate, confirming the decline in savings to GDP ratio observed in Table 7.2. This may also partially explain the rapid rise in market capitalization in the Egyptian stock market since unattractive saving interest rates may have channelled the savings to the stock markets and other alternative investment avenues.

7.3 Data, methodology and empirical findings

7.3.1 Sample data

We used data for Egyptian banks obtained from BankScope, an international database covering over 29,000 banks worldwide. The sample of 45 Egyptian banks during the period 1992–2007 provided a total of 423 annual bank observations. Further, to examine the link between financial sector development and economic growth, we collected macroeconomic data for Egypt from the World Development Indicators database of the World Bank.

7.3.2 Research methodology

As indicated in the literature review section, few studies have conducted a systematic examination of the interaction between financial sector reforms, competition, efficiency and economic growth. Our research framework addresses this issue in three stages. First, we measure industry competition and the productive efficiency of the Egyptian banking sector, which provides a complete picture of finance development in Egypt. Second, we explore the determinants of competition and efficiency of the Egyptian banking sector, with a particular focus on the impact of financial reforms. Finally, we investigate the link between competitive conduct, productive efficiency and economic growth.

7.3.3 Empirical results

This section provides the results of the empirical analysis in three steps. First, we measure two important indicators of financial sector development, industry competition and productive efficiency. For each indicator we calculate five different empirical measures to gain a complete understanding of the development of the Egyptian banking sector. Second, we explore the factors determining the variation in industry competition and individual banks' productive efficiency, with particular focus on the impact of financial reforms in Egypt. Finally, we examine the link between financial sector development indicators and economic growth in Egypt.

7.3.3.1 Banking sector competitiveness

The Herfindahl index is a simple and widely used measure for determining the degree of concentration in a given industry. The more concentrated the industry, the higher the value of the index and the lower the extent of competition. Table 7.3 reports the performance and market structure for Egyptian banks and shows the values of the Herfindahl index for various years and for a number of variables for the banking sector in Egypt. According to the variables BHHI, which represents median values of income concentration based on the proportions of interest

Table 7.3 Performance and market structure of Egyptian bank sector, 1992–2007

Year	BHHI	BROA	BROE	BOVH	CR4L	CR4D	SHHI	FBPR
1992	0.761	0.008	0.107	0.020	0.750	0.759	0.321	0.011
1993	0.747	0.019	0.162	0.016	0.746	0.755	0.201	0.011
1994	0.704	0.018	0.193	0.018	0.739	0.751	0.176	0.012
1995	0.668	0.017	0.241	0.016	0.742	0.749	0.115	0.019
1996	0.674	0.016	0.198	0.017	0.690	0.734	0.095	0.022
1997	0.656	0.016	0.188	0.016	0.673	0.719	0.092	0.024
1998	0.637	0.017	0.171	0.018	0.646	0.669	0.081	0.023
1999	0.680	0.016	0.174	0.018	0.549	0.636	0.079	0.024
2000	0.685	0.010	0.106	0.018	0.458	0.597	0.115	0.049
2001	0.665	0.008	0.079	0.018	0.477	0.617	0.112	0.050
2002	0.683	0.003	0.031	0.016	0.485	0.630	0.109	0.050
2003	0.572	0.005	0.047	0.016	0.492	0.628	0.112	0.059
2004	0.624	0.003	0.044	0.016	0.482	0.587	0.111	0.065
2005	0.638	0.007	0.058	0.016	0.499	0.598	0.128	0.089
2006	0.701	0.003	0.058	0.015	0.500	0.594	0.131	0.180
2007	0.654	0.014	0.109	0.016	0.478	0.615	0.119	0.196

Note: BHHI = sector median of income concentration Herfindahl–Hirschman index based on banks' segment income; BROA = sector median return on assets; BROE = sector median return on equity; BOVH = sector median overhead expense over total assets; CR4L = market share of largest four banks by loans; CR4D = market share of largest four banks by deposits; SHHI = sector Herfindahl–Hirschman index based on individual banks' total assets; FBPR = foreign bank penetration rate defined as ratio of foreign banks' assets over total assets of bank sector.

income, fee income and other operating income, and SHHI, which provides a measure of concentration based on the total assets of individual banks, it can be concluded that the degree of concentration in the Egyptian banking industry appears to be declining. Results indicate that the Egyptian banking sector has become more competitive over time. The declining values of CR4L and CR4D in Figure 7.4 suggest that both the market share and the share of deposits of the four largest banks seem to have declined over time. Other measures, such as BROA, BROE and BOVH, which indicate the operating efficiency of Egyptian banks, also confirm that with the increase in competition, banks have had to reduce their overheads and their returns on total assets and equity capital. The foreign bank penetration ratio (FBPR) has also increased over time. A big jump in the ratio in 2006 was on account of the acquisition of the fourth-largest public sector bank, Bank of Alexandria, by Sanpaolo IMI.

7.3.3.2 Degree of competition based on Panzar-Rosse model

We estimate the H-statistic, which is the sum of the elasticities of two input prices of a multi-product revenue equation, following the methodology suggested in Kasekende et al. (2009). The results indicate monopolistic competition ($0 < H < 1$) in the Egyptian banking sector for

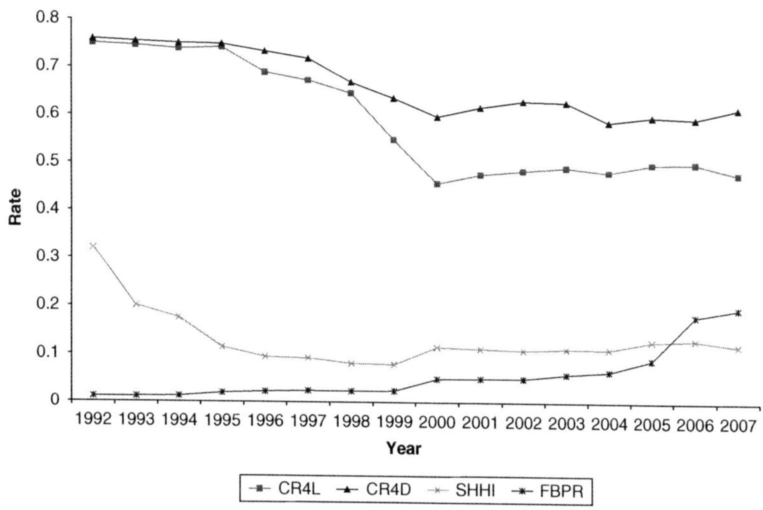

Figure 7.4 Evolution of Egyptian banking sector's market structure, 1992–2007
Note: CR4L = four-bank concentration ratio by loan; CR4D = four-bank concentration ratio by deposits; SHHI = sector concentration ratio; FBPR = foreign bank penetration rate defined as ratio of foreign banks' assets over total assets of bank sector

the sample period. To determine whether the competitive behaviour of different types of banks differ, we estimate the *H*-statistic for disaggregated samples based on the ownership types (i.e. government-owned banks, private banks, foreign banks and domestic banks). The ownership classification is based on the identity of owners holding more than 50 per cent shares. The estimated *H*-statistics for different types of banks show that government banks with an *H*-statistic of 0.425 are generally less competitive than private banks with an *H*-statistic of 0.547. This may be due to the fact that there are just four public sector banks; all of these are significant players and are able to use their monopolistic position. Not surprisingly, foreign banks with *H*-statistics of 0.487 are less competitive than domestic banks with *H*-statistics of 0.582. This may be because many foreign banks are relative newcomers in the markets and they tend to face higher costs than domestic banks in building relationships with local businesses in generating income. In other words, it takes foreign banks a significant amount of time to acquire knowledge of local financial markets.

The time series pattern of average industry competition, demand elasticity, and the Lerner index, reported in Table 7.4 and Figure 7.5, show that over the whole sample period, the 95 per cent upper bound of θ (industry competition) never exceeds the value of 1, and the 95 per cent lower bound of θ is always above 0. Therefore, it can be concluded that the Egyptian banking sector seems to be characterized by a super competition situation. The Lerner index shows a similar V pattern over time. This is because the average industry demand elasticity in Egypt has been very stable at around 1.15 over the sample period. The evidence on theta suggests that competition in the Egyptian banking sector initially improved between 1992 and 1996 as seen from the downward trend of theta values. The competition status remains stable between 1996 and 2002. However, there is an upward trend from 2002 which reverses after 2005.

The changes in competition in the Egyptian banking sector can be interpreted in the context of financial reforms in Egypt. The period 1992–1996 was the first stage of financial reforms implemented in Egypt, which comprised the elimination of the interesting rate ceiling in 1992 and lending limits in 1993. These policy changes seem to have a significant and positive impact on competition within the banking sector. In the second stage of financial reform (1996–2002), the Egyptian government continued the financial liberalization by privatizing the government's stake in commercial banks and by easing industry regulations. In this period, bank competition seemed to respond well

Table 7.4 Empirical measures of competitive conditions in Egyptian banking sector, 1992–2007

Year	Average competition (θ)	Industry demand elasticity (η)	Lerner index (θ/η)
1992	0.581	1.171	0.496
1993	0.660	1.171	0.563
1994	0.644	1.156	0.557
1995	0.524	1.156	0.453
1996	0.456	1.155	0.395
1997	0.438	1.155	0.379
1998	0.418	1.164	0.359
1999	0.445	1.164	0.383
2000	0.473	1.164	0.407
2001	0.475	1.164	0.408
2002	0.484	1.118	0.433
2003	0.552	1.118	0.494
2004	0.605	1.108	0.546
2005	0.699	1.108	0.630
2006	0.692	1.108	0.624
2007	0.677	1.108	0.611

Notes: θ = Time series of industry average degree of competition; η = industry demand elasticity; and θ/η = Lerner index.
The three empirical measures of competitive conditions are based on estimation results of the three-equations system following the conjectural variation approach.

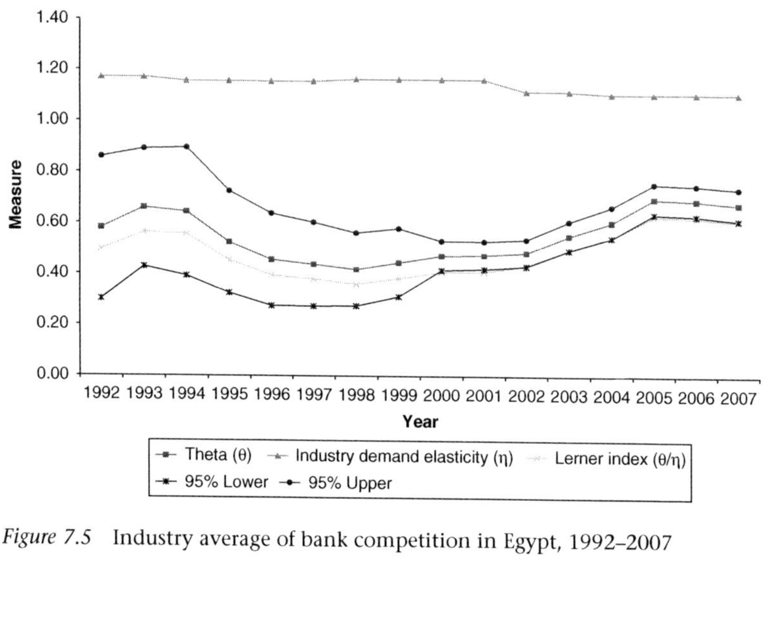

Figure 7.5 Industry average of bank competition in Egypt, 1992–2007

in the first three years, but then it seems to stabilize. Notably, the magnitude of the impact of policies pursued during 1996–2002 on the competitive behaviour in the banking sector seems to be less than in the first stage of financial reforms.

The post-2002 period in our sample period is the third stage of financial reform, involving enhancement of monitoring mechanisms and comprehensive restructuring of the financial sector. In particular, Egyptian banks were required to raise their capital adequacy ratio to meet Basel II standards in 2003. Also, because of this, the number of banks were reduced and the remaining banks may have had to increase their capital requirements in a short time, which could have caused significant disruptions in banks' normal business. Hence, some banks may have temporarily scaled back their business activities to meet the new capital adequacy requirements. After the initial transition period, the banking sector seems to have benefitted from a lower bankruptcy risk due to higher capital reserves and more efficient use of resources. This could explain the decrease in industry competition between 2003 and 2005, and the subsequent improvement in competitive behaviour.

Another approach to investigate the status of industry competition is to examine whether abnormal profit persists. To test this, we conduct an empirical analysis of bank competition with the Persistence of Profitability (POP) model, which directly examines the extent of persistent profitability over time. Results (not reported, available on request) suggest that the persistent overcharge parameter of Egyptian banks is around 0.810 in the sample period. This number is quite high compared with those obtained in other studies. For example, Goddard et al. (2004) report a POP parameter of 0.439 for banks in the six largest European countries. This difference in the POP measure may not be surprising, as the banking sector in developed countries is more competitive than in developing countries such as Egypt. The size of the impact on POP is significant and confirms that large banks in Egypt are able to extract higher abnormal profits than small banks. Our results also show that foreign banks make lower abnormal profits than domestic banks while government banks take higher abnormal profits than private banks.

7.3.3.3 *Productive efficiency of Egyptian banks*

We use the Data Envelopment Analysis (DEA) approach to calculate productive efficiency for Egyptian banks. The results show that the mean value of various efficiency measures is around 0.70. Alternatively speaking, the average x-inefficiency is about 30 per cent. Figure 7.6 presents how average bank efficiency scores obtained from different approaches have behaved over time. The patterns of different efficiency measures

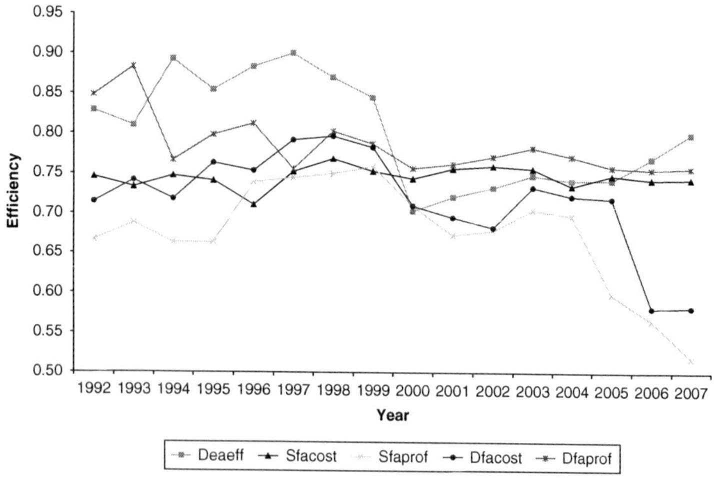

Figure 7.6 Average efficiency score of Egypt's banking sector over time, 1992–2007

are very distinct. The DEAEFF efficiency score shows a V pattern over time. It starts at 0.828 in 1992, then drops to 0.703 in 2000, and gradually goes up to 0.800 in 2007. In contrast, the average scores of cost efficiency (SFACOST and DFACOST) are generally stable at around 0.760 over the whole sample period. Finally, the average scores of profit efficiency (SFAPROF and DFAPROF) are in the region of 0.75 during most of the sample period and abruptly drop to below 0.60 after 2005.

The average inefficiency score falls in the range of results reported in earlier studies. Berger et al. (1993) report that the average x-inefficiency of US banks is about 20–25 per cent. Altunbas et al. (2001) documented similar results for European banks. Kirkpatrick et al. (2008) examine the bank efficiency for 89 commercial banks in Sub-Saharan Africa and find that the average x-inefficiency score varies from 19.29 to 33.65 for different measures.

The conflicting messages from the pattern, as seen in Figure 7.6, may reflect the comprehensiveness of financial reform in the Egyptian banking sector. For example, it is evident that all efficiency measures, except DFACOST, showed an upward trend from 1992 to 1997, indicating that bank efficiency in the Egyptian banking sector improved during first-stage financial reforms. The trends diverged after 1997 as financial reforms became more intensive. As seen in Table 7.1, many commercial banks were privatized or restructured, or underwent mergers and acquisitions under the guidance of the Egyptian government. Although the banking sector may have generally benefitted from reforms in the long term, the banks involved could have faced significant disruption in business activities during the restructuring process as well as high reorganization costs. This may explain why the profit efficiency measures display a noticeable downward trend after 1999. As net profit is used as the dependent variable of multiproduct function to estimate profit efficiency, all possible restructuring charges are included when calculating net profit figures and thus affect our estimates of profit efficiency significantly.

We further examine whether efficiency measures differ across various types of banks, as this has interesting regulatory implications. The results reported in Table 7.5, Panel A, show a comparison of the efficiency measures between government and private banks. In general, private banks are more profit efficient than government banks. The difference in SFAPROF (or DFAPROF) between private and government banks is highly significant. Private banks are more efficient than government banks in terms of DEAEFF, but the difference is not statistically significantly. In contrast, government banks are marginally more cost efficient than private banks and, despite the difference in cost efficiency, is not statistically significant. In Panel B, we compare the efficiency measures between domestic and foreign banks. Although the differences in profit, cost and efficiency measures are not statistically significant, domestic banks are marginally more efficient than foreign banks. This is consistent with our earlier argument that for many foreign banks, Egypt is a new market and hence they may incur higher business development costs which reduces their efficiency relative to the domestic banks.

Test results (not reported here, available on request) related to the determinants of competition status in the banking sector confirm that financial reform policies in Egypt have had a positive impact on competition behaviour in the banking sector. The coefficient of REF96 is –0.202 and significant at the 1 per cent level. The coefficient of REF02 is –0.052 but it is not statistically significant. As theta is inverse to industry competition, the negative coefficients of the two reform indicators confirm that financial reforms have improved competition. There is a steady decline over the whole sample period in the market share of the four largest banks as a result of privatization.

7.3.3.4 Competitiveness, efficiency and economic growth

In the third and final stage of our analysis, we examine the relationship between industry competition, productive efficiency and economic growth with an endogenous growth approach. The results (not reported

Table 7.5 Productive efficiency scores of Egyptian banks by ownership type

Statistic	DEAEFF	SFAPROF	DFAPROF	SFACOST	DFACOST
Panel A: private versus government banks					
Mean for private banks	0.780	0.686	0.723	0.746	0.774
Mean for government banks	0.767	0.525	0.551	0.767	0.784
t-Stat. for group difference	0.580	5.710	5.870	−0.910	−0.420
Prob > *t*	0.559	< 0.001	< 0.001	0.362	0.673
z-Stat. for group difference	−0.621	−5.329	−5.505	0.656	0.170
Prob > *z*	0.267	< 0.001	< 0.001	0.256	0.433
Panel B: domestic versus foreign banks					
Mean for domestic banks	0.781	0.673	0.708	0.752	0.779
Mean for foreign banks	0.771	0.667	0.704	0.732	0.759
t-Stat. for group difference	0.580	0.240	0.190	1.140	1.100
Prob > *t*	0.560	0.814	0.849	0.256	0.271
z-Stat. for group difference	−0.352	−0.582	−0.570	−0.810	−0.844
Prob > *z*	0.363	0.280	0.284	0.209	0.199

Notes: DEAEFF = productive efficiency measure with data envelopment analysis approach; SFAPROF = profit efficiency measure with stochastic frontier approach; DFAPROF = profit efficiency measure with distribution free approach; SFACOST = cost efficiency measure with stochastic frontier approach; and DFACOST = cost efficiency measure with distribution free approach.

Significance of group difference tested with *t*-statistic for parametric approach and with Wilcoxon rank sums z-scores for non-parametric approach.

here, available on request) suggest that there is a significant relationship between productive efficiency and economic growth in the short run. However, test results for long-run causality are insignificant and in some cases bear unexpected signs. We believe that this may be due to the lack of availability of Egyptian data for longer time periods, since cointegration results can be very sensitive to the presence of outliers. However, the absence of a long-term relationship is not entirely surprising as, in a comprehensive study of 50 countries, Claessens and Laeven (2004) show that the competitiveness measure is negatively associated with countries' growth and that the effects of banking system competitiveness on growth vary with the level of countries' financial sector development.

7.4 Regulatory lessons

Our results have several important policy implications. First and foremost, our evidence confirms that financial sector reforms have had a positive and significant impact on the competitiveness and efficiency of the Egyptian banking sector. Second, our findings strengthen the argument for improving competitiveness and production efficiency of the financial sector as there is clear evidence that this leads to improved economic growth, at least in the short run. Finally, the impact of the reform process cannot be immediate, as restructuring and reorganizing large state-owned banks carry implicit costs. The efficiency gains from financial reforms are therefore likely to be realized over a longer period. Nevertheless, findings presented in this chapter suggest that Egyptian policymakers should continue with their reform programme with renewed vigour.

Although Egypt's banking sector has become competitive over time, it remains concentrated and segmented and the public sector banks have retained their dominance relative to more mature markets such as the UK. The privatization programme of banks needs to be pursued with renewed vigour while simultaneously ensuring effective compliance with regulations. Furthermore, Egypt needs to ensure that improvements in the judicial framework keep pace with rapid increases in bank lending. Prudential regulation of the banking sector is crucial given the increased privatization to ensure private market discipline. At the same time, Egypt will need to consider whether it is prudent to use homogeneous control measures in view of the increased heterogeneity in types of banks. Egypt should also continue to improve corporate governance standards and compliance that will help to strengthen the supervision and transparency of the banking sector. Although the problem of nonperforming assets has been largely mitigated through the privatization of public sector banks, there are still concerns with regard to the adequacy of capital and management efficiency, especially in small private banks. Finally, the second phase of Egyptian banking sector reforms that started in July 2009 should continue with the speedy implementation of Basel II to ensure compatibility of the regulations with international standards.

7.5 Conclusions

This chapter examined the impact of financial reforms on the competitiveness and efficiency of the banking sector in Egypt that could offer important regulatory policy lessons for other African economies. The issue of competition in the financial services sector in the African context has many important implications for improvements in efficiency, financial stability and effective regulation and supervision. Egypt is identified as one of the highly reforming countries and hence thorough research using Egyptian banking sector data is likely to offer useful regulatory lessons and implications for stimulating productivity and growth. This is particularly important since policymakers need to be informed of the outcomes and relevance of financial reforms, particularly in the wake of the global financial crisis.

The findings suggest that the degree of competition in Egypt's banking sector is comparable with other African markets. The evidence suggests that competition in the Egyptian banking sector initially improved between 1992 and 1996 but declined during 1996–2002, before increasing once again from 2002. There is a steady decline over the whole sample period in the market share of the four largest banks as a result of privatization. Further, financial reforms seem to have reduced costs in the Egyptian banking sector over time and there is evidence of persistent overcharging by Egyptian banks, which is higher compared to developed countries. The difference is not surprising as the banking sector in developed countries is more competitive than in developing countries such as Egypt. Further analysis suggests that government banks are generally less competitive than private banks, and foreign banks are less competitive than domestic banks. Foreign banks exhibit lower abnormal profits than domestic banks while government banks show higher abnormal profits than private banks. However, the differences in abnormal profits are not statistically significant. In summary, the results using different methodologies for measuring competitiveness suggested evidence that the Egyptian banking sector has become more competitive over time.

We found that the average x-inefficiency of Egyptian banks is around 30 per cent, which is similar to those reported for other African countries. However, we do find somewhat conflicting results for cost and profitability measures, but attribute this to the comprehensiveness of financial reform in the Egyptian banking sector since reforms introduced at different points in time may have had mixed effects due to restructuring and reorganizing costs. We further examined whether efficiency measures differ across different types of banks since this has interesting regulatory policy implications. The results suggested that, generally, private banks are more profit efficient than government banks. In contrast, government banks are marginally more cost efficient than private banks. However, the differences in profit, cost and efficiency measures are not statistically significant.

Overall, our findings confirm that financial reform policies in Egypt have had a significant positive impact on competition and the productive efficiency of the banking sector, which, in turn, seem to have contributed to improved economic growth in the short term.

References

Altunbas, Y., E.P.M. Gardener, P. Molyneux and B. Moore. 2001. 'Efficiency in European Banking'. *European Economic Review*, 45: 1931–55.

Beck, T., A. Demirgüç-Kunt and R. Levine. 2002. 'Bank concentration and crises'. World Bank and University of Minnesota. mimeo.

Berger, A.N., W.C. Hunter and S.G. Timme. 1993. 'Efficiency in financial institutions: A review and preview of research, past, present and the future'. *Journal of Banking and Finance*, 17: 221–49.

Central Bank of Egypt. 2007. *Central Bank of Egypt Annual Report 2007*. Cairo: Central Bank of Egypt.

Cairo Stock Exchange. 2008. *Cairo and Alexandria Stock Exchange Report 2008*. Cairo: Cairo Stock Exchange.

Claessens, S. and L. Laeven. 2004. 'What drives bank competition? Some international evidence'. *Journal of Money, Credit and Banking*, 36: 563–84.

Goddard, J., P. Molyneux and O.S. Wilson. 2004. 'The profitability of European banks: A cross-sectional and dynamic panel analysis'. *The Manchester School*, 72: 363–81.

Kasekende, L., K. Mlambo, V. Murinde and T. Zhao. 2009. 'Restructuring for competitiveness: The financial services sector in Africa's largest economies'. In World Economic Reform (ed.), *Africa Competitiveness Report 2009*, Chapter 3, pp. 49–81.Washington, D.C.: The World Bank.

Kirkpatrick, C., V. Murinde and M. Tefula. 2008. 'The measurement and determinants of x-inefficiency in commercial banks in Sub-Saharan Africa'. *The European Journal of Finance*, 14: 625–39.

8
Banking System and Financial Reforms in Algeria

Taoufik Rajhi and Hatem Salah

8.1 Introduction

The 2008 international financial crisis once again brought to the fore the importance of competitiveness in national financial and banking services to guarantee resource mobilization for the productive sector and the financing of economic growth. Nonetheless, it is true that the competitiveness of financial services depends on national policies targeting efficiency and the promotion of competition in the banking sector, increasing financial stability, introducing efficient financial regulation and improving the quality of supervision and governance of the national financial system.

Viewed from this angle, banking sector competitiveness is crucial for stimulating a country's economic development. Indeed, a competitive financial sector channels available financial savings towards the productive sector and encourages the promotion of the private sector and economic growth. This is why financial reform has been underway in most African countries for several decades, with the aim of, among other things, increasing the competitiveness of their financial systems.

African countries which embarked on financial reform have admittedly not had identical experiences, nor have they achieved the same degree of success. Each country constitutes a model in its own right, depending on its size, the maturity of its economy, depth of financial reforms undertaken and the effectiveness of the policies adopted to liberalize various sectors of activity and to promote specific mechanisms as instruments for resource allocation and economic regulation. At this level of analysis, two issues are worth examining. The first relates to understanding the mechanisms through which financial sector deepening influences economic growth development in African countries. The second deals with lessons drawn from other countries in respect of financial policy, with a view to embarking on a different path of financial and banking restructuring and consolidation; one which could be more satisfactory for Africa, as its design would be supported by a new financial architecture.

Algeria was similar to other countries in setting out on the path of financial reform to strengthen the role of credit allocation market mechanisms, improve the institutional capacity to mobilize savings and effective monetary policy, and encourage competition among financial institutions.

These reforms were initially directed at the banks and later extended with the establishment of the Algeria Stock Exchange in 1997 and the first privatization programme. In the latter case, Algeria also decided to reform the supervision and regulatory authority by granting it greater autonomy.

The country applied these financial reforms sequentially. First, interest rates were liberalized, credit controls abolished and new financial instruments created for the budget. Thereafter, in 1995 and 2001,[1] monetary policy was streamlined, financial sector deepening was stepped up and prudential and supervision regulations were strengthened. The aim of this new regulatory framework was to ensure the withdrawal of the Algerian state from certain competitive economic activities. As a final measure, Algeria liberalized the capital account.

It might be useful to reflect on the nature of the financial reforms undertaken by Algeria and their results and, more particularly, to ascertain whether these reforms resulted in greater efficiency in the commercial banks and increased banking competitiveness in Algeria. It also needs to be determined whether the Algerian economy was able to exploit the positive externalities stemming from an efficient financial services sector and whether it benefited from spillover effects from the rest of the world as a result of its economy's greater financial openness. Finally, based on the Algerian experience, it is important to look at these lessons to see how they could benefit all African countries, which for years have been undertaking quite extensive financial reforms in an attempt to render their economies more competitive.

To this end, we will begin by analysing the evolution of banking depth indicators in Algeria. In particular, we will study the evolution of indicators on banking access, credit to the private productive sector and real interest rates, as well as progress in the profitability of banks through the development of their banking and intermediary financing margins and return on assets or equity.

will discuss and analyse the prospects for the reforms for Algeria to strengthen the soundness of its bank- ›mote competition among banks, develop its financial , consolidate financial supervision and upgrade the financial infrastructure. We will then examine the issue of financial integration in the Maghreb region and the contribution this could make to developing the financial system and increasing its efficiency and resilience in times of crisis.

8.2 Financial development and undersized bank intermediation in Algeria

In most emerging countries, the banking system occupies a key position in financing the economy and forms the cornerstone of the financial system of those economies. As an African country, Algeria is no exception to the rule. To judge its level of financial development, indicators need to be devised for its banking development and effectiveness. Banking development in the literature generally refers to measurement indicators related to deposit collection activity or the banking sector's capacity to grant credit (Honohan and Beck, 2007). Although these two development measurements are closely correlated, they differ in their aims and measurements. The volume of resources collected by the banking system in the form of deposits is particularly interesting in terms of monetary policy and inflation projection. In contrast, the credit activity of banks is fundamental to funding the productive sector and accelerating economic growth (Beck et al., 2000, 2004). Similarly, the willingness of banks to lend to the private sector indicates the maturity of the banking system and its capacity to channel available savings towards productive uses.

8.2.1 Undersized bank intermediation

The usual indicators for this type of problem are based on ratios to GDP of either liquid assets (M3) or quasi-money (M2), or of credit granted by the banking sector to the private sector. Although the drawback of these ratios lies in the fact that they are correlated, they do not have equal economic importance. M2/GDP or M3/GDP ratios provide more information about the accessibility to banking services and financial savings mobilization, while the credit/GDP ratio highlights the role of banks in financing the productive sector.

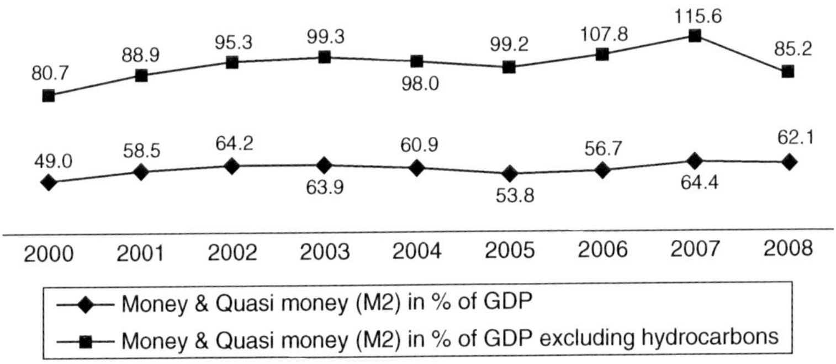

Figure 8.1 Trend of M2/GDP (in per cent), 2000–2008
Source: Bank of Algeria, Annual Report (2008).

8.2.1.1 *Toward better resource collection*

With the exception of 2008, the progression of the M2/GDP ratio indicates constant expansion within the banking sector in Algeria (Figure 8.1). On average, the ratio is 59 per cent for the period 2000–2008. However, this does not properly reflect the development of banking, as part of budgetary savings is paid into an income regulation fund and therefore does not feature in M2. If one takes this into account when calculating the same ratio in relation to GDP, excluding oil and gas, the banking development indicator is at an average of 97 per cent between 2000 and 2008. Compared with other countries, Algeria is at the forefront.

The second indicator of banking development is the ratio between GDP and liquid assets (M3), which, on average, ranges from 54 per cent to 89 per cent in GDP terms, excluding oil and gas (Figure 8.2). This ratio is 32 per cent on average for Africa, 49 per cent for the East Asian and Pacific region and 100 per cent for high-income countries.[2] Here again, compared with other countries, the banking system in Algeria is slightly ahead in terms of available financial resource mobilization. This is a determining factor in encouraging sustainable economic growth.

8.2.1.2 *More favourable credit allocation to private sector*

Compared with the modest position occupied by the stock exchange in Algeria, banks constituted the main source of finance for the country's economic sector in the period 2000–2007. Figure 8.4 clearly shows that credit to the economy averages 42 per cent of GDP, excluding oil and gas (the oil and gas sector finances itself), with an average annual growth rate of 1.2 per cent. This is borne out by the constant expansion

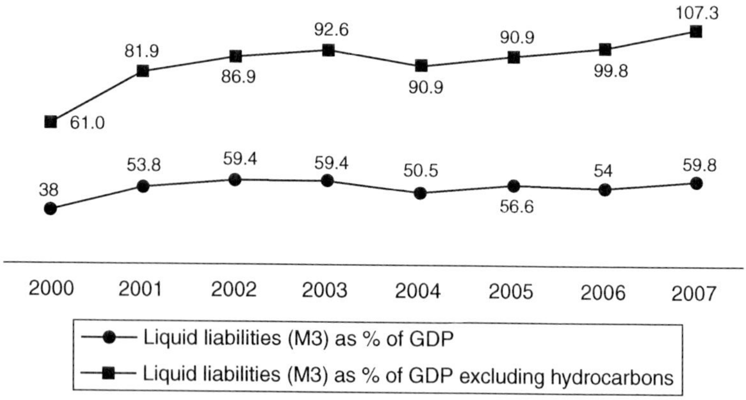

Figure 8.2 Trend of M3/GDP (in per cent), 2000–2007
Sources: World Development Indicators, World Bank (2008); Bank of Algeria (2008).

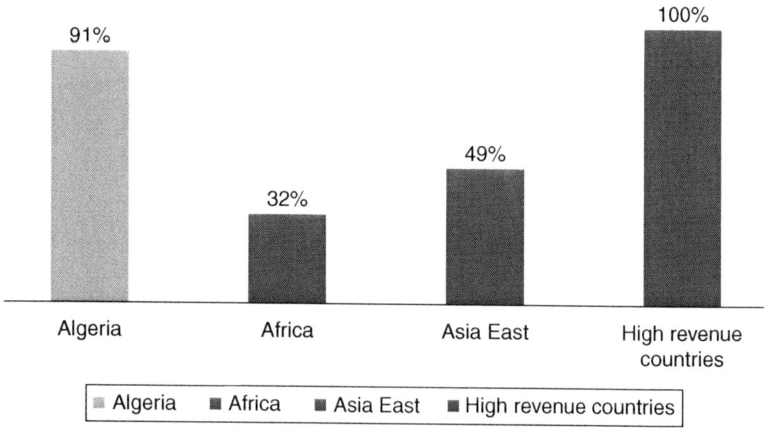

Figure 8.3 Banking development in Africa
Sources: Honohan and Beck (2007); Bank of Algeria, 2000–2007 Annual Reports.

of bank intermediation in Algeria and its importance in financing the economy. Another relevant banking development indicator pertains to outstanding bank loans to the private sector in relation to GDP. As indicated in Figure 8.5, this ratio increased annually by 9 per cent; and in 2008 it stabilized at 23 per cent of GDP, excluding oil and gas.

This ratio is still very low, especially when compared with Algeria's neighbours (almost 40 per cent in Morocco and 60 per cent in Tunisia).

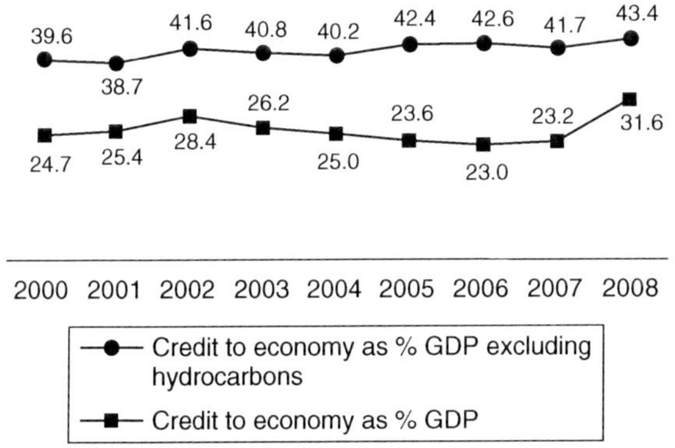

Figure 8.4 Trend of credit to the economy as a percentage of GDP
Source: Bank of Algeria Annual Report 2008.

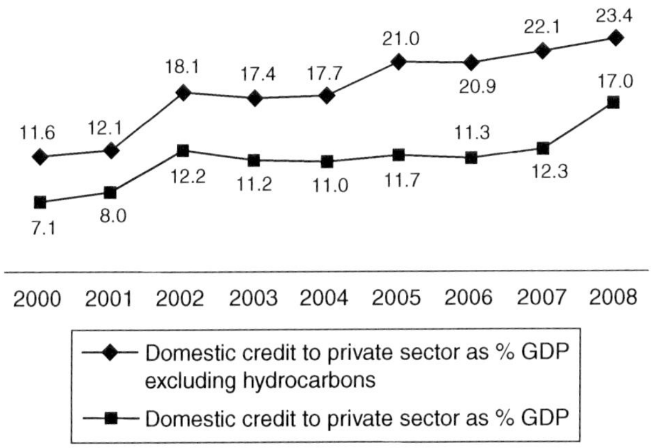

Figure 8.5 Trend of ratio of credit to private sector in Algeria as a percentage of GDP
Source: Bank of Algeria Annual Report 2008.

At this level, Algeria is below average, at about 18 per cent for 2005,[3] and behind South Asian and high-income countries, with levels in 2005 of 30 per cent and 107 per cent, respectively.[4] The ratio of bank credit granted to the private sector in Algeria is at almost the same level as that of low-income countries outside Africa, at 21 per cent in 2005 (Honohan and Beck, 2007). This classification of Algeria seems relatively unchanged, despite a slight increase in the ratio between 2005 and 2008 (Figure 8.6). However, it seems that this ratio has tended to increase

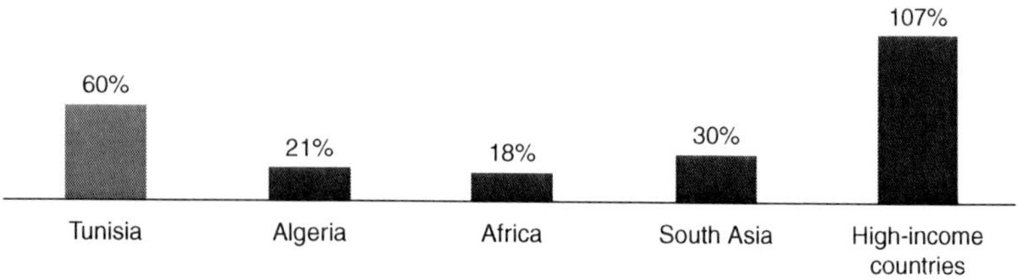

Figure 8.6 Banking credit to private sector as a percentage of GDP: comparative analysis
Sources: Honohan and Beck (2007); Central Bank of Tunisia (2007).

significantly since 2000, indicating that Algeria is catching up with other countries in the region.

Referring to the dispersion indicators for 2000–2008, Algeria does not yet seem to have brought its banking development under control. During that period, Algeria showed a relatively high average dispersion of about 4 per cent, compared with Tunisia's 1.3 per cent[5] dispersion. However, even if banking development in Algeria is perhaps not advancing with the required steadiness and stability, financial instability is contained and does not create a risk to the country's economic growth.

8.2.1.3 Enhancing banking depth and greater access to banking services

In 2008 the Algerian banking system comprised six public banks, 14 private banks with foreign capital, one bank specialized in agricultural finance and six financial institutions.[6] A large number of bank agencies exist in the banking sector in Algeria; the network consisted of 1339 agencies in 2007. This affords satisfactory coverage of the Algerian territory in both rural and urban areas, and encourages the penetration of banking services. However, the rate of banking access in Algeria from the point of view of network development remains low, with one bank agency for 28,300 inhabitants (Figure 8.7). Theoretically, the geographic proximity of a bank is crucial for developing retail banking activity because it affords greater accessibility of banking products to a wider section of the population. Yet access to banking services remains relatively low in Algeria compared with other countries at the same level of development (Figure 8.8).

In Tunisia, the ratio is one banking agency to 11,000 inhabitants, while in Morocco there is one agency for every 15,000 inhabitants. In Morocco's case, the average should be interpreted with caution, given the disparities between the rural and urban areas. Furthermore, the

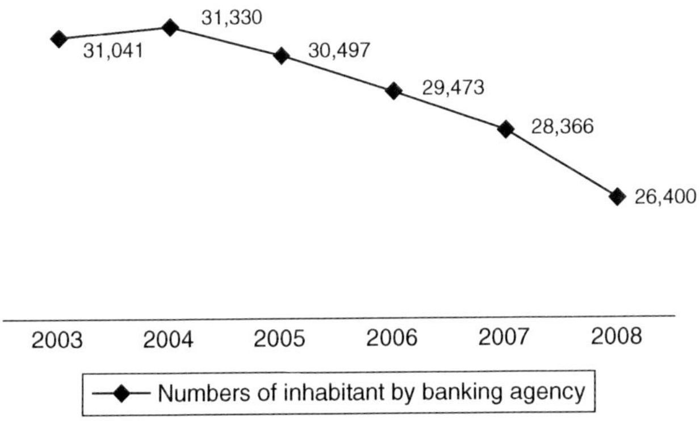

Figure 8.7 Trend in access to banking products in Algeria
Source: Maghreb Union of Banks with calculations by authors.

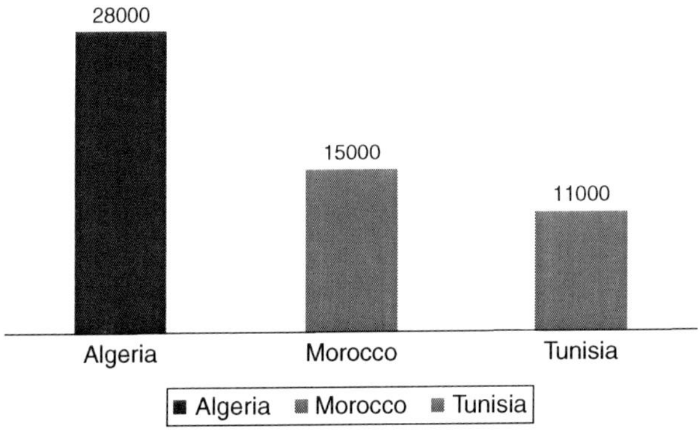

Figure 8.8 Comparative analysis of access to banking services in Maghreb, 2006
Source: Maghreb Union of Banks with calculations by authors.

network of banking agencies in Morocco is strongly concentrated in Casablanca, which has 60 per cent of the country's agencies.

If one considers the banking access rate in terms of the percentage of households with at least one bank account, it would seem that Algeria lacks a complete and sophisticated banking system, as the banking access rate is below 20 per cent, compared with 30 per cent in Morocco in 2009. This places Algeria third among Maghreb countries.

Algeria should, therefore, adopt an even more vigorous footprint and territorial grid strategy because geographic proximity continues to define the bank-client relationship, despite the development of online onic banking indicator: comparative analysis

	lectronic payment terminals	Number of ATMs installed	Number of bank cards in circulation
	4,000	836	700,000
Tunisia, 2007	8,577	1,100	1,900,000

Source: Maghreb Union of Banks.

or remote banking. Indeed, the bank-client relationship is built on geographic proximity, as it adds local character to banking markets. Moreover, localization constitutes a channel of horizontal differentiation for the bank and grants it the power of local monopoly (Chiappori et al., 1995). In the new theory of financial intermediation, the proximity of the client is also understood in terms of informational distance, allowing the bank to reduce informational asymmetry in its relationship with clients, in addition to improving its client monitoring within the framework of its credit activity (Degryse and Ongena, 2008; Sussman and Zeira, 1995).

The development of electronic banking is still lower than expected, despite the efforts of *Algéria Poste* and the technical support of Société d'Automatisation des Transactions Interbancaires et de Monétique (SATIM).[7] Payment cards issued by the banks remain insufficient, with approximately 700,000 cards in circulation for a population of 34 million. In 2006, the number of ATMs stood at 886 units, with the number of Electronic Payment Terminals (EPTs)[8] at 4000 units. By comparison, in 2007 Tunisia had 1.9 million payment cards in circulation for a population of 10 million inhabitants. The country also had 8577 installed EPTs and 1100 ATMs (see Table 8.1).

8.3 Some measurement of banking efficiency in Algeria

The banking system in Algeria has always been dominated by public banks. The Algerian state set up these banks to fund activities it considered strategic, such as housing, agriculture and industry. However, their continued existence was threatened by the credit distribution policies adopted in the 1980s and 1990s, as manifested by problems of asset quality, solvency and liquidity. The banks were obliged to increase their intermediation margins while at the same time increasing the risk premium. Furthermore, an analysis of the profit trend of both public and private Algerian banks confirms that they have a relatively high profitability rate compared to banks in the rest of the world. The reason for this lies in the deteriorating quality of assets and the weak level of competition among banks, the largest of which are government-owned.

8.3.1 Return on equity and assets

8.3.1.1 Return on equity

For the period 2002–2007, Algerian commercial banks posted a relatively high return on equity (ROE) compared with the African average, which is approximately 20.1 per cent.[9] However, the ROE trend is quite uneven between the group of public banks and those with foreign shareholding. The ROE of public banks steadily increased to settle at 23.6 per cent in 2007. By contrast, the ROE of private banks with foreign shareholding is much higher, compared with public banks, at 28 per cent in 2007 (Figure 8.9). Moreover, it is higher than the 26.7 per cent ROE average for foreign banks in Africa (Honohan and Beck, 2007), which was above the 8.6 per cent ratio of banks with foreign shareholding in the rest of the world. In other words, foreign banks in Algeria show a profit level three times higher than their counterparts operating elsewhere in the world (Figure 8.10). Foreign banks seem to be more efficient than other banks and managed to cross economic boundaries due to their cultural and linguistic proximity to the host country, as they are mostly banks originating from France or the Arabian world.

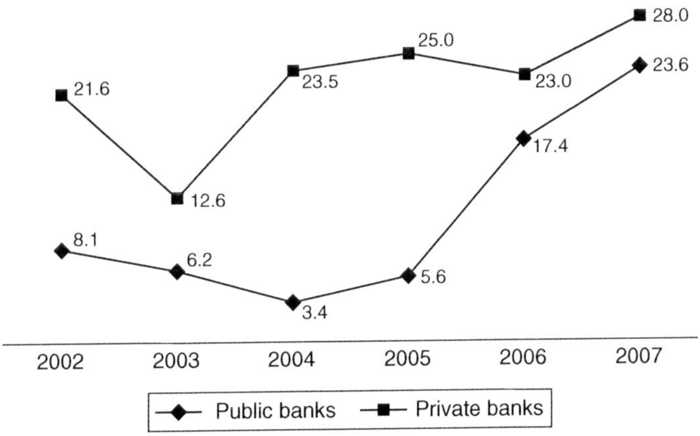

Figure 8.9 Trend in ROE
Source: Bank of Algeria, 2002–2007 Annual Reports.

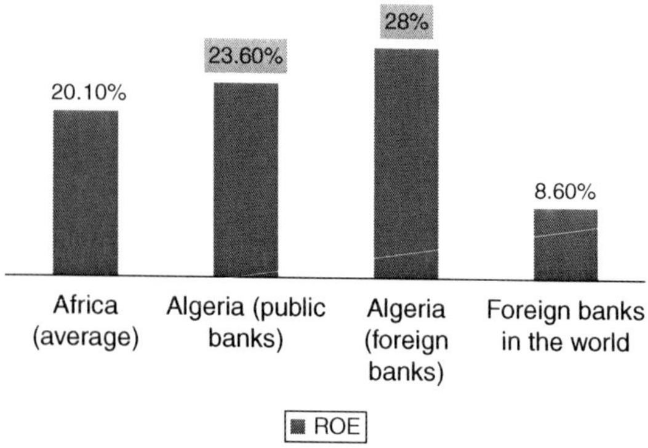

Figure 8.10 Comparative analysis in Africa, 2005
Source: Bank of Algeria, 2002–2007 Annual Reports ; Honohan and Beck (2007).

8.3.1.2 Return on assets

The improvement in the return on assets of public banks stems mainly from the rate of return on productive assets, which is measured by the ROA ratio (net results/total assets). It shows net progress, as illustrated in Figure 8.11, which highlights the strong performance of private banks with foreign shareholding (an average of 2.05 per cent) in terms of return on productive assets. In contrast, public banks were handicapped

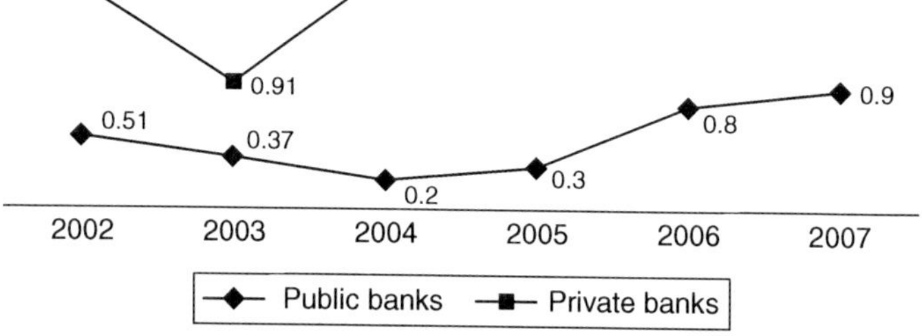

Figure 8.11 ROA trend
Source: Bank of Algeria, 2000–2007 Annual Reports.

by the return on their assets, which barely exceeds 0.9 per cent. In general, return on bank assets in Algeria remains low in comparison with the 2.1 per cent average in Africa. This low return on assets is probably attributable to the behaviour of the group of public banks, which registers a high ratio of non-performing loans and a low intermediation margin because of the low lending rate.

The relative improvement in return on assets may also be explained by the improvement in the gross operating coefficient measured by the ratio of total charges/total pre-tax profit. The constant decrease in Algerian bank charges during the period 2002–2007 explains the improvement in the return on assets (Figure 8.12).

8.3.2 Pricing of banking products and mark-ups

During the period 2002–2007 the margins of private and public banks, which were already unequal, took off in opposite directions. Private banks continued to progress favourably, registering an average 5 per cent growth, while margins for public banks were much lower, averaging about 2.8 per cent.

The gap in margins continues to grow between the two bank categories: from 0.6 points in 2002, it increased to 4.4 points in 2007. The weak margin posted by public banks is mainly attributable to the poor performance at the intermediation level. Private banks have seen their margins increase due to an improvement in their intermediary financing margins (Figures 8.13 and 8.14).

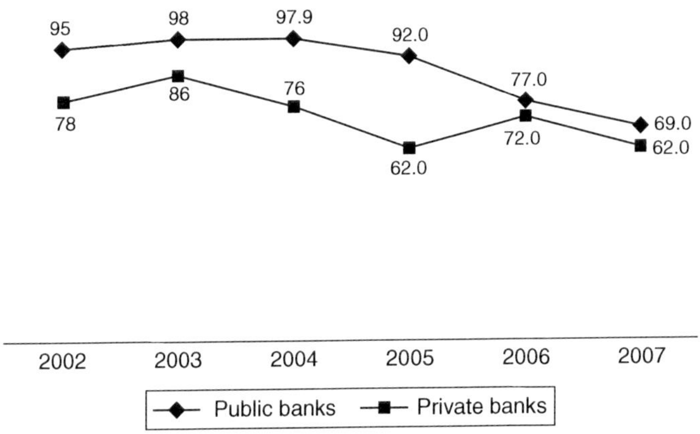

Figure 8.12 Gross operating coefficient trend
Source: Bank of Algeria, 2000–2007 Annual Reports.

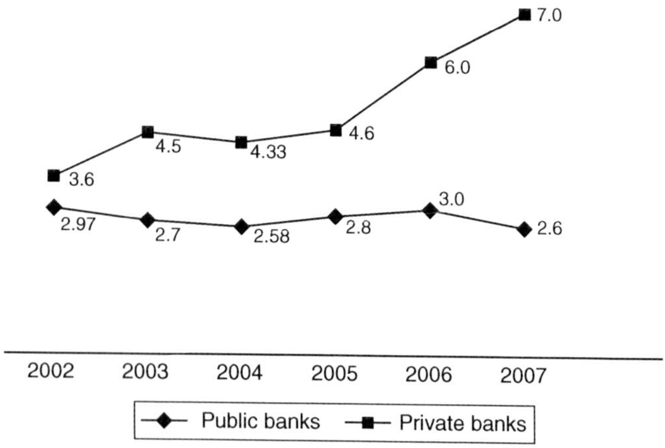

Figure 8.13 Banking margin
Source: Bank of Algeria, 2000–2007 Annual Reports.

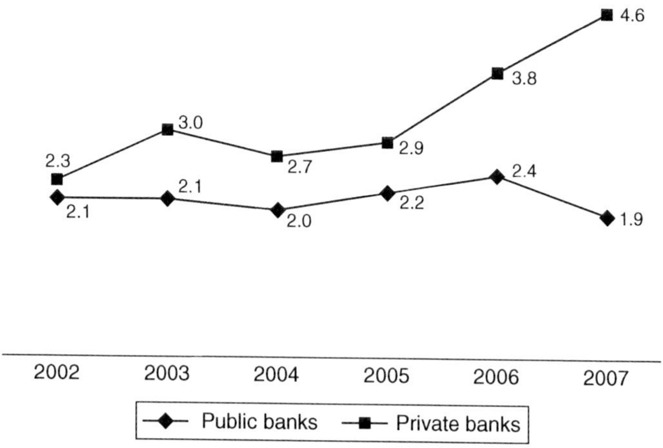

Figure 8.14 Intermediation margin
Source: Bank of Algeria, 2000–2007 Annual Reports.

A breakdown of the intermediation margin reveals that client activity predominates in the overall banking sector, contributing 80.28 per cent and 45.87 per cent of the intermediate margin of private and public banks, respectively, with divergent trends in 2007. The share of client activity in the interest margins of private banks remained high for the last three years (80.28 per cent in 2007), while the share of this activity

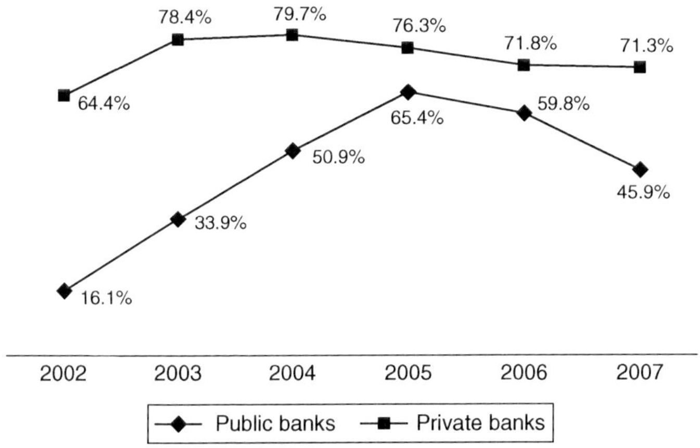

Figure 8.15 Relative weight of client operations in intermediate margin composition
Source: Bank of Algeria, 2002–2007 Annual Reports.

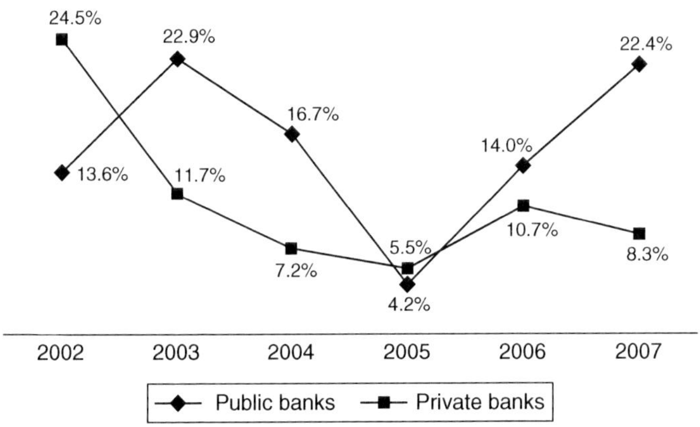

Figure 8.16 Relative weight of operations with financial institutions in intermediation margin composition
Source: Bank of Algeria, 2002–2007 Annual Reports.

in the interest margins of public banks drops considerably, registering 45.87 per cent in 2007 (Figures 8.15 and 8.16).

The level of non-performing loans in public bank assets partially explains this trend, as non-performing debts do not generate interest margins. The margins reported for public and private banks in

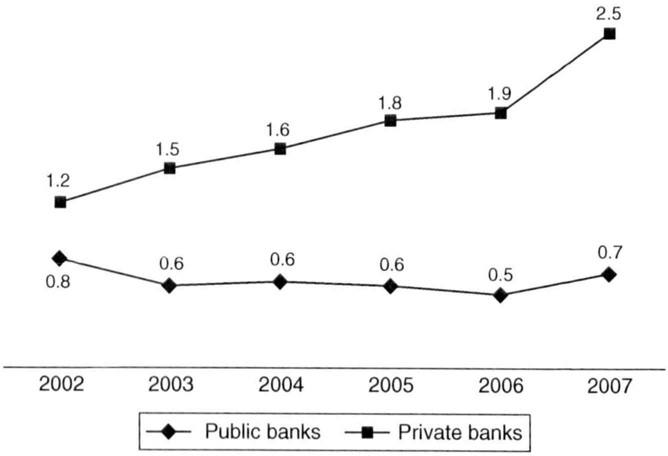

Figure 8.17 Margin excluding intermediation
Source: Bank of Algeria, 2004–2007 Annual Reports.

Figure 8.17 illustrate the above argument and point to some segmentation in the credit market in Algeria.

In contrast, public banks enjoy a relatively large share of operations with banking institutions and share-trading operations, compared to private banks. Public bank margins related to these two activities are high and on the increase (54.11 per cent in 2007), while those of private banks are far lower. Private banks, however, have margins on other interests and similar products (9.20 per cent in 2007), whereas public banks hardly ever attain such margins. Given the context of limited opportunities for client operations, the improvement of bank liquidity in 2006 and 2007 particularly occurred in public banks which partially rechannelled their activities towards operations with financial institutions, especially with the Bank of Algeria (liquidity mopping operations and the facilitation of interest-bearing deposits). Thus, the capacity of commercial bank productive assets to generate net banking earnings is considerably higher in private banks than public ones. The predominance of client operations in private bank intermediation margins – more lucrative than operations with financial institutions – and the higher level of non-performing loans in the assets of public banks explain the unequal banking margin levels of the two bank groups.

The profit margin, which measures the share of banking margin retained by banks after considering management costs (in particular, provision for overheads and credit risk), is similar for both groups of

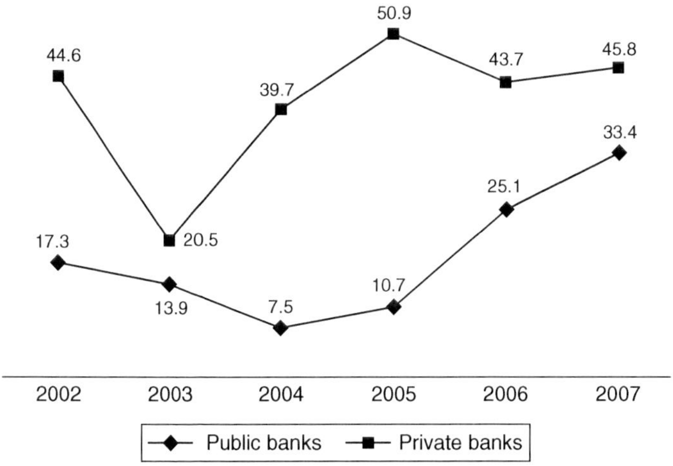

Figure 8.18 Bank profit margin
Source: Bank of Algeria, 2000–2007 Annual Reports.

banks (Figure 8.18). For public banks, it displays a constant upward trend in the period 2002–2007, increasing from 7.5 per cent in 2004 to 33.4 per cent in 2007. For private banks, this margin, which is slightly higher than that for public banks, rose from 40 per cent in 2004 to 46 per cent in 2007.

The profit margin gap between public and private banks points to better credit risk management by the private banks. At the same time, the increase in the profit margin of public banks in 2007 (8.28 points) indicates a gradual improvement in the appraisal, management and monitoring of credit risks owing to, among others things, the assistance and intensification of portfolio checks by the Bank of Algeria and the Banking Commission.

The increase in the profit margin of public banks is the result of cross-effects: a reduction of credit risk provisioning and a reasonable increase in overheads.

Overall, the improvement of public bank profitability during the period 2005–2007 can be attributed to the substantial increase in their financial leverage, indicating growth in the volume of activity in relation to equity capital, which remained virtually stable. However, this improvement was slightly reduced because of the decrease in the banking margin rate, reflecting a reduction in return on assets in a situation of excess liquidity. The second reason for this improvement is the reduction of the share of provisioning for banking risks in the GNP following the decrease in annual reserves.

8.3.3 Real interest rate and risk premium

Algeria has not yet succeeded in achieving positive real interest rates, in contrast to other countries in the region such as Egypt, Morocco and Tunisia. From this point of view, it would appear that the financial reforms undertaken by Algeria to date have not yet yielded positive real deposit rates,[10] given that they settled at a negative level of about -3 per cent in 2008 (Figure 8.19). Financial repression persists in the country and financial saving remains discouraging. Yet, Figure 8.19 shows that not only have the lending rates in Algeria turned positive between 2000 and 2007, but that they are in continuous decline (3.3 per cent in 2008 as against 9.6 per cent in 2000). Freely determined interest rates and the widespread use of indirect monetary policy instruments have ensured positive lending rates, thus helping to bring about optimum credit allocation.

It should, however, be noted that these positive lending rates favour the lenders, in particular the banks, and are detrimental to savers (depositors), as these rates result in an increase in real terms in the income of the lenders (the banks) and a rise in the cost of credit for the borrowers.

Moreover, commercial banks in Algeria are not in a position to calculate the return on their long-term risks. There are several reasons for this difficulty in determining the cost of long-term funding. Firstly, the banks' inadequate accounting and information systems do not allow them to calculate the precise cost of resources or to assess the cost of risk based on cost accounting. Secondly, banks come up against the opacity

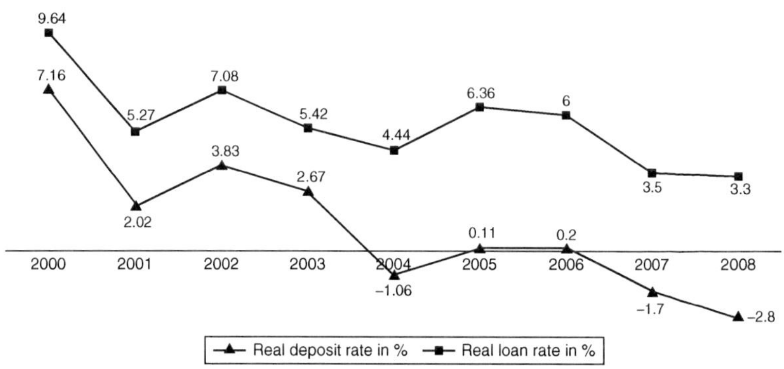

Figure 8.19 Fluctuations in real borrowing and lending rates
Source: IMF (2009).

of their clients' accounts, as a result of which they are unable to determine the profitability of a given project and its associated risk premium. Finally, the banks' difficulties are linked to the interest rate situation in Algeria. On the one hand, banks have no short-term reference rates (in the absence of central bank rediscounting operations) or long-term rates, given the instability of risk-free rates (sudden changes in Treasury bond rates). On the other hand, the interest rate curve causes a problem because it is inverted: short-term rates are higher than long-term ones. By way of illustration, for small consumer credits of 12 months or less, the percentage rates (including the nominal rate, charges and commissions) are from 25 per cent to 30 per cent, whereas long-term rates of over 15 years are 5 per cent (Figure 8.20).

8.3.4 Risks incurred by banks and non-performing loans

Similar to other countries in the region, the level of non-performing loans in Algeria's commercial banks remains high: 30 per cent in 2006 for public banks (the category dominating the banking sector). In actual fact, this rate previously was far higher (50 per cent in 2000), but due to the state initiative to streamline public banks, it was brought down to a more reasonable level (Figure 8.21). However, it is worth noting that the international norm for non-performing loans is 6 per cent, therefore, the effort to clean up the public bank portfolio continues. It is high time that public banks should no longer be requested to finance public corporations on the brink of bankruptcy solely for the purpose of preserving jobs. The very existence of the banking sector in Algeria is at stake and its survival has already cost society dearly (30 per cent of GDP).[11] The clean-up effort to date has been considerable, but has not yet been completed. It is vital for Algeria's economy that the same degree of determination be applied to mopping up debt from the banks' balance sheets and stepping up provisioning for those debts. Such action

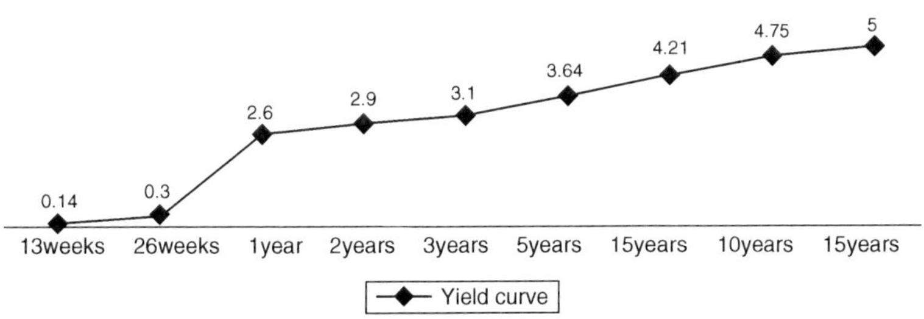

Figure 8.20 Bond market rates
Source: Bank of Algeria, Annual Report (2008).

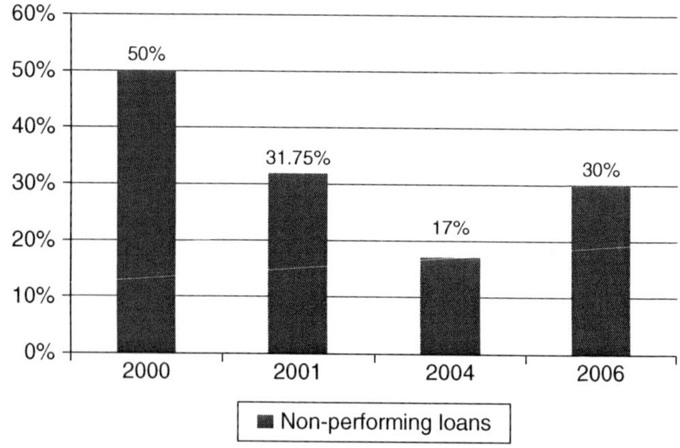

Figure 8.21 Trend of non-performing loans in Algerian banks
Source: World Bank, IMF (2006); Global Financial Stability Report: Market Development.

is crucial to restore competitiveness and increase the profitability of the public banking sector.

In the short term, this requires factoring companies to be set up with state assistance. In the medium and long term, the overall operating model of banks needs to be reviewed, especially regarding stricter rules for granting credit.

8.3.5 Competition and market discipline

A study of the banking sector in Algeria regarding the intensity of internal rivalry and threats of product substitution or new entrants shows that this sector is barely competitive. However, competition among banks constitutes one of the main mechanisms of economic governance that 'disciplines' the attitude of banks and their executives and encourages them to adopt control measures aimed at minimizing the cost of obtaining external capital (Levine, 2004).

Two indicators are commonly used to assess the intensity of competition in the banking sector, namely the asset concentration rate and the Herfindahl–Hirschman index. Regarding the former, estimates are often based on the percentage of assets (or asset components) held by the top three banks (Top 3) or the top five banks (Top 5). Based on these indicators, and referring to Figure 8.22 which traces the trend of the concentration ratio, a clear tendency emerges towards concentration in the Algerian banking sector. Indeed, in 2001 the top three banks in Algeria held just 69 per cent of the total balance sheet whereas by 2007 the

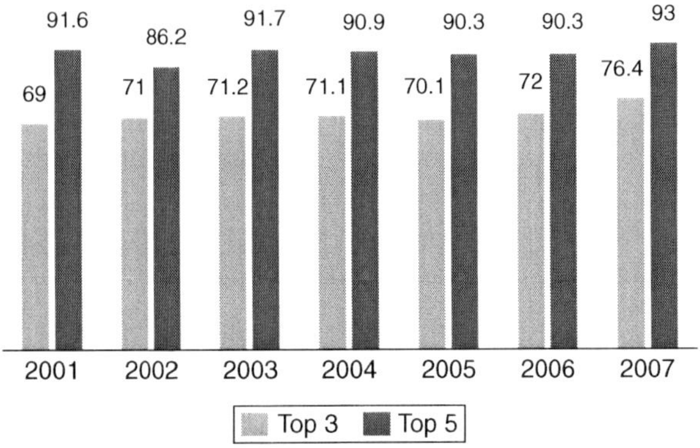

Figure 8.22 Concentration rate of Top 3 and Top 5 banks in Algeria
Source: Calculations by the authors.

proportion had increased to 76.4 per cent. One finds an almost identical configuration in the Top 5 ratio: in 2007 these banks alone held 93 per cent of the total banking sector balance sheet, compared with 91.6 per cent in 2001.

The only observable difference here is that the concentration rate measured in terms of the top five banks seems to be more irregular. However, both measurement methods produce the same result, namely a tendency towards concentration. Moreover, the same observation is confirmed by the other concentration indicator, namely the Herfindahl–Hirschman index. In fact, this index increased from 0.19 in 2000 to 0.26 in 2007, showing a 37 per cent rise (Figure 8.23).

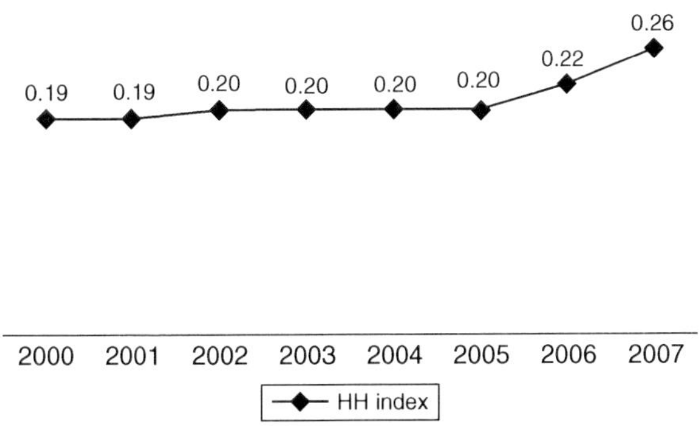

Figure 8.23 Herfindahl–Hirschman concentration index trend
Source: Calculations by the authors.

Table 8.2 Bank concentration rates in some African countries

	Algeria	Egypt	Morocco	Tunisia
Percentage of deposits held by the top 5 banks	94%	63.1%	75%	64.5%
Percentage of assets held by the top 5 banks	95%	61.8%	66.5%	64.8%

Source: Barth et al. (2003).

Moving to a comparative analysis of countries of the North African region, Table 8.2 shows that Algeria has the highest concentrated banking sector, with 95 per cent of assets being held by the top five banks as against 75 per cent in Morocco, 65 per cent in Tunisia and 63 per cent in Egypt.[12] In this regard, the Algerian experience seems paradoxical in terms of financial reform, given that the financial liberalization process appears to coincide with a renewal of concentration.

To conclude this analysis of the structure of the Algerian banking sector, three notable tendencies are observed:

1. Concentration in the banking sector has increased, despite the process of financial liberalization initiated by Algeria.
2. Competition intensity has increased in terms of the number of banks in the banking sector, following the entry of a growing number of private banks with foreign shareholding. However, the banking margin rates remain high, especially in private banks.
3. The absence of an alternative to bank financing has given the banks in Algeria undeniable market power.

8.4 Summary of main results

In terms of banking development and compared with other countries in Africa, the banking system in Algeria shows definite progress in mobilizing available financial resources, such as M2/GDP (97 per cent average for 2000–2008) or M3/GDP (89 per cent average for 2000–2008). It should be noted that this ratio averages 32 per cent in Africa, 49 per cent in the East Asia/Pacific region and 100 per cent in high-income countries.[13] This development is a determining factor that encourages sustained economic growth.

By contrast, financial intermediation, as measured by the ratio of credit granted to the private sector, remains weak in Algeria despite reforms in support of the sector. Compared with other African countries, Algeria is below the average of about 18 per cent in 2005 and behind South Asian countries or those with high incomes, whose 2005 rates stood at 30 per cent and 107 per cent, respectively. The ratio of bank credit granted to the private sector in Algeria is at almost the same level as that in non-African low-income countries, which was 21 per cent in 2005. It appears that this classification of Algeria has not changed much, as the ratio has increased only slightly between 2005 and 2008.

The accessibility of banking services is relatively low in Algeria compared to countries that are at the same level of development. Indeed, financial inclusion from the point of accessibility to banking products still remains low because of the insufficient development of the agency network (Algeria had one bank agency per 28,300 inhabitants in 2007). Geographic proximity is crucial for the development of retail banking as it affords greater access to banking products for a large section of the population.

In terms of ROE, Algerian banks have been shown to perform better, on average, than comparable countries in Africa. Private banks with foreign shareholding in particular have the highest ROE rate, at 28 per cent. This figure is quite high, three times higher than the average for banks with foreign shareholding operating elsewhere in the world. With regard to ROA, banks in Algeria are at a disadvantage given the burden of non-performing loans, which translates into fairly low rates of ROA, mainly in the public sector, compared to the African average. To understand this disparity between the private and public sector, it is necessary to refer to the constitutive structure of the intermediation margin. A breakdown of this margin reveals the strong predominance (80 per cent) of highly lucrative client activity in the private bank sector.

Compared with other developing countries, the Algerian experience of financial liberalization presents several special features. The benefits of the announced liberalization, both internal and external, are gradually making themselves felt in terms of growing competition and improvement in the performance of Algerian public sector banks. Indeed, the competitiveness of banking markets in Algeria is increasing, with banks displaying greater competitiveness and efficiency. The market power of public banks in the past is gradually weakening. However, the state's prominent role in the sector as well as the slow rate of reform, particularly in the privatization programme and non-performing loans, are responsible for the disappointing results. Finally, financial openness in the form of an increased presence of foreign banks has so far not

) improved banking performance in Algeria, despite the foreign presence has real capacity to influence the rest given the marginal position occupied by this sector at

8.5 Prospects for reform and recommendations

Algeria has already seen the benefit of reforms. However, several challenges remain to enhance the financial system to be more efficient and to operate in a more competitive environment. We will propose a few pointers to reform, which could allow the Algerian financial system to play its full role in financing the productive sector.

8.5.1 Undertake further reforms to modernize Algeria's financial sector

8.5.1.1 Increase soundness of banking system

The soundness of the banking system in Algeria can only be increased if the ratio of outstanding debt can be reduced. The Algerian state has already begun buying up outstanding bank loans granted to public corporations. This clean-up should continue by increasing provisioning, consolidating the banks' capital and reviewing procedures for partially cancelling dead credit. It is up to the banks to declare losses on loans in time and constitute the required provisions. For their part, the supervision authorities should examine, together with the failed banks, the necessary measures necessary to restore their solvency and profitability:

(a) *Clean up the outstanding debt on banks' balance sheets and ensure a better balance between classified claim and provisioning.*
(b) *Reduce the moral hazard borne by public banks,* which are often tempted to grant financing without paying much attention to their clients' solvency, as they are ensured of state intervention should the necessity arise.
(c) *Scrupulously respect internationally accepted prudential rules.* The supervision authorities would first need to have real *de jure* and *de facto* independence and be assured of the strong support of the political powers. The staff of the supervision entity must have the required skills in respect of the financial practices of financial institutions. Lastly, it is important to improve banks' ability to accelerate the establishment of a new prudential framework.

8.5.1.2 Strengthen competition among banks

Intensifying competition among banks is meant to improve their effectiveness, enhance financial stability, increase the range of supplied products and allow households and firms access to financial services. However, the shareholding structure of banks, which in Algeria is mainly public, impedes competition and financial deepening. Hence, it is important to identify those reforms necessary to eliminate obstacles that limit competition, as is done below. A strategy of strengthening competition and efficiency must also explore other areas, in particular the regulatory and supervision framework, as well as developing other non-banking sources of funding:

(a) *Privatize certain public banks in favour of foreign investors with a good reputation in the international marketplace* to encourage the transfer of know-how in the banking profession, financial engineering and modern management and product design technologies. There is no doubt that the 2009 financial crisis slowed the process of privatization of public banks in Algeria because of a fear by the authorities of ceding these banks to untrustworthy buyers. The government drew up a strategy whereby the state's stake in the capital of public banks would be reduced once these banks had been cleaned up and their portfolios cleared. It is now imperative to review the list of banks which could be privatized, to decide on when they should be privatized and to whom they should be sold.

(b) *Restructure and strengthen the governance of the remaining public banks* so that they remain competitive in the face of the serious threat posed by foreign banks. The state will need to transform itself into an active, modern shareholder. First of all, it would need to improve the portfolio diversification of public banks, which sometimes depends heavily on a single clientor on a single sector. The state should upgrade management methods, for example by implementing management-by-objectives where the public bank manager is obliged to reach targets set in accordance with the bank's strategy.

(c) *Promote a much wider private banking sector* by harmonizing competition conditions among the public and private actors, that is, create a level playing field. In a similar vein, gradually remove the remaining restrictions hindering the establishment of foreign banks and encourage Algerian banks to become established abroad in order to support the development of banking activities in the Maghreb region.

(d) *Build a strategy for the creation of 'national champions'* with the aim of setting up national banking groups capable of being leaders in international competition in terms of competitiveness, size, capitalization and profit.

8.5.1.3 Deepen financial markets

It is necessary to improve the scope and liquidity of capital markets: Algerian capital markets concentrate on issuing government securities although the share market is practically non-existent. Modernizing these markets will facilitate financial intermediation and risk management and, in the medium term, support cross-border capital flows. The relevant programme should include measures to strengthen the regulation and oversight of the stock markets, drawing up a comprehensive curve of interest rates, extending the investor base and increasing market transparency, all of which would encourage investors to acquire a stake:

(a) *Strengthen the regulation and supervision of stock markets*: reforms should be undertaken to strengthen the legal, regulatory and institutional framework governing share markets. The main thrust should be the adoption of international norms and best practices, as drawn up by the International Organisation of Securities Commissions, which also sets out the aims and principles of financial regulation.
(b) *Deepen the financial market and draw up a comprehensive interest rate curve*: it is obvious that managing public debt is decisive in deepening financial markets because of the role it plays in building up an interest rate curve. Such a curve is required in the banking industry for two reasons: firstly, it serves as a basis to calculate banking margins, and secondly, it allows clients to be offered exit rates, depending on maturity. Similarly, it is useful for evaluating financial assets. From this point of view, it is up to the government to issue securities with varying maturity dates on a regular basis and at the market rate. In Algeria, the government's issuing strategy consists of issuing a small number of lines with large deposits, which allows a rate curve to be compiled. However, each point featured on this curve is not yet sufficiently comprehensive or accurate.
(c) *Revitalize the capital market to render it attractive to both issuers and subscribers*. To do so, various investors should be encouraged to enter the market, especially institutional investors (in particular pension funds and insurance companies). Their presence in the financial market would increase its liquidity and depth. Possible

recommendations to achieve this would be to exempt long-term savings products from taxation, for example savings account shares (which have proved very successful in Tunisia), harmonizing competition conditions among banks that mobilize long-term savings, and encouraging foreign institutional investors to invest in the Algerian market.

(d) *Revitalize the money market by establishing an appropriate interbank market*, regulated by the central bank and that is less dependent on liquidity fluctuations linked to income from the hydrocarbons sector. One worthwhile reform would be to make it more binding for banks to provide liquidity to the central bank, thereby encouraging them to approach the interbank market. The other reform would be to set up a range of negotiable debt securities to integrate the short-, medium- and long-term markets.

(e) *Further liberalization of the foreign exchange markets* in step with the pace of liberalization of the capital account and increasing the risk management capacity of banks.

8.5.1.4 Consolidate financial supervision

The Algerian authorities have made commendable progress in strengthening supervision and financial regulation. However, a new series of reforms needs to be undertaken in order to improve the effectiveness of prudential control in Algeria, in line with the basic principles of Basel I and II. A plan of action should be designed to deal with the shortcomings of prudential regulation, such as the operational and financial autonomy of the regulatory agencies and the efficiency with which the supervision is exercised. Indeed, the lack of independence of the Bank of Algeria, the interventionism of the Ministry of Finance, the weight of public banks in the banking sector, where the state has the majority stake, and the role played by public corporations in the Algerian business world, means that there is often a contradictory situation, with the state being both judge and party to the developments in the sector. The problem of technical capacity is further compounded by legitimate political control. Some recommendations include the following:

(a) *Increase the independence of the supervision agencies and clearly define the legal conditions for removing their chairs and members of the board of directors.*

(b) *Clearly distinguish between the role of the Ministry of Finance and that of the regulatory authority*. Clearly demarcating the powers and prerogatives of each supervision agency and their relations with the Ministry of Finance is likely to guarantee the independence of these authorities and their ability to assume their responsibilities without interference. In Algeria, the Ministry of Finance has extensive powers in granting licences to financial institutions, setting the regulatory framework by which they are governed and imposing penalties. The question which arises is how to prevent the extensive powers of the ministry from undermining the authority and prerogatives of the supervision agencies. Might it not be judicious to transfer the right of granting licences to the supervision agencies?

(c) *Provide oversight bodies with appropriate financial resources,* thereby enabling them to recruit, retain and train qualified staff.
(d) *Draw up prudential regulations in line with international standards* by adopting a supervision approach which concentrates more on risk and the improvement of coordination among the various supervision agencies.
(e) *Develop financial supervision skills in non-traditional banking activities* (e.g. micro-credit and Islamic financing) in order to reduce the possible accumulation of risk in these activities and thus protecting the rest of the banking sector against the spread of such risks.

8.5.1.5 Upgrade financial infrastructure

The development and stability of financial systems require a modern financial infrastructure that is favourable to the various finance professions. The Algerian authorities would need to extend the reforms already underway to the judicial and legal fields, accounting standards and audits as well as the securities regulatory and delivery systems. Lastly, it is imperative to establish private credit bureaux that contribute to greater market transparency and better credit risk management, which are conducive to financial intermediation. Specific steps could include the following:

(a) *Strengthen the law on bankruptcy* and establish independent commercial courts which are able to enforce commercial law.
(b) *Revise the principle of foreclosure and reform the rules and procedures on collaterals.* These measures are likely to encourage banks to commit more actively to the long-term financing of the productive sector.
(c) *Specify the legal definition of property rights,* especially in matters involving land, and render the rules on mergers and transfers more

flexible. This should allow bank guarantees to be instit
encourage foreign investors to establish themselves in the c

(d) *Strengthen corporate and banking governance.*
(e) *Adopt international standards on audits and the publication of financial statements.* This should afford certain financial companies and institutions access to external financing.
(f) *Establish public credit registers and facilitate the creation of private credit bureaux.* The aim of such facilities would be to improve the collection, accessibility, scope, disclosure and quality of credit information. The information will be both positive (amount of credit and modalities of repayment at due date) and negative (late payments, number and amount of repayment). Establishing a credit bureau would allow for improved financial information in respect of the banks' clientele, not only big corporations but also SMEs, microenterprises, private clients and clients benefiting from microcredit, by setting up (i) a more complete and accurate database on the debt levels and solvency of banking clients and microcredit associations; and (ii) a system for consolidating, processing and analysing all identity and financial data concerning the indebtedness of the clients of credit institutions. Once the credit bureau is operational, one could expect (i) an improved rate of access to bank financing and a reduction in credit cost due to a decrease in the risk premium; (ii) greater access by agents to quality information which is reliable, comprehensive, complete and standardized throughout the entire banking system; (iii) opening up to a clientele previously excluded from banking, due to improved risk assessment; and (iv) a reduction in outstanding debts and better protection of lenders' rights.
(g) *Speed up the modernization of payment systems.*

8.5.2 Regional financial integration to deepen financial markets and improve their efficiency and resilience in a crisis

The benefits of financial integration are well developed in economic literature. They are assessed in terms of consumption smoothing, the counter-cyclicality of capital flows, the positive effect of foreign direct investment (FDI) on growth and productivity factors, and the technological externalities acquired with the establishment of foreign banks. The financial integration of the Maghreb region should give rise to better allocation of available resources to the benefit of investment and trade, further deepening of domestic financial markets and improving risk-sharing. Overall, the region's economy should grow more quickly and with increased resilience. Similarly, a Maghreb characterized by the seamless movement of goods, services and capital would be a most attractive market for national and foreign investors. Specifically, a well-integrated Maghreb region could benefit more from potential association agreements with the European Union. It could also become an attractive destination for investors from other regions, including Middle-Eastern oil-exporting countries. Lastly, regional financial integration could play a catalytic role for wider financial integration with the rest of the world by giving new impetus to the financial sector reforms required to prepare the region's financial systems for greater competition, while at the same time minimizing the risk of financial instability.

8.5.2.1 *Possible short-term measures*

(a) *Remove financial obstacles to intra-Maghreb trade*, in particular by allowing the banks of the Maghreb region to establish branches or subsidiaries in the region.
(b) *Accelerate the establishment of the Maghreb Bank for Investment and Foreign Trade.*
(c) *Ensure close coordination among central banks.*
(d) *Continue implementing payment systems* with a view to their harmonization.

8.5.2.2 *Possible medium-term measures*

(a) *Strengthen macroeconomic stability within each country* by adapting the appropriate macroeconomic frameworks so as to contain the volatility of capital flows.
(b) *Minimize the risk of financial instability*, in particular by strengthening banks' own equity.
(c) *Harmonize market infrastructure* at the regulatory and supervision level, harmonize payment and financial information systems and, finally, financial contracts.
(d) *Gradually liberalize the capital account.* Such a strategy would encourage capital movement (including the establishment of foreign banks) within the countries of the Maghreb region and increase financial integration. It is likely that such financial opening would expose national financial systems to the volatility of world financial markets, but instituting the attendant and mitigated measures should limit the risk of financial instability.

(e) *Encourage the regional integration of stock markets* by means of information and technology sharing and intra-Maghreb cross-investment.
(f) *Raise the level of regional coordination and cooperation* among the Treasury administrators of each country and the central banks so as to regulate the region's market liquidity more effectively by guaranteeing long-term government financing.

8.5.2.3 Possible long-term measures

(a) *Create benchmark banking performance indicators for Algeria* rather than an average indicator for the region.
(b) *Create and design long-term performance assessment and monitoring indicators* for banks in Algeria.

8.6 Concluding remarks

The aim of the research in this chapter is to measure the competitiveness of Algeria's financial services. First, it deals with a comparative analysis of the main indicators of banking development, thereby contextualizing the Algerian experience and comparing it with other African countries. Finally, we analyse the prospects for reforms that Algeria needs to undertake in order to increase the soundness of its banking system, promote competition among banks, extend financial markets, consolidate financial oversight, scale up the financial infrastructure and achieve financial integration in the Maghreb region.

Notes

1. In 1995, Algeria sought to promote competition among various economic actors, following the publication of Decree No. 95–22 of 26 August 1995, which set out the first instructions on privatizing public corporations, and Decree No. 01–04 of 20 August 2001, which set out the organization, management and privatization of public economic institutions.
2. See, for example, Figure 8.3. Figures taken from the study by Honohan and Beck (2007) of 127 countries for the period 2004–2005.
3. Figures taken from Honohan and Beck (2007).
4. Figures taken from Honohan and Beck (2007).
5. Figures taken from Ben Larbi and Ohanessian (2006) for the period 2000–2004. The 4 per cent dispersion for Algeria is calculated for the period 2000–2008. Dispersion in relation to average bank credit ratio in per cent GDP, excluding oil and gas, would be only 3.5 per cent for the period 2000–2004. Credit to the private sector ratio as per cent of GDP gives a dispersion of 2 per cent for the period 2000–2004.

6. According to the regulations in Algeria, credit institutions do not collect deposits from the public.
7. Official records indicate that SATIM has been driving electronic banking in Algeria (see, for example, Bank of Algeria, 2008).
8. The other important development is the use of EPTs.
9. Average rate calculated for 2000–2004, Honohan and Beck (2007).
10. Interest rates have been progressively liberalized; first in 1995 with Instruction 07–95 setting out the conditions applicable to banking operations, where the attrition rate was cancelled but with the Bank of Algeria being allowed to set a maximum banking margin, and later in 2001 when this upper limit was abolished, thereby allowing credit institutions to define their conditions according to their own commercial policies.
11. According to the Bank of Algeria report (2009), the Algerian Government bought back non-performing loans held by public corporations and other debts to the state amounting to 484 billion Dinars between 1990 and 1998. The process was intensified between 2000 and 2007, with the government buying back debts owed by companies which had been wound up or dismantled and debts owed by agriculture and savings banks for a total of 756.6 billion Dinars. In total, this initiative to streamline public banks could cost the Algerian State 1,240.6 billion Dinars in the period 1990–2007.
12. By way of illustration, this index is 0.30 for the USA, 0.41 for Lebanon and 0.61 for France.
13. Figures taken from the study by Honohan and Beck (2007) on 127 countries for the period 2004–2005.

References

Bank of Algeria. 2008. *Bank of Algeria Annual Reports 2008*. Algiers: Bank of Algeria.

Barth, J.R., G. Caprio Jr. and R. Levine. 2003. 'Bank supervision and regulation: What works best?' *Journal of Financial Intermediation*, 12: 205–48.

Beck, T., A. Demirgüç-Kunt and R. Levine. 2004. 'Finance, inequality, and poverty.' Policy Research Working Paper No. 3338. Washington, D.C.: World Bank.

Beck, T., R. Levine and N. Loayza. 2000. 'Finance and the sources of growth'. *Journal of Financial Economics*, 58 (1–2): 261–300.

Ben Larbi, S. and R. Ohanessian. 2006. 'Liberalisation of financial systems and economic growth in the countries of the Maghreb: An exploratory study'. *Financial Development Techniques*, 85 (December): 43–60.

Central Bank of Tunisia. 2007. *Central Bank of Tunisia Annual Report, 2007*. Tunis: Central Bank of Tunisia.

Chiappori, P.A., D. Perez-Castrillo and T. Verdier. 1995. 'Spatial competition in the banking system, localization, cross-subsidies and the regulation of deposit rates'. *European Economic Review*, 39: 889–918.

Degryse, H. and S. Ongena. 2008. 'Competition and regulation in the banking sector: A review of the empirical evidence on the sources of bank rents'. *Handbook of Financial Intermediation and Banking*, Amsterdam: Elsevier, pp. 483–554.

Honohan, P. and T. Beck. 2007. 'Making finance work for Africa'. Washington D.C.: World Bank.

IMF. 2009. *International Financial Statistics Yearbook*, 2009. Washington, D.C.: International Monetary Fund.

Levine, R. 2004. 'The corporate governance of banks: A concise discussion of concepts and evidence'. World Bank Policy Research Working Paper No. 3404.

Sussman, O. and J. Zeira. 1995. *Banking and Development.* Discussion Paper No. 1127. London: CEPR.

World Bank. 2008. *World Development Indicators, 2008*. Washington D.C.: World Bank.

Index